MINERAL TEXTILE

By

Meenakshi Rastogi

SONALI PUBLICATIONS
NEW DELHI-110002

Edition 2017

ISBN 978-81-8411-226-9

Published by

SONALI PUBLICATIONS

4228/1, Ansari Road,
New Delhi-110 002 (India)
Phone: 23266109, 23279245
Fax: 91-11-23253475
E-mail: sonalipub@yahoo.co.in

Printed at:

Preface

Asbestos and basalt fibre are used for vinyl tiles, sheeting, and adhesives, "transite" panels and siding, acoustical ceilings, stage curtains, and fire blankets.Glass Fibre is used in the production of spacesuits, ironing board and mattress covers, ropes and cables, reinforcement fibre for composite materials, insect netting, flame-retardant and protective fabric, soundproof, fireproof, and insulating fibres.Metal fibre, metal foil, and metal wire have a variety of uses, including the production of cloth-of-gold and jewelry. Hardware cloth is a coarse weave of steel wire, used in construction.

Asbestos is a naturally occurring silicate mineral with long, thin fibrous crystals. The word *asbestos* is derived from a Greek adjective meaning inextinguishable. The Greeks termed asbestos the *miracle mineral* because of its soft and pliant properties, as well as its ability to withstand heat.Asbestos is known to have toxicity. The inhalation of toxic asbestos fibers can cause serious illnesses, including malignant mesothelioma, lung cancer, and asbestosis (also called pneumoconiosis). Since the mid 1980s, many uses of asbestos have been banned in several countries.Asbestos became increasingly popular among manufacturers and builders in the late 19th century because of its resistance to heat, electricity and chemical damage, its sound absorption and tensile strength. When asbestos is used for its resistance to fire or heat, the fibers are often mixed with cement or woven into fabric or mats. Asbestos was used in some products for its heat resistance, and in the past was used on electric oven and hotplate wiring for its electrical insulation at elevated temperature, and in buildings for its flame-retardant and insulating properties, tensile strength, flexibility, and resistance to chemicals.

Basalt fiber or **fibre** is a material made from extremely fine fibers of basalt, which is composed of the minerals plagioclase, pyroxene, and olivine. It is similar to carbon fibre and fiberglass, having better physicomechanical properties than fiberglass, but being significantly cheaper than carbon fibre. It is used as a fireproof textile in the aerospace and automotive industries and can also be used as a composite to produce products such as tripods.

Fibreglass, (also called *fibreglass* and *glass fibre*), is material made from extremely fine fibers of glass. It is used as a reinforcing agent for many polymer products; the resulting composite material, properly known as fiber-reinforced polymer (FRP) or glass-reinforced plastic (GRP), is called "fiberglass" in popular usage. Glassmakers throughout history have experimented with glass fibers, but mass manufacture of fiberglass was only made possible with the invention of finer machine tooling. In 1893, Edward Drummond Libbey exhibited a dress at the World's Columbian Exposition incorporating glass fibers with the diameter and texture of silk fibers. This was first worn by the popular stage actress of the time Georgia Cayvan.

What is commonly known as "fiberglass" today, however, was invented in 1938 by Russell Games Slayter of Owens-Corning as a material to be used as insulation. It is marketed under the trade name **Fibreglass,** which has become a genericized trademark. A somewhat similar, but more expensive technology used for applications requiring very high strength and low weight is the use of carbon fiber.

A **space suit** is a complex system of garments, equipment and environmental systems designed to keep a person alive and comfortable in the harsh environment of outer space. This applies to extra-vehicular activity (EVA) outside spacecraft orbiting Earth and has applied to walking, and riding the Lunar Rover, on the Moon.

Some of these requirements also apply to pressure suits worn for other specialised tasks, such as high-altitude reconnaissance flight. Above Armstrong's Line (around 19,000 m/62,000 ft), the atmosphere is so thin that pressurised suits are needed. Hazmat suits that superficially resemble space suits are sometimes used when dealing with biological hazards. The first space suits were made by the B. F. Goodrich Company of Akron, Ohio.

Composite materials (or *composites* for short) are engineered materials made from two or more constituent materials with significantly different physical or chemical properties which remain separate and distinct on a macroscopic level within the finished structure.

Cloth of gold is a fabric woven with a gold-wrapped or spun weft - referred to as "a spirally spun gold strip". In most cases, the core yarn is silk wrapped with a band or strip of high content gold filé. In rarer instances, fine linen and wool have been used as the core.Cloth of gold is not to be confused with various gold embroidery techniques that date to the early Middle Ages, though the type of goldwork thread called "passing" is identical to the weft thread of cloth of gold. It is mentioned on both Roman headstones for women and in the Book of Psalms (psalm 45, verse 14) as a fabric befitting a princess. The Ancient Greek reference to the Golden Fleece is seen by some as a reference to gold cloth. Cloth of gold has been popular for ecclesiastical use for many centuries, and that is the most common use of this material today.Few extant examples have survived in Roman provincial tombs. Later producers of cloth of gold include the Byzantine Empire and Medieval Italian weavers. A similar *cloth of silver* was also made. It is still made in India and Italy today.Modern metallic fabrics made in the West are known as lamé."Cloth of gold" is a familiar name occasionally applied to the venomous Conus textile species of cone shell, presumably because of its Byssus or fine hair. Byssus from some species has been made into a very fine cloth.

Jewellery is an item of personal adornment, such as a necklace, ring, brooch or bracelet, that is worn by a person. It may be made from gemstones or precious metals, but may be from any other material, and may be appreciated because of geometric or other patterns, or meaningful symbols. Earrings and other body rings are also considered to be jewellery, while body art is not. Also, items affixed to a garment, such as buttons, are not considered to be jewellery, even if they are unusual and highly decorative. Also, items such as belts and handbags etc. are not considered to be jewellery, and are considered to be accessories.

The word *jewellery* is derived from the word *jewel*, which was anglicised from the Old French "*jouel*" circa the 13th century. Further tracing leads back to the Latin word "*jocale*", meaning plaything. Jewellery is one of the oldest forms of body adornment; recently found 100,000 year-old beads made from *Nassarius* shells are thought to be the oldest known jewellery.

Jewellery is sometimes seen as wealth storage or functionally as holding a garment or hair together. It has from very early times also been regarded as a form of personal adornment. The first pieces of jewellery were made from natural materials, such as bone, animal teeth, shell, wood and carved stone. More exotic jewellery was probably made for wealthy people or as indications of social status. In some cases people were buried with their jewellery.

Jewellery has been made to adorn nearly every body part, from hairpins to toe rings and many more types of jewellery. While high-quality jewellery is made with gemstones and precious metals, such as silver or gold, there is also a growing demand for art jewellery where design and creativity is prized above material value. In addition, there is the less costly costume jewellery, made from lower value materials and mass-produced. Other variations include wire sculpture (wrap) jewellery, using anything from base metal wire with rock tumbled stone to precious metals and precious gemstones.

The objective of this book is to provide the whole knowledge about what kind of Mineral textiles are and in which form they exists, by which user can understand all the aspects of this book.

Thanks

Contents

1

Introduction

Basalt and Asbestos fibre are used for vinyl tiles, sheeting, and adhesives, "transite" panels and siding, acoustical ceilings, stage curtains, and fire blankets.

Glass Fibre is used in the production of spacesuits, ironing board and mattress covers, cables and ropes, reinforcement fibre for composite materials, insect netting, flame-retardant and protective fabric, soundproof, insulating and fireproof fibres.

Metal foil, Metal fibre and metal wire have a variety of uses, including the production of cloth-of-gold and jewelry. Hardware cloth is a coarse weave of steel wire, used in construction.

Mineral Fibres

Fibreglass, made from specific glass, and optical fibre, made from purified natural quartz, are also man-made fibres that come from natural raw materials.

Metallic fibres can be drawn from ductile metals such as copper, gold or silver and extruded or deposited from more brittle ones, such as nickel, aluminum or iron.

Carbon fibres are often based on carbonised polymers, but the end product is pure carbon. There are two sorts of man-made fibres: synthetic fibres and regenerated fibres.

Synthetic fibres generally come from synthetic materials such as petrochemicals. But some types of synthetic fibres are manufactured from natural cellulose, including rayon, modal, and the more recently developed Lyocell. Cellulose-based fibres are of two types, regenerated or pure cellulose such as from the cupro-ammonium process and modified or derivitized cellulose such as the cellulose acetates.

Mineral and Fashion Textile Designs

Fashion designers commonly rely on textile designs to set their fashion collections apart from others. Marisol Deluna, Nicole Miller, Lilly Pulitzer, the late Gianni Versace and Emilio Pucci can be easily recognized by their signature print driven designs.

Mineral Textile Weaving

Plain weave—It (also called **tabby weave or taffeta weave**) is the most basic of the three fundamental farms of textile weaves. It is strong and hard-wearing, used for fashion and furnishing fabrics.

In plain weave the warp and weft are aligned so that they form a simple criss-cross pattern. Each weft thread crosses the warp threads by going over one, then under the next, and so on. The next weft thread goes under the warp threads that its neighbor went over, and vice versa.

Balanced plain weaves are fabrics in which the warp and weft are made of threads of the same weight (size) and the same number of threads per inch.

Basketweave is a variation of plain weave in which two or more threads are bundled and then woven as one in the warp or weft, or both.

A balanced plain weave can be identified by its checkerboard-like appearance. It is also known as one-up-one-down weave or over and under pattern.

Some examples of fabric with plain weave are chiffon, taffeta, and organza.

Satin weave—It is one of the three important textile weaves. (The other two are plain and twill weave.) The satin weave is distinguished by its lustrous, or 'silky', appearance. Satin describes the way the threads are combined, and the yarn used may be silk or polyester, among others, giving different fabrics.

The satin weave is characterized by four or more cool fill or weft yarns floating over a warp yarn or vice versa, four warp yarns floating over a single weft yarn. This explains the even sheen, as unlike in other weaves, the light reflecting is not scattered as much by the fibres, which have fewer tucks.

Twill —Twill is a type of fabric woven with a pattern of diagonal parallel ribs.

It is made by passing the weft thread over one or more warp threads and then under two or more warp threads and so on, with a "step" or offset between rows to create the characteristic diagonal pattern. Because of this structure, twills generally drape well. Examples of twill fabric are chino, gabardine, tweed, serge, drill and denim,.

Harris Tweed is a luxury twill handwoven on the Isle of Harris, Outer Hebrides, Scotland.

In a twill weave, each weft or filling yarn floats across two or more warp yarns in a progression of interlacings by one to the right or left, forming a distinct diagonal line. This diagonal line is also known as a wale. A float is the portion of a yarn that crosses over two or more yarns from the opposite direction.

A twill weave needs three or more harnesses, depending on its complexity. A twill weave is the second most basic weave that can be made on a fairly simple loom.

Twill weave is often design and the denominator indicates the number of harnesses that are lowered when a filling yarn is inserted, in this example one. The fraction 2/1 would be read as "two up, one down". The minimum number of harnesses needed to produce a twill can be determined by totaling the numbers in the fraction. For the example described, the number of harnesses is three.

Technically twill fabrics have a front and a back side, unlike plain weave, where the two sides are the same. The front side of the twill is the technical face and the back is called technical back. The technical face side of a twill weave fabric is the side with the most pronounced wale. It is usually more durable, more attractive, and most often used as the fashion side of the fabric. Usually this side is the side visible during weaving. If there are warp floats on the technical face (if the warp crosses over two or more wefts), there will be filling floats (the weft will cross over two or more warps) on the technical back. If the twill wale goes up to the right on one side, it will go up to the left on the other side. Twill fabrics have no up and down as they are woven.

Sheer fabrics are seldom made with a twill weave. Because a twill surface has interesting texture and design, printed twills (where a design is printed on the cloth) are much less common than printed plain weaves. When twills are printed, they are most likely to be lightweight fabrics. Soil shows less on the uneven surface of twills than it does on smooth surfaces, such as plain weaves. Thus, twills are often used for sturdy work clothing or durable upholstery because soils and stains are less noticeable on this fabric. for example, Denim, is a twill.

The fewer interlacings in twills permit the yarns to move more freely, and thus they are softer and more pliable, and drape better. Twills also recover better from wrinkles than plain-weave fabrics. When there are fewer interlacings, yarns can be packed closer together to produce high-count fabrics. In twills and higher counts, the fabric is much durable and air- and water-resistant.

There are even-sided twills and warp-faced twills. Even-sided twills include foulard or surah, serge, twill flannel, sharkskin, herringbone, and houndstooth. Warp-faced twills include lining twill, jean, denim, drill, covert, gabardine, chino, cavalry twill, and fancy twill.

Mineral Textile Spinning

An ancient textile art in which plant, animal or synthetic fibres are twisted together to form yarn. For thousands of years, fibre was spun by hand using simple tools, the spindle and distaff. Only in the High Middle Ages did the spinning wheel increase the output of individual spinners, and mass-production only arose in the 18th century with the beginnings of the Industrial Revolution. Hand-spinning remains a popular handicraft.

Characteristics of spun yarn vary based on the material used, fibre length and alignment, quantity of fibre used, and degree of twist.

Modern powered spinning, originally done by water or steam power but now done by electricity, is vastly faster than hand-spinning.

The spinning jenny, a multi-spool spinning wheel invented circa 1764 by James Hargreaves, dramatically reduced the amount of work needed to produce yarn, with a single worker able to work eight or more spools at once. At roughly the same time, Richard Arkwright and a team of craftsmen developed the spinning frame, which produced a stronger thread than the spinning jenny. Too large to be operated by hand, a spinning frame powered by a waterwheel became the water frame.

Samuel Crompton combined elements of the spinning jenny and water frame to create the spinning mule, in 1779. This produced a stronger thread, and was suitable for mechanisation on a grand scale.

In the 20th century, new techniques including Open End spinning or rotor spinning were invented to produce yarns at rates in excess of 40 meters per second.

Mineral Textile Knitting

A method by which thread or yarn may be turned into cloth. Knitting consists of loops called stitches pulled through each other. The active stitches are held on a needle until another loop can be passed through them.

It may be done by hand or by machine. By hand, there are numerous styles and methods. Flat knitting, which can be done on two st:aight needles or a circular needle, produces a length of cloth, while circular knitting, which is done on circular or double-pointed needles, produces a seamless tube.

Different yarns and knitting needles may be used to achieve different end products by giving the final piece a different colour, texture, weight, or integrity. Using needles of varying sharpness and thickness as well as different varieties of yarn adds to the effect.

Circular and Finger Knitting are the two type of Knitting. Circular knitting (also called "knitting in the round") is a form of knitting that creates a seamless tube. Knitting is worked in rounds (the equivalent of rows in flat knitting) in a spiral. Originally, circular knitting was done using a set of four or five double-pointed knitting needles. Later, circular needles were invented. A circular needle resembles two short knitting needles connected by a cable between them. Flat knitting, on the other hand, is used, in its most basic form, to make flat, rectangular pieces of cloth. It is done with two straight knitting needles and is worked in rows, horizontal lines of stitches.

Circular knitting is employed to create pieces that are circular or tube-shaped, such as hats, socks, mittens, and sleeves. Flat knitting is usually used to knit flat pieces like scarves, afghans, blankets, and the backs and fronts of sweaters.

There is also such a thing as finger knitting. It is not done like knitting on needles, it is done on your fingers. This produces a tube like piece.

Process—There are many hundreds of different knitting stitches used by knitters. A piece of knitting begins with the process of *casting on* (also known as "binding on"), which involves the initial creation of the stitches on the needle. Different methods of casting on are used for different effects: one may be stretchy enough for lace, while another provides a decorative edging—*Provisional* cast-ons are used when the knitting will continue in both directions from the cast-on. There are various method employed to "cast on," such as the "thumb method" (also known as "slingshot" or "long-tail" cast-ons), where the stitches are created by a series of loops that will, when knitted, give a very loose edge ideal for "picking up stitches" and knitting a border; the "double needle method" (also known as "knit-on" or "cable cast-on"), whereby each loop placed on the needle is then "knitted on," which produces a firmer edge ideal on its own as a border; and many more. The number of active stitches removed or added.

Most Western-style knitters follow either the English style (in which the yarn is held in the right hand) or the Continental style (in which the yarn is held in the left hand). A third but less common method, called combination knitting, may also be used.

Once the knitted piece is finished, the remaining live stitches are "cast off." Casting (or "binding") off loops the stitches across each other so they can be removed from the needle without unravelling the item. Although the mechanics are different from casting on, there is a similar variety of methods.

In knitting certain articles of clothing, especially larger ones like sweaters, the final knitted garment will be made of several knitted pieces, with individual sections of the garment knit separately and then sewn together. Seamless knitting, where a whole garment is knit as a single piece, is also possible. Elizabeth Zimmermann is probably the good-known proponent of seamless or circular knitting techniques. Smaller items, such as hats and socks, are usually knit in one piece on double-pointed needles or circular needles.

Mineral Textile : Preservation

Textile preservation refers to the processes by which textiles are cared for and maintained to be preserved from future damage. The field related the category of art conservation as well as library preservation, depending on the type of collection. In this case, the concept of textile preservation applies to a wide range of artifacts, including tapestries, carpets, quilts, clothing, flags and curtains, as well as objects which ''contain'' textiles, such as upholstered furniture, dolls, and accessories such as parasols, fans, gloves and hats or bonnets. Many of these artifacts require specialized care, often by a professional conservator. The goal of this article is to provide a general overview of the textile preservation process, and to serve as a jumping-off point for further research into more specialised care. Always contact a professional conservator if you are unsure of how to proceed in the preservation process.

Collections—Historic textile collections can largely be divided into three categories: museums, historic societies/locations, and private collections. The needs of each of these locations will vary. A private collection, for instance, is less likely to have as high a traffic flow as a museum, and may thus be able to take preservation steps that a working museum cannot (such as keeping lights to a minimum for longer periods of time). The different venues may also have different problems that arise, such as the fact that many historic homes do not have climate control, and rely strongly on natural light to display their furnishings, both of which may contribute to textile wither.

Environment—The chief cause for decay in textiles is almost always the environment in which they are stored. Light, humidity and temperature can all contribute to a textile's health or deterioration, depending on their intensity. Additionally, pests, chemicals, and pollutants may also cause damage to an antique fabric. Airborne chemicals, such as smog or cigarette smoke are also harmful to the textiles, and should be avoided if at all possible: high-efficiency air filters should be installed throughout the building to reduce the presence of airborne chemicals that may stain, weaken, or discolor fabrics.

Light—Light can have a variety of effects on textiles over time. In some cases, it may contribute to discoloration or fading but of more concern is the damage which the fibres may suffer under prolonged exposure to non-visible light, such as ultraviolet and infrared lighting. Ideally, textiles should be stored or displayed in as little light as possible, and preferably in total darkness. However, as this is impractical for display and care of the piece, knowing the limits of lighting as well as the safest amounts of lighting, become important.

Natural light is the more common source of ultraviolet light, and as such, care should be taken to avoid exposure to direct sunlight at all costs, and indirect sunlight whenever possible. This may mean displaying or storing textiles in an area without windows, or with blackout curtains, which can be pulled whenever the room is not in use. If a room relies on natural light, coatings or UV screens can be applied to the windows to block harmful rays while still allowing light to pass through. These filters should be checked periodically, however, as they have a limited lifespan and may need to be replaced every few years .

Halogen and fluorescent produced light can also produce large amounts of UV radiation, though filters which fit over the bulbs are available to limit the damaging light. These filters will need to be replaced when the bulbs are changed, so maintenance staff should be aware of them and their use.

One advantage of fluorescent lights is that they produce little heat, which may also be harmful to textiles. Incandescent lights produce a large amount of heat in addition to large quantities of infrared radiation, which is likewise damaging to the fibres in antique textiles. If incandescent lights must be used, they should be placed far enough away from display cases that their heat does not affect the contents.

In the case of particularly delicate textiles, display organizers might consider motion-activated or timed lighting, or lighting controlled though a visitor-activated switch, which would allow the textiles to remain in darkness when they are not under view. All textiles should be displayed on a rotating schedule, allowing them a few months of display, then the rest of the year in dark storage, to prolong their life.

Climate—Humidity and heat can both contribute and a textile's deterioration. However, excessive dryness may also cause damage, especially to elastic fibres, such as wool, which rely on some amount of moisture to maintain their flexibility (Putnam and Finch). Additionally, temperature and humidity should be kept as constant as possible; changes in either of these may cause the textile fibres to expand and contract, which, over time, can also cause damage and deterioration to the textile. For this reason, both storage and display areas should be fitted with monitoring equipment to gauge the temperature and humidity of rooms, display cases, enclosed storage facilities, and work areas.

Ideally, around 70 degrees Fahrenheit, temperature should be kept though some slight fluctuation in either direction is permissible, as long as it occurs gradually. For instance, temperature may be slightly lower in winter to save energy costs, but the change should be affected slowly, so as not to place the fibres under undue stress.

As for humidity, the preservationist or conservator should aim for a relative humidity of 50%, though, as with temperature, some small fluctuation is allowable, as long as it occurs gradually (Mailand). In enclosed display or storage cases, humidity can be somewhat maintained through the use of silica gel crystals. These crystals should not be placed in contact with the textiles, but may be placed in breathable muslin bags and hung inside the case to maintain a constant humidity; they should be monitored periodically, however, to be sure that they are working.

In areas where climate control is unavailable (such as in historic buildings), the conservator can still moderate the temperature and relative humidity through use of fans, humidifiers and dehumidifiers, and portable cooling or heating units.

In addition to humidity and temperature, air flow is also a concern for textile preservation. Textiles should never be sealed in plastic or other air-tight casing unless it is part of a treatment or cleaning process. Proper circulation, combined with the suggested humidity, will help to prevent the growth of mold and mildew, which may weaken or stain antique textiles.

Pests—Another significant threat to textile collections are Pests, as there are a number of creatures which can cause damage to fibres. Among the most common are clothes moths, carpet beetles, silverfish, firebrats and rodents.

Clothes moths are attracted to protein fibres, and so are especially drawn to silk, wool, and feathers. An infestation might 'dentified through the evidence of white cocoons (or the remnants) on the textiles, or of sighting the insects themselves. Roughly centimetres long and white in colour.

thes moths, carpet beetles are likewise drawn to be quite destructive. Evidence of an infestation may take of the form of chewed holes, carcasses, or larvae, which appear as small pale worm-like insects.

Firebrats and Silverfish are related insects which consume starch, usually found in sizing or other treatments applied to fabrics, as well as plant-based textiles such as linen and cotton. Both are attracted to dark, moist climates, though silverfish prefer cooler temperatures, while firebrats tend towards warmer. Both are about 12 millimetres in length and either light or dark in colouring, depending on which form is present.

Rodent infestations can be identified in the usual ways, such as seeing droppings, nests, or comparatively large chewed areas of textile where they have caused damage.

In all cases, chemical means of pest control should be avoided if possible, not only due to harm to humans who come in contact with them, but because the chemicals may cause damage to the very textiles the conservator is trying to save. For rodents, snap traps may be effective, and if needed, a professional exterminator should be called. Poison bated traps should be avoided, as the rodent could die somewhere inaccessible, and provide a breeding ground for further pests. Also, in the case of a rodent infestation, all access points to the room (such as cracks or holes) through which they might be entering should be located and sealed if possible.

For insects, keeping clean storage, display, and work environment is the good method of prevention. Also, sticky traps (replaced often) around doors, windows, and display cases may be useful for monitoring the insect population. Furthermore, the population of carnivorous insects, such as spiders, should be observed. While such insects are not harmful to textiles by themselves, they can indicate another population of insects which are.

If the infestation can be limited to one or a few pieces, the insects may be killed through freezing of the object. The textile should be wrapped in plastic and vacuum-sealed, then brought to a freezing temperature as quickly as possible, to prevent the insects from adjusting to the cold. The object may be left frozen for several days, but should be brought slowly back up to room temperature to avoid further damage. Note that while this method should kill adults, it may not destroy any eggs that are present.

If chemical means must be employed, it would be best to consult with a professional conservator to be certain that the treatment will not harm the textiles themselves.

Even if no marks of an infestation are present, textiles should still be inspected periodically to be certain that there is no outbreak that has gone unobserved. Additionally, when dealing with a new acquisition which shows signs of insect damage, the specimen should be quarantined until it can be determined whether the insects are still present before introducing it to the rest of the collection.

Mineral Textile Instability—In some cases, the textiles are weakened not by outside causes such as pests or light, but by chemical reactions taking place within the fabric itself, such as the oxidation of iron-based mordants over time, which can cause darkening and discolouration in the surrounding fibres.

One example which is cited frequently throughout the literature is the case of "shattered silk." During the late nineteenth and early twentieth centuries, many silk manufacturers treated their fabrics with metallic salts (usually containing tin and iron) to give them a heavier, more luxurious feel. However, as these fabrics have aged, the metals in the fibres have accelerated their wither and caused them to become extremely brittle. The shredded or "shattered" effect this causes is the reason for the name. In this case, the environment of the textile contributes very little to the deterioration from the metallic salts, though exposure to light may accelerate it even further.

Textile preservationists should be familiar with their collections and the history and provenance of their pieces. Chemical tests can reveal the types of dyes and mordants used, as well as any other treatments applied to the fabric. Such knowledge can lead to the prevention of further decay by learning which pieces need to be handled with particular care.

Mineral Textile Handling—It goes without saying that fragile and/or valuable textiles should be handled with care, and as little as necessary in any given circumstance. However, should handling be necessary, there are precautions which can be taken to ensure the safety of the textile.

Because our hands contain acids and oils in the skin, clean cloth gloves should be worn when handling textiles. If gloves are unavailable, then frequent hand-washing should be undertaken to ensure that no damage is caused. For similar reasons, the working, display, and storage areas should be free of food, drink, and cigarette smoke, which can also stain or damage the fabric. Finally, to avoid ink stains, only pencils should be used for sketching or writing in the work space.

To avoid pulls and snags, remove any jewelry that may catch in the fabric's weave, and wear clothing free of large buckles or other objects which may snag the textile. Long hair should also be tied back to allow a clear view of the working area, even when the head is bent over the table.

Working with the textiles, it should be placed on a clean, flat surface which is larger than the textile itself, so that the whole piece is supported evenly. Although it is supported, never place anything on top of the textile while it is in the flat position.

When moving the textile, it is important to maintain the flat, even support of the work space. If the piece is small enough (a handkerchief or sampler, for instance), it may be placed on an acid-free board or similar support and carried as if on a tray. If the piece is too large for this (a carpet or tapestry, for example), the piece may be rolled around an acid-free tube and carried by two people to its new location.

Finally, clothing and antique costumes should never be worn, as the mere process of putting the clothes on and taking them off will cause damage. Additionally, the model may not fit the costume precisely (remember that clothing was for a long time made to fit a specific person, not mass-produced in approximate sizes), causing strain where there should be none and slack where there likewise should be none.

Cleaning of Mineral Textile

Vacuuming—One of the safest and easiest ways to clean

textiles is to vacuum them. The fabric is placed on a clean, flat work surface. If the specimen is particularly delicate, or simply as a precaution, a fibreglass screen edged with twill tape may be placed over the textile. The screen allows dirt and dust to pass through, but prevents individual threads from being pulled loose or unravelled further by the suction. Using a vacuum attachment and the lowest power setting, move the suction over the screen until the entire area has been cleaned. If needed, move the screen to a new area and begin again. Always remember to vacuum both sides of the textile, as dirt may filter through to the other side. Hanging textiles will need to be vacuumed less often than horizontal pieces, as there are some places where dust can collect.

Wet Deaning—One of the key standards of preservation is that of reversibility: anything done to preserve a piece should be able to be undone with minimal damage to the piece itself. Because wet cleaning is a chemical process, it is not reversible, and so should be used only when absolutely necessary.

Before cleaning a textile, certain questions should be asked to determine both the best treatment for that particular combination of textile and soil, and to ascertain whether the piece is able to be cleaned, or may sustain damage during the process.

What is the chemical composition of the textile? In other words, does it have a high acid content? Where there chemicals used in its production that might contribute to how it reacts to water? Or how it may react to cleaning chemicals?

What are the characteristics of the fibres? For instance, linen and cotton, being plant fibres, are both stronger wet than dry, and so may be able to withstand a more mechanical stress than something like silk. Wool can absorb large amounts of water, but mats if washed in high temperatures. All silks become brittle with age, but weighted silks (see Textile Instability above) decay more quickly, and thus must be handled with extreme care. Additionally, some silks, once wet, can be permanently spotted. Learn the basic characteristics of the far of fibres you have, and how they have been treated before undertaking any type of cleaning.

What colourants have been used, and how will they react to cleaning? This can apply not only to dyes but to mordants as well. Different parts of the world may have different dye processes, so here is where knowledge of when and where a textile originated, as well as a working knowledge of chemistry, can come in handy. If in doubt as to the wash ability of a dye, apply a drop or two of water to an inconspicuous place and blot with a clean white cloth. If the dye transfers to the cloth, even in small amounts, the textile should not be washed.

Are there finishes or surface treatments that must be preserved? For example, is the fabric painted? If so, it should never be washed; some other cleaning method should be used.

What types of soils are there? The older the stain, the more difficult it is to remove. After a certain point, it may be best to leave the soil or stain, or displace it only partially, in order to preserve the rest of the piece. Additionally, soils which may not be detectable to the naked eye might be present in the textile; flags, for instance, may be highly acidic due to long exposure to air pollutants, and should be treated by a professional conservator.

What cleaner is most effective and safest? Commercial detergents should never be used on antique textiles, whatever their claims of gentleness: the chemicals used in most clothes detergents are too harsh for old fibres to withstand. A wide range of speciality detergents are available from conservation suppliers, though most sources suggest Ivory dish soap as a last-minute substitution if needed. Never use chemical spot cleaners, as they are likewise too harsh for old fibres to tolerate. This is especially important for pieces in situ, as this may endanger other nearby pieces as well (the wooden part of an upholstered piece of furniture, for instance).

What additives and cleaning aids are needed? This can include physical supplies (screens, water, a vacuum cleaner), as well as chemical (cleaning agents, water softener, etc.).

How long can the specimen be exposed to the cleaner? Prolonged exposure may cause additional damage to the fibres.

What mechanical action can be used? The older and more fragile a textile, the less movement it will be able to tolerate during the cleaning process, so this should be considered before undertaking a cleaning.

After the best cleaning process has been determined, the piece should be prepared for washing. Usually, this involves vacuuming to remove any surface dirt. Backing and linings should also be removed, vacuumed, and washed separately. This is not only to prevent colour bleeding, but to prevent trapping dirt between the layers, which may cause discolouration from the inside. Additionally, different fibres react differently to cleaning, and fabrics may shrink or stretch, which, if still attached together, may cause rippling and distortion in the lining and outer layer of the textile.

As with moving or working with dry pieces, the textile should be washed in a flat, fully supported position. Usually this is achieved through the use of screens like the ones used in vacuuming, though these may be supported in a frame of some kind for added stability. The textile should be sandwiched between two screens. If the piece is particularly delicate or fragile, it may be wrapped in netting, then placed between the screens.

The cleaning solution should be prepared using distilled water. If that is unavailable, softened water may be substituted. The main concern is to avoid hard water, which will leave deposits of minerals in the fibres. The solution should be placed in a container large enough for the textile to lie flat in. For large pieces, it may be necessary to construct a temporary basin outside or in a large room: Finch and Putnam suggest using boards or bricks to constrict a frame, then lining it with a large piece of plastic, weighted on the sides, and strong enough to support the water that will be poured into it. If a smaller basin is used, it should be of stainless steel, ceramic or a stable plastic.

The screen-encased textile is lowered into the solution. The textile can then be washed by pressing a soft sponge directly down onto the fibres. DO NOT RUB the sponge, as this will cause unnecessary abrasion at a moment when the textile is already weak from the water. The textile may be submerged for no more than an hour, and should be rinsed at least four times after it is cleaned (Mailand).. The final rinse should always be with distilled water. The textile should be placed to dry on a flat surface or screen, in a well-ventilated room away from heat.

Mineral Textile : Dry Cleaning

Dry cleaning is generally only used for oil stains, as it is a very stressful process of the textile. Commercial dry cleaners should never be used, as the chemicals used in the process are too strong for old fabrics to withstand without damage. If dry cleaning is absolutely necessary, consult a professional conservator.

Ironing and Steaming of Mineral Textile

Ironing and steaming textiles should be done with caution, as the heat may affect the viability of the fibres. More importantly, the fabric should always be cleaned before either of these processes is used, since heat can trap dirt and stains in the fibres to such an extent that the stain becomes permanent. Always use the lowest setting for either of these procedures [22]. If a garment relies on folds to maintain its proper shape (such as pleats), it may be better to finger-press the folds into place when the garment is damp and allow it to dry that way, rather than subject it to the added stress of ironing.

Mineral Textiles Storage

As stated in the Climate section, the best storage environment for textiles is dark, clean, cool, and moderately dry, with a constant temperature and relative humidity. Ideally, there should be no strain on any one particular area of cloth. There are three basic kinds of storage for textiles, and the choice of which to use relics on the type of textile and the space available. Flat, Ralled and hanging are the three types.

Flat Storage—Flat storage is the best option for exceptionally fragile pieces because it provides the most even support for the fibres. Enamelled metal shelves or drawers may be used, or acid-free boxes. The textiles can be placed in the boxes or drawers flat, if at all possible. If folding becomes necessary, acid-free tissue paper should be used to form soft rolls around which the folds can be shaped, to prevent creases from forming. Even so, folded textiles should be removed and refolded differently every few months, to permit even wear on the piece.

Rolled Storage—For exceptionally large textiles, such as draperies, tapestries, carpets and quilts, rolled storage is the best option. Like the upholstery section of a fabric store, the rolled storage area should consist of racks, each containing horizontally suspended acid-free or fabric-covered tubes around which the fabrics can be wrapped, being sure to line the selvages up with the edges of the roll. Textiles with a decorative side (such as velvets and embroidered textiles) should always be rolled with the decorative side facing out. This is because the inner layer, especially if there is a lining, may crease, stretch, or fold while it is on the roll. The rolled textiles can then be covered with a muslin wrapper to protect it from dust.

Hanging Costume Storage—For costumes, flat storage may create more problems than it solves, since it is impossible to store them in this manner without forming creases and folds. Therefore, unless the costume is so weakened that it cannot support its own weight, hanging storage is perhaps the good option. Costumes which are unusually heavy (heavily beaded gowns, for instance), or those whose fabric may distort easily (such as some stretch fabrics, or those cut on the bias) should also be stored in flat storage. Garments suitable for hanging should be placed on plastic hangers which have been padded to mimic the shape of human shoulders, and covered with a cloth or plastic cover with an open bottom to allow air circulation while keeping the costume clean. Wooden hangers may have a high acid content, which may cause discolouration or decay to the costume. Likewise, metal hangers do not provide sufficient support, and may lead to distortion of the garments' shoulders. So, both forms of hanging should be avoided.

If sufficient space is available, selected garments may be stored on dummies to better keep their shape. If this method is used, dummies should be fitted out with the proper undergarments, such as bustles or panniers, to provide adequate support for the garments as they were intended to be worn. However, while the main concern of a display may be to make the garment look attractive on the dummy, storage need have no such considerations. Loose, unsupported parts of the garment (such as sleeves or shirts) should be loosely stuffed with acid-free tissue paper to provide extra support.

Costume accessories can be placed in a variety of ways. Generally, bonnets and gloves should be loosely stuffed with acid-free tissue and placed in archival-quality boxes or under cover. Fans and parasols may be stored in half-open positions, which provide the least amount of stress on the fabrics.

Display of Mineral Textile

The conditions required for display of textiles are largely those that have already been discussed in the Storage and Environment sections. Cool, dry, and dark, are to be preferred, with clean surroundings and frequent checks to be certain that the textiles are remaining in good condition. Lighting should be kept to a minimum, and textiles should be rotated through display, so that each is only exposed to light for a some months at a time before being returned to darkness or taken for cleaning/conservation work. Textiles should be vacuumed before and after display.

2

Basalt Fibre and Asbestos

Asbestos is a naturally occurring silicate mineral with long, thin fibrous crystals. The word asbestos is derived from a Greek adjective meaning inextinguishable. The Greeks termed asbestos the miracle mineral because of its pliant and soft properties, as well as its ability to withstand heat.

Asbestos is known to have toxicity. The inhalation of toxic asbestos fibres can cause serious illnesses, including malignant mesothelioma, asbestosis, and lung cancer (also called pneumoconiosis). Since the mid 1980s, many uses of asbestos have been banned in several countries.

Asbestos became increasingly popular among manufacturers and builders in the late 19th century due to its resistance to electricity, heat and chemical damage, its sound absorption and tensile strength. When asbestos is used for its resistance to heat or fire, the fibres are often mixed with cement or woven into fabric or mats. Asbestos was used in few products for its heat resistance, and in the past was used on electric oven and hotplate wiring for its electrical insulation at elevated temperature, and in buildings for its flame-retardant and insulating properties, flexibility, tensile strength and resistance to chemicals.

Types and Associated Fibres

Six minerals are defined as "asbestos" including: chrysotile, crocidolite, amosite, tremolite, anthophyllite and actinolite.

White

Chrysotile, CAS No. 12001-29-5, is obtained from serpentine rocks which are common throughout the world. Its idealized chemical formula is $Mg_3(Si_2O_5)(OH)_4$. Chrysotile fibres are curly as opposed to fibres from amosite, crocidolite, tremolite, actinolite, and anthophyllite which are needlelike. Chrysotile, along with other types of asbestos, has been restricted in dozens of countries and is only allowed in the United States and Europe in very limited circumstances. Chrysotile has been used more than any other type and accounts for about 95% of the asbestos found in buildings in America. Applications where chrysotile might be used include the use of joint compound. It is more flexible than amphibole kinds of asbestos; it can be spun and woven into fabric. The most common use is within corrugated asbestos cement roof sheets typically used for outbuildings, warehouses and garages. It is also found as flat sheets used for ceilings and sometimes for floors and walls. Numerous other items have been made containing chrysotile including brake linings, cloth behind fuses (for fire protection), pipe insulation, in floor tiles and in rope seals to boilers.

Brown

Amosite, CAS No. 12172-73-5, is a trade name for the amphiboles belonging to the *Cummingtonite - Grunerite* solid solution series, commonly from Africa, named as an acronym from Asbestos Mines of South Africa. One formula given for amosite is $Fe_7Si_8O_{22}(OH)_2$. It is found most frequently as a fire retardant in ceiling tiles and thermal insulation products.

Blue

Crocidolite, CAS No. 12001-28-4 is an amphibole found primarily in southern Africa, but also in Australia. It is the fibrous form of the amphibole riebeckite. One formula given for crocidolite is $Na_2Fe^{2+}{}_3Fe^{3+}{}_2Si_8O_{22}(OH)_2$. Notes: chrysotile commonly occurs as soft friable fibres. Asbestiform amphibole may also occur as soft friable fibres but some varieties such as amosite are commonly straighter. All forms of asbestos are fibrillar in that they are composed of fibres with widths less than 1 micrometer that occur in bundles and have very long lengths. Asbestos with particularly fine fibres is also referred to as "amianthus". Amphiboles such as tremolite have a crystal structure containing strongly bonded ribbonlike silicate anion polymers that extend the length of the crystal. Serpentine (chrysotile) has a sheetlike silicate anion which is curved and which rolls up like a carpet to construct the fibre.

Other Materials

Other regulated asbestos minerals, such as tremolite asbestos, CAS No. 77536-68-6, $Ca_2Mg_5Si_8O_{22}(OH)_2$; actinolite asbestos (or *smaragdite*), CAS No. 77536-66-4, $Ca_2(Mg, Fe)_5(Si_8O_{22})(OH)_2$; and anthophyllite asbestos, CAS No. 77536-67-5, $(Mg, Fe)_7Si_8O_{22}(OH)_2$; are less commonly used industrially but can still be found in a variety of construction materials and insulation materials and have been reported in the past to occur in a few consumer products.

Other natural and not currently regulated asbestiform minerals, such as richterite, $Na(CaNa)(Mg, Fe^{++})_5 (Si_8O_{22}) (OH)_2$, and winchite, $(CaNa)Mg_4(Al, Fe^{3+})(Si_8O_{22})(OH)_2$, may be found as a contaminant in products such as the vermiculite containing zonolite insulation manufactured by W.R. Grace and Company. These minerals are thought to be no less harmful than tremolite, amosite, or crocidolite, but since they are not regulated, they are referred to as "asbestiform" rather than asbestos although may still be related to hazardous and diseases.

Asbestos Producer Nations

In 2006, 2.3 million tons of asbestos was mined worldwide, in 11 or 12 countries. The largest producer was china about 40%

world share followed by China, Kazakhstan, and Canada (the last of which produces 10% of the world's asbestos).

Uses

Historic—Asbestos was named by the ancient Greeks, although the naming of minerals was not very consistent yet at that time (it should be noted that the modern Greek word stands for lime, not for the material known as asbestos in English). The ancients already recognized certain hazards of the material. Strabo the Greek geographer and the Roman naturalist Pliny the Elder noted that the material damaged lungs of slaves who wove it into cloth.Charlemagne, the first Holy Roman Emperor, is said to have had a asbestos table cloth.

Wealthy Persians, Who bought asbestos imported over the Hindu Kush, amazed guests by cleaning the cloth by simply exposing it to fire. According to Biruni in his book of Gems, any cloths made of asbestos were called shastakeh. Some of the Persians believed the fibre was fur from an animal that lived in fire and died when exposed to water.

Marco Polo While traveling to China described observing miraculous garments that were cleaned by being placed in fires. These garments were without a doubt made from asbestos.

Some archeologists believe that ancients made shrouds of asbestos, wherein they burned the bodies of their kings, in order to preserve only their ashes, and prevent their being mixed with those of wood or other combustible materials commonly used in funeral pyres. Others assert that the ancients used asbestos to make perpetual wicks for sepulchral or other lamps. In more recent centuries, asbestos was indeed used for this purpose. Although asbestos causes skin to itch upon contact, ancient literature indicates that it was prescribed for diseases of the skin, and particularly for the itch. It is possible that they used the term asbestos for alumen plumosum, because the two terms have often been confused throughout history.

Asbestos became more widespread during the industrial revolution; in the 1860s it was used as insulation in the U.S. and Canada. Development of the first commercial asbestos mine began in 1879 in the Appalachian foothills of Quebec. By the mid 20th century uses included fire retardant coatings, bricks, concrete, pipes and fireplace cement, fire, heat, and acid resistant gaskets, ceiling insulation, pipe insulation, fireproof drywall, roofing, flooring, lawn furniture, and drywall joint compound.

Approximately in the United States 100,000 people have died, or will die, from asbestos exposure related to ship building. In the Hampton Roads area, a shipbuilding center, mesothelioma occurrence is seven times the national rate. Thousands of metric tons of asbestos were used in World War II ships to wrap the pipes, line the boilers, and cover engine and turbine parts. There were approximately 4.3 million shipyard workers in the United States during WWII; for every thousand workers about fourteen died of mesothelioma and an unknown number died from asbestosis.

Asbestos fibres were once used in automobile brake pads and shoes. Since the mid-1990s, a majority of brake pads, new or replacement, have been manufactured instead with linings made of carbon, ceramic, metallic and Aramid fibre (Twaron or Kevlar—the same material used in bulletproof vests).

Kent, the first filtered cigarette on the market, used crocidolite asbestos in its "Micronite" filter from 1952 to 1956.

The first documented death related to asbestos was in 1906. In the early 1900s researchers began to notice a large number of early deaths and lung problems in asbestos mining towns. By the 1930s, England regulated ventilation and made asbestosis an excusable work related disease, about ten years sooner than the U.S. The term Mesothelioma was not used in medical literature until 1931, and was not associated with asbestos until sometime in the 1940s.

The United States government and asbestos industry have been criticized for not acting quickly enough to inform the public of dangers, and to reduce public exposure. In the late 1970s court documents proved that asbestos industry officials knew of asbestos dangers and tried to hide them.

In Japan, particularly after World War II, asbestos was used in the manufacture of ammonium sulfate for purposes of rice production, sprayed upon the ceilings, iron skeletons, and walls of railroad cars and buildings (during the 1960s), and used for energy efficiency reasons as well. Production of asbestos in Japan peaked in 1974 and went through ups and downs until about 1990, when production began to drop severely.

Specific Products

Serpentine Group—Serpentine minerals have a layered or sheet structure. Chrysotile is the only asbestos mineral in the serpentine group. In the United States, chrysotile has been the most commonly used type of asbestos. According to the U.S. EPA Asbestos Building Inspectors Manual, chrysotile accounts for approximately 95% of asbestos found in buildings in the United States. Chrysotile is often present in a wide range of materials, including:

- joint compound
- mud and texture coats
- vinyl floor tiles, sheeting, adhesives
- roofing tars, felts, siding, and shingles
- "transite" panels, siding, countertops, and pipes
- fireproofing
- caulk
- gaskets
- brake pads and shoes
- clutch plates
- stage curtains
- fire blankets
- interior fire doors
- fireproof clothing for firefighters
- thermal pipe insulation

In the Australia and European Union it has recently been ristricted as a potential health hazard and is not used at all. Japan is moving in the same direction, but more slowly. Revelations that hundreds of workers had died in Japan over the previous few decades from diseases related to asbestos sparked a scandal in mid-2005. Tokyo had, in 1971, ordered companies handling asbestos to install ventilators and check health on a regular basis; however, the Japanese government did not ban crocidolite and amosite until 1995, and a full-fledged ban on asbestos was implemented in October 2004.

Amphibole Group

In the amphibole group five types of asbestos are found: amosite, crocidolite, anthophyllite, actinolite and tremolite. Amosite, the second most likely type to be found in buildings, according to the U.S. EPA Asbestos Building Inspectors Guide, is the "brown" asbestos.

Crocidolite and amosite were formerly used in many products until the early-1980s. The use of all types of asbestos in the amphibole group was banned in much of the Western world by the mid-1980s, and by Japan in 1995. These products were mainly:

Ceiling Tiles and Low Density Insulation Board

Asbestos-cement sheets and pipes for construction, casing for water and electrical/telecommunication services

Thermal and chemical insulation (i.e., fire rated doors, limpet spray, lagging and gaskets)

Health Related Issues

Chrysotile asbestos, like all other forms of industrial asbestos, has produced tumors in animals. Mesotheliomas have been observed in people who were occupationally exposed to chrysotile, family members of the occupationally to make known, and residents who lived close to asbestos factories and mines. Brown asbestos, like all asbestos, is hazardous. Amosite is the most hazardous of the asbestos minerals due to its hollow straight fibre structure that can stay airborne for up to 72 hours. It also does not get trapped by water as easily as the serpentine fibres do of crysotile. Tremolite often contaminates chrysotile asbestos, thus creating an extra hazard.

Asbestos exposure becomes a health concern when high concentrations of asbestos fibres are inhaled over a long time period. People who become ill from asbestos are almost always those who are exposed on a day-to-day basis in a job where they work directly with the material. As a person's exposure to fibres increases, either by breathing more fibres or by breathing fibres for a longer time, that person's risk of disease also increases. Disease is very unlikely to result from a single, high-level exposure, or from a short period of exposure to lower levels.

Other Asbestos-related Diseases

Asbestos warts – caused when the sharp fibres lodge in the skin and are overgrown causing benign callus-like growths.

Pleural plaques – discrete fibrous or partially calcified thickened area which can be seen on X-rays of individuals exposed to asbestos. They do not become malignant or cause other lung impairment.

Diffuse pleural thickening – similar to above and can sometimes be associated with asbestosis. Usually no symptoms shown but if extensive may cause lung impairment.

As Contaminant

Most respirable asbestos fibres are invisible to the unaided human eye because their size is about 3.0-20.0 μm in length and can be as thin as 0.01 μm. Human hair ranges in size from 17 to 181 μm in width. Fibres ultimately form because when these minerals originally cooled and crystallized, they formed by the polymeric molecules lining up parallel with each other and forming oriented crystal lattices. These crystals thus have three cleavage planes, just as other minerals and gemstones have. But in their case, there are two cleavage planes that are much weaker than the third direction. When sufficient force is applied, they tend to break along their weakest directions, resulting in a linear fragmentation pattern and hence a fibrous form. This fracture process can keep occurring and one larger asbestos fibre can ultimately become the source of hundreds of much smaller and thinner fibres.

As asbestos fibres get lighter and smaller, they more easily become airborne and human respiratory exposures may result. Fibres will eventually settle but may be re-suspended by air currents or other movement.

Friability of a product containing asbestos means that it is so weak and soft in structure that it can be broken with simple finger crushing pressure. Friable materials are of the most initial concern due to their ease of damage. The forces or conditions of usage that come into intimate contact with most non-friable materials containing asbestos are substantially higher than finger pressure.

Environmental Asbestos

Asbestos can be found naturally in the air outdoors and in some drinkable water, including water from natural sources. Studies have shown that members of general (non-occupationally exposed) population have tens of thousands to hundreds of thousands of asbestos fibres in each gram of dry lung tissue, which translates into millions of fibres and tens of thousands of asbestos bodies in each person's lungs.

Asbestos from natural geologic deposits is known as "Naturally Occurring Asbestos" (NOA). Health risks associated with exposure to NOA are not yet completely understood, and current US federal regulations do not address exposure from NOA. Many populated areas are in proximity to shallow, natural deposits which occur in 50 of 58 California counties and in 19 other U.S. states. In one study, data was collected from 3,000 mesothelioma patients in California and 890 men with prostate cancer, a malignancy not known to be related to asbestos. The study found a correlation between the incidence of mesotheliomas and the distance a patient lived from known deposits of rock likely to include asbestos, the correlation was not present when the incidence of prostate cancer was compared with the same distances. According to the study, risk of mesothelioma declined by 6 percent for every 10 kilometers that an individual had lived away from a likely asbestos source.

Portions of El Dorado County, California are known to contain natural asbestos formations near the surface. The USGS studied amphiboles in soil and rock in the area in response to an EPA sampling study and subsequent criticism of the EPA study. The study found that many amphibole particles in the area meet the counting rule criteria used by the EPA for chemical and morphological limits, but do not meet morphological requirements for commercial-grade-asbestos. The executive summary pointed out that even particles that do not meet requirements for commercial-grade-asbestos can be a health problem and suggested a collaborative research effort to assess health risks associated with "Naturally Occurring Asbestos".

Large portions of Fairfax County, Virginia were also found to be underlain with tremolite. The county monitored air quality at construction sites, controlled soil taken from affected areas, and required freshly developed sites to lay 6 inches (150 mm) of clean, stable material over the ground.

History of Health Concerns and Regulation

Prior to 1900—By the first century AD, Greeks and Romans had already observed, at least in passing, that slaves involved in the weaving of asbestos cloth were afflicted with a sickness of the lungs.

Early concern in the modern era on the health effects of asbestos exposure can be found in several sources. Among the earliest were reports in Britain. The annual reports of the Chief Inspector of Factories reported as early as 1898 that asbestos had 'easily demonstrated' health problems.

At about the same time, what was probably the first study of mortality among asbestos workers was reported in France. While the study describes the cause of death as chalicosis, a generalized pneumoconiosis, the circumstances of the employment of the fifty workers whose death prompted the study suggest that the main cause was asbestos or mixed asbestos-cotton dust exposure.

1900s–1910s—Further awareness of asbestos-related diseases was found in the early 1900s, when London doctor H. Montague Murray conducted a post mortem exam on a young asbestos factory worker who died in 1899. Dr. Murray gave testimony on this death in connection with an industrial disease compensation hearing. The post-mortem confirmed the presence of asbestos in the lung tissue, prompting Dr. Murray to express as an expert opinion his belief that the inhalation of asbestos dust had at least contributed to, if not actually caused, the workers death.

The record in the United States was similar. Early observations were largely anecdotal in nature and did not definitively link the occupation with the disease, followed by more compelling and larger studies that strengthened the association. One such study, published in 1918, noted:

All of these processes unquestionably involve a considerable dust hazard, but the hygienic aspects of the industry have not been reported upon. It may be said, in conclusion, that in the practice of American and Canadian life insurance companies, asbestos workers are commonly declined on account of the assumed health-injurious conditions of the industry .

1920s and 1930s—Widespread recognition of the occupational risks of asbestos in Britain was reported in 1924 by a Dr. Cooke, a pathologist, who introduced a case description of a 33-year old female asbestos worker with the following: 'Medical men in areas where asbestos is manufactured have long suspected the dust to be the cause of chronic bronchitis and fibrosis...." Dr. Cooke then went on to report on a case in 1927 involving a 33-year old male worker who was the only survivor out of ten workers in an asbestos carding room. In the report he named the disease "asbestosis."

Dr. Cooke's second case report was followed, in the late 1920s, by a mega public health investigation (now known as the Merewether report after one of its two authors) that examined some 360 asbestos-textile workers (reported to be about 15% of the total comparable employment in Britain at the time) and found that about a quarter of them suffered from pulmonary fibrosis .

This investigation resulted in improved regulation of the manufacturing of asbestos-containing products in the early 1930s. Regulations included industrial hygiene standards, medical examinations, and inclusion of the asbestos industry into the British Workers' Compensation Act.

The first known US workers' compensation claim for asbestos disease was in 1927. In 1930, the first reported autopsy of an asbestosis sufferer was conducted in the United states and later presented by a doctor at the Mayo Clinic, although in this case the exposure involved mining activities somewhere in South America.

A major asbestos company Johns–Manville produced a repart in 1930, for internal company use only, about medical reports of asbestos worker fatalities. In 1932, A letter from U.S. Bureau of Mines to asbestos manufacturer Eagle-Picher stated, in relevant part, "Now it is known that asbestos dust is one of the most dangerous dusts to which man is exposed". In 1933, Metropolitan Life Insurance Co. doctors found that 29% of workers in a Johns-Manville plant had asbestosis. Likewise, in 1933, Johns-Manville officials settled lawsuits by 11 employees with asbestosis on the condition that the employees' lawyer agree to never again "directly or indirectly participate in the bringing of new actions against the Corporation." In 1934, officials of two large asbestos companies, Johns-Manville and Raybestos-Manhattan, edited an article about the diseases of asbestos workers written by a Metropolitan Life Insurance Company doctor. The changes downplayed the danger of asbestos dust. In 1935, officials of Johns-Manville and Raybestos-Manhattan instructed the editor of Asbestos magazine to publish nothing about asbestosis. In 1936, a group of asbestos companies agreed to sponsor research on the health effects of asbestos dust, but required that the companies maintain jatle control over the disclosure of the results.

1940s—In 1942, an internal Owens-Corning corporate memo referred to "medical literature on asbestosis . . . . scores of publications in which the skin and lung hazards of asbestos are discussed." Either in 1942 or 1943, the president of Johns-Manville, Lewis H. Brown, said that the managers of another asbestos company were "a bunch of fools for notifying employees who had asbestosis." When one of the managers asked, "do you mean to tell me you would let them work until they dropped dead?" the response is reported to have been, "Yes. We save a lot of money that way." In 1944, a Metropolitan Life Insurance Company report found 42 cases of asbestosis among 195 asbestos miners.

1950s—In 1951, asbestos companies removed all references to cancer before allowing publication of research they sponsored. In 1952, Dr. Kenneth Smith, Johns-Manville medical director, recommended (unsuccessfully) that warning labels be attached to products having asbestos. Later, Smith testified: "It was a business decision as far as I could understand . . . the corporation is in business to provide jobs for people and make money for stockholders and they had to take into consideration the effects of everything they did and if the application of a caution label identifying a product as hazardous would cut into sales, there would be serious financial implications." In 1953, National Gypsum's safety director wrote to the Indiana Division of Industrial Hygiene, recommending that acoustic plaster mixers wear respirators "because of the asbestos used in the product." Another company official noted that the letter was "full of dynamite" and urged that it be retrieved before reaching its destination. A memo in the files noted that the company "succeeded in stopping" the letter, which "will be modified."

1960s–early 1980s—Asbestos was used to fireproof roofing and flooring, for heat insulation, and for a variety of other purposes

Modern Regulation

United States—In 1989 the United States Environmental Protection Agency (EPA) issued the Asbestos Ban and Phase Out Rule which was subsequently overturned in the case of Corrosion Proof Fittings v. U.S. Environmental Protection Agency, 1991. This ruling leaves many consumer products that may still legally contain trace amounts of asbestos. For a clarification of products which legally contain asbestos read the EPA's clarification statement.

The EPA has proposed a concentration limit of seven million fibres per liter of drinking water for long fibres (lengths greater than or equal to 5 μm). The Occupational Safety and Health Administration (OSHA), has set limits of 100,000 fibres with lengths greater than or equal to 5 μm per cubic meter of workplace air for 8-hour shifts and 40-hour work weeks.

New Zealand

In 1984, the import of raw amphibole (blue and brown) asbestos into New Zealand was banned. The import of chrysotile (white) asbestos was banned in 2002.

Australia

A complete ban on asbestos containing material in Australia was introduced in 1991 although few building materials in storage were still being used in the years that followed. Queensland began regulation of asbestos removal and disposal in 2005. Handlers of asbestos materials must have a B-Class license for bonded asbestos and an A-Class license for friable asbestos.

The town of Wittenoom, in Western Australia was built around a (blue) asbestos mine. The town has since been closed, and is contaminated. However one couple remains there, refusing to leave the area and refusing to believe in current medical advice.

Contamination of other Products

Vermiculite and Asbestos—Vermiculite is a hydrated laminar magnesium-aluminum-iron silicate which resembles mica. It can be used for many industrial applications and has been used as a replacement for asbestos. Some ore bodies of vermiculite have been found to contain small amounts of asbestos. One vermiculite mine operated by W. R. Grace and Company in Libby, Montana exposed workers and community residents to danger by mining contaminated vermiculite, in 1999 the EPA began cleanup efforts and now the area is a superfund cleanup area. The EPA has determined that harmful asbestos is released from the mine as well as through other activities that effect soil in the area.

Asbestos and Talc—Talc is sometimes contaminated with asbestos. In 2000, tests in a certified asbestos-testing laboratory found the tremolite form of amphibole asbestos in three out of eight major brands of children's crayons (oil pastels) that are made partly from talc —Prang, Crayola, and Rose Art. In Crayola crayons, the tests found asbestos levels from 0.05% in Carnation Pink to 2.86% in Orchid; in Prang crayons, the range was from 0.3% in Periwinkle to 0.54% in Yellow; in Rose Art crayons, it was from 0.03% in Brown to 1.20% in Orange. Overall, 32 different types of crayons from these brands contained more than trace amounts of asbestos, and eight others contained trace amounts. The Art and Creative Materials Institute, a trade association which tests the safety of crayons on behalf of the makers, initially insisted the test results must be incorrect, although they later said they do not test for asbestos. In May 2000, Crayola said tests by materials analyst, Richard Lee, of two of its crayons were negative for asbestos, although it later emerged that Lee had testified in lawsuits over 250 times on behalf of the asbestos industry, which paid him US$7 million. In June 2000, Binney & Smith, the maker of Crayola, and the other makers agreed to stop using talc in their products, and changed their product formulations in the United States. The mining company, R T Vanderbilt Co of Gouverneur, New York, which supplied the talc to the crayon makers, insists there is no asbestos in its talc "to the best of our knowledge and belief", but tests by the United States Mine Safety and Health Administration found asbestos in all four talc samples that it tested in 2000.

Asbestos in Construction

In Developed Countries—The use of asbestos in new construction projects has been rostricted for health and safety reasons in many developed countries, including the European Union, Japan, Australia, and New Zealand. A notable exception is the United States, where asbestos continues to be used in construction such as cement asbestos pipes. Until the mid-1980s, white asbestos was used in the manufacture of Artex a decorative stipple finish.

Prior to the ban, asbestos was widely used in the construction industry. Many older buildings contain asbestos. In the United States, there is a minimum standard for asbestos surveys as described by

ASTM Standard E 2356-04. The U.S. Environmental Protection Agency includes some but not all asbestos-contaminated facilities on the Superfund National Priorities list (NPL). Renovation and demolition of asbestos contaminated buildings is subject to EPA NESHAP and OSHA Regulations. Asbestos is not a material covered under CERCLA's innocent purchaser defense. In the UK, the removal and disposal of asbestos and of substances containing it are covered by the Control of Asbestos Regulations 2006.

In developing Countries

Some developing countries, such as China and India, have continued widespread use of asbestos. The most common is corrugated asbestos-cement sheets or "A/C Sheets" for roofing and for side walls. Millions of homes, schools, factories or sheds and shelters continue to use asbestos. Cutting these sheets to size and drilling holes to receive 'J' bolts to help secure the sheets to roof framing is done on site. There has been no significant change in production and use of A/C Sheets in developing countries following the highly restrictions in developed nations.

Litigation

Asbestos litigation is the longest, most expensive mass tort in U.S. history, involving more than 8,400 defendants and 730,000 claimants as of 2002 according to the RAND Corporation, and at least one defendant reported claim counts in excess of 800,000 in 2006.

Current trends indicate that the worldwide rate at which people are diagnosed with the disease will likely increase by the next decade. Analysts have estimated that the total costs of asbestos litigation in the USA alone is over $250 billion.

The Federal legal system in the United States has been faced with numerous counts of asbestos related suits, which often included multiple plaintiffs with similar symptoms. The concern with these court cases are the staggering numbers, which in 1999 recorded 200,000 cases pending in the Federal court system of the United States . Further, it is estimated that within the next 40 years, cases may balloon to seven hundred thousand cases. These numbers help explain how there are thousands of current pending cases.

Litigation of asbestos materials has been a difficult entity to muster due to the multiple factors which play a role in each case. The company that often is being exposed for their negligence of working conditions and the worker or in many cases, workers who were exposed to asbestos and did not know that they were, or knew and now fear future medical problems, have current symptoms or were upset for the negligence of the company. Companies sometimes counter saying that health issues do not currently appear in their worker or workers, or sometimes are settled out of court. The Research and Development (RAND) think-tank has appropriated certain legal information which is readily available for proclaimed victims of natural resource accidents. This information, although sometimes deemed radical, has helped more workers, regardless of health condition, earn compensation by companies. RAND, along with the Institute for Civil Justice (ICJ) have been proponents of the organization of past cases in order to determine one aspect of fair compensation for workers.

1999 saw the introduction of the Fairness in Asbestos Compensation Act. This Act was used as a tool in order to determine which of the numerous federal cases were true, and if the plaintiff's were actually suffering from asbestos related illness. This process was necessary as thousands of false insurance claims were costing companies billions and ultimately many companies were forced to file for bankruptcy. While companies filed for bankruptcy, this limited payouts to those who were actually affected by the material. What the 1999 Act ultimately determined was "a judgment that those resources should be spent on delivering complete and prompt compensation to those who are, and will become, impaired by asbestos disease, and not dissipated on payments to those who are not sick and may never become sick, on punitive damages that seek retribution for the decisions of long-dead executives for conduct that took place decades ago and on the extraordinary transaction costs (Professor Christopher Edley, Jr.)." With this litigation, it was recommended by many that the framework of the Act was set in a manner that was fair towards many parties.

There is no effective way to allocate funding to each claimant with the fair treatment of companies in question. Although a majority of companies involved with numerous asbestos cases are household names, they are also at the highest risk while faced with workers health concerns. The 1999 Act has effectively helped save money, time and aggravation for both sides of every asbestos case. There are some cases of bankruptcy and some cases of fraudulent medical concerns. Notable concerns with bankruptcy include the fact that once a company is forced to divide funding amongst its workers, it has a limited budget which lags on the economy and ultimately cannot contribute back the way it once was. This was a prominent reason for the hesitation of any strict enforcement policy. However, the Act of 1999 helps to alleviate exuberant payouts to unqualified claimants, all while legally and safely protecting those who were, are and will be affected by asbestos related illnesses.

Litigation exists outside the United States in England, Ireland, Scotland, the Netherlands, Australia, France, and Japan among other nations. See the companion article for further information.

The volume of the asbestos liability has concerned manufacturers and insurers and reinsurers. The amounts and method of allocating compensation have been the source of many court cases, and government attempts at resolution of existing and future cases.

Critics of Safety Regulations

According to Natural Resources Canada, chrysotile asbestos is not as dangerous as once thought. According to their fact sheet, "...current knowledge and modern technology can successfully control the potential for health and environmental harm posed by chrysotile". In May of 1998, Canada requested consultations with the European Commission concerning France's 1996 prohibition of the importation and sale of asbestos.

Canada claimed that the French measures contravened provisions of the Agreements on Sanitary and Phytosanitary Measures and on Technical Barriers to Trade, and the GATT 1994.

The EC said that substitute materials had been developed in place of asbestos, which are safer to human health. It stressed that the French measures were not discriminatory, and were fully justified for public health reasons. The EC said that in the July consultations, it had tried to convince Canada that the measures were justified, and that just as Canada broke off consultations, it was in the process of submitting substantial scientific data in favour of the asbestos ristriction.

Critics of Canada's support of the use of chrysotile asbestos argue that Canada is ignoring the problems associated with the material. The CFMEU pointed out that selling asbestos is illegal in Canada, but it is exported and most exports go to developing countries. Canada has pressured countries, including Chile, and the UN to avoid asbestos ristriction.

Asbestos regulation critics include Junkscience.com author and Fox News columnist Steven Milloy and the asbestos industry. Sometimes critics argue that increased regulation does more harm than good and that replacements to asbestos are inferior. An example is the suggestion by Dixy Lee Ray and others that the shuttle Challenger exploded because the maker of O-ring putty was pressured by the EPA into ceasing production of asbestos-laden putty. However, scientists point out that the putty used in Challenger's final flight did contain asbestos, and failures in the putty were not responsible for the failure of the O-ring that led to loss of the shuttle.

In the fistr forty floors of the world trade center towers. Asbestos was used causing an airborne contamination among lower Manhattan after the towers collapsed in the attacks on September 11th, 2001. Steven Milloy suggests that the World Trade Center towers could still be standing or at least would have stood longer had a 1971 ban not stopped the completion of the asbestos coating above the 64th floor . This was not mentioned in the National Institute of Standards and Technology's report on the towers' collapse. All fireproofing materials, regardless of what they are made of are required to find a fire-resistance rating prior to installation. All fibre-based lightweight commercial spray fireproofing materials are vulnerable to kinetic energy impacts that are outside of the fire testing upon which their ratings are based, including asbestos-based materials, and would have been removed in mega areas by the impact of the planes.

Substitutes for Asbestos in Construction

Fibreglass insulation was invented in 1938 and is now the most commonly used type of insulation material. The safety of this material is also being called into question, as research indicates that the composition of this material causes similar toxicity as asbestos.

In Europe stone- and glasswool are the main insulators in homes.

Many companies that produced asbestos-cement products that were reinforced with asbestos fibres have developed products incorporating organic fibres. One such product was known as Eternit and another "Everite" now use "Nutec" fibres which consist of organic fibres, silica and portland cement. Another substitute is cement-bonded wood fibre. Stonefibres are used in gaskets and friction materials.

Polybenzimidazole is another potential fibre or PBI fibre. Polybenzimidazole fibre is a synthetic fibre with high melting point of 760 °C that also does not ignite. Due to its exceptional thermal and chemical stability, it is often used by fire departments and space agencies.

Disposal and Recycling

In most developed countries, asbestos is typically disposed of as hazardous waste in landfill sites.

Asbestos can also be recycled by transforming it into harmless silicate glass. A process of thermal decomposition at 1000-1250 °C produces a mixture of non-hazardous silicate phases, and at temperatures above 1250 °C it produces silicate glass. Microwave thermal treatment can be used in an industrial manufacturing process to transform asbestos and asbestos-containing waste into porcelain stoneware tiles, porous single-fired wall tiles, and ceramic bricks.

Basalt Fibre

Basalt fibre or fibre is a material made from extremely fine fibres of basalt, which is composed of the minerals plagioclase, olivine and pyroxene. It is similar to carbon fibre and fibreglass, having better physicomechanical properties than fibreglass, but being significantly cheaper than carbon fibre. It is used as a fireproof textile in the aerospace and automotive industries and can also be used as a composite to produce products such as tripods.

Manufacture

The manufacture of basalt fibre requires the melting of the quarried basalt rock to about 1,400°C (2,500°F). The molten rock is then extruded through small nozzles to produce continuous filaments of basalt fibre. There are three main manufacturing techniques, which are centrifugal-blowing, centrifugal-multiroll and die-blowing. The fibres typically have a filament diameter of between 9 and 13 μm which is far enough above the respiratory limit of 5 μm to make basalt fibre a suitable replacement for asbestos. They also have a high elastic modulus, resulting in excellent specific tenacity --three times that of steel.[verification needed]

History

In the year of 1923, the first attempts to produce basalt fibre was in United States of America. These were further developed after World War II by researchers in the USA, Europe and the Soviet Union especially for military and aerospace applications. Since declassification in 1995 basalt fibres have been used in a wider range of civilian applications.

3

Fibreglass

Fibreglass, (also called fibreglass and glass fibre), is material made from extremely fine fibres of glass. It is used as a reinforcing agent for many polymer products; the resulting composite material, properly known as fibre-reinforced polymer (FRP) or glass-reinforced plastic (GRP), is called "fibreglass" in popular usage. Glassmakers throughout history have experimented with glass fibres, but mass manufacture of fibreglass was only made possible with the invention of finer machine tooling. In 1893, Edward Drummond Libbey exhibited a dress at the World's Columbian Exposition incorporating glass fibres with the diameter and texture of silk fibres. This was first worn by the popular stage actress of the time Georgia Cayvan.

What is commonly known as "fibreglass" today, however, was invented in 1938 by Russell Games Slayter of Owens-Corning as a material to be used as insulation. It is marketed under the trade name Fibreglas, which has become a genericized trademark. A somewhat similar, but more expensive technology used for applications requiring very high strength and low weight is the use of carbon fibre.

Process of Formation

Glass fibre is formed when thin strands of silica-based or

other formulation glass is extruded into many fibres with small diameters suitable for textile processing. Glass, even as a fibre, has little crystalline structure (see amorphous solid). The properties of the structure of glass in its softened stage are very much like its properties when spun into fibre. One definition of glass is "an inorganic substance in a condition which is continuous with, and analogous to the liquid state of that substance, but which, as a result of a reversible change in viscosity during cooling, has attained so high a degree of viscosity as to be, for all practical purposes, rigid."

The technique of heating and drawing glass into fine fibres has been known for millennia; however, the use of these fibres for textile applications is more recent. Until this time all fibreglass had been manufactured as staple. When the two companies joined to produce and promote fibreglass, they introduced continuous filament glass fibres. Owens-Corning is still the major fibreglass producer in the market today.The first commercial production of fibreglass was in 1936. In 1938, Owens-Illinois Glass Company and Corning Glass Works joined to form the Owens-Corning Fibreglas Corporation. Two types of fibreglass most commonly used are S-glass and E-glass E-glass has good insulation properties and it will maintain its properties up to 1500 degree F(815 deg C). S-glass has a high tensile strength and is stiffer than E-glass.

Base

The basis of textile-grade glass fibres is silica, SiO2. In its pure form it exists as a polymer, (SiO2)n. It has no true melting point but softens at 2000°C, where it starts to degrade. At 1713°C, most of the molecules can move about freely. If the glass is then cooled quickly, they will be unable to form an ordered structure. In the polymer, it forms SiO4 groups which are configured as a tetrahedron with the silicon atom at the center and four oxygen atoms at the corners. These atoms then form a network bonded at the corners by sharing the oxygen atoms.

The vitreous and crystalline states of silica (glass and quartz) have similar energy levels on a molecular basis, also implying that the glassy form is extremely stable. In order to induce crystallization, it must be heated to temperatures above 1200°C for long time periods.

Although pure silica is a perfectly viable glass and glass fibre, it must be worked with at very high temperatures, which is a drawback unless its specific chemical properties are needed. It is usual to introduce impurities into the glass in the form of other materials to lower its working temperature. These materials also impart various other properties to the glass which may be beneficial in different applications. The first kind of glass used for fibre was soda lime glass or A glass. It was not very resistant to alkali. A new type, E-glass was formed that is alkali free (<2%) and is an alumino-borosilicate glass. This was the first glass formulation used for continuous filament formation. E-glass still makes up most of the fibreglass production in the world. Its particular components may differ slightly in percentage, but must fall within a specific range. The letter E is used because it was originally for electrical applications. S-glass is a high-strength formulation for use when tensile strength is the most important property. C-glass was developed to resist attack from chemicals, mostly acids which destroy E-glass. T-glass is a North American variant of C-glass. A-glass is an industry term for cullet glass, often bottles, made into fibre. AR-glass is alkali-resistant glass. Most glass fibres have limited solubility in water but are very dependent on pH. Chloride ions will also attack and dissolve E-glass surfaces. A recent trend in the industry is to reduce or eliminate the boron content in the glass fibres.

Since E-glass does not really melt, but soften, the softening point is defined as "the temperature at which a 0.55 – 0.77 mm diameter fibre 235 mm long, elongates under its own weight at 1 mm/min when suspended vertically and heated at the rate of 5°C per minute". The strain point is reached when the glass has a viscosity of 1014.5 poise. The annealing point, which is the temperature where the internal stresses are reduced to an acceptable commercial limit in 15 minutes, is marked by a viscosity of 1013 poise.

Properties

Glass fibres are useful because of their high ratio of surface area to weight. However, the increased surface area makes them much more susceptible to chemical offence.

By trapping air within them, blocks of glass fibre make good thermal insulation, with a thermal conductivity of the order of 0.05 W/(mK).

Glass strengths are usually tested and reported for "virgin" fibres: those which have just been manufactured. The freshest, thinnest fibres are the strongest because the thinner fibres are more ductile. The more the surface is scratched, the less the resulting tenacity. Because glass has an amorphous structure, its properties are the same along the fibre and across the fibre. Humidity is an important factor in the tensile strength. Moisture is easily adsorbed, and can worsen microscopic cracks and surface defects, and lessen tenacity.

In opposite to carbon fibre, glass can undergo more elongation before it breaks. There is a correlation between bending diameter of the filament and the filament diameter. The viscosity of the molten glass is very important for manufacturing success. During drawing (pulling of the glass to reduce fibre circumference), the viscosity should be relatively low. If it is too high, the fibre will break during drawing. However, if it is too low, the glass will form droplets rather than drawing out into fibre.

Glass-reinforced Plastic

Glass-reinforced plastic (GRP) is a composite material or fibre-reinforced plastic made of a plastic reinforced by fine glass fibres. Like graphite-reinforced plastic, the composite material is commonly referred to by the name of its reinforcing fibres (fibreglass). Chemosetting plastics are normally used for GRP production—most often polyester (using butanone as a catalyst), but epoxy or vinylester are also used. The glass can be in the form of a chopped strand mat (CSM) or a woven fabric.

As with many other composite materials (such as reinforced concrete), the two materials act together, each overcoming the deficits of the other. Whereas the plastic resins are strong in compressive loading and relatively weak in tensile strength, the glass fibres are very strong in tension but have no strength against compression. By combining the two materials, GRP becomes a material that resists both compressive and tensile forces well. The two materials may be used uniformly or the glass can be specifically placed in those portions of the structure that will experience tensile loads.

Uses

Uses for regular fibreglass include mats, thermal insulation, electrical insulation, reinforcement of various materials, tent poles, sound absorption, heat- and corrosion-resistant fabrics, high-strength fabrics, arrows, bows and crossbows, translucent roofing panels, automobile bodies, electrical insulation and boat hulls.

Fibreglass Molding

Fibreglass molding is a process in which fibreglass reinforced resin plastics are formed into useful shapes.

Mold Making

The fibreglass mold process begins with an object known as the buck or plug. This is an exact representation of the object to be made, and can be made from a variety of different materials. Certain types of foam are commonly used.

After the plug has been formed, it is sprayed with a mold release agent. The release agent will allow the mold to be separated from the plug once it is finished. The mold release agent is a special wax, and/or PVA (Polyvinyl alcohol). Polyvinyl Alcohol, however, is said to have negative effects on the last mold's surface finish.

Once the plug has its release agent applied, gelcoat is applied with a roller, brush or specially-designed spray gun. The gelcoat is pigmented resin, and gives the mold surface a harder, more durable finish. Once the release agent and gelcoat are applied, layers of fibreglass and resin are laid-up onto the surface. The fibreglass used will typically be identical to that which will be used in the final product. In the laying-up process, a layer of fibreglass mat is applied, and resin is applied over it. A special roller is then used to remove air bubbles. If left in the curing resin, air bubbles would significantly reduce the strength of the finished mold. The fibreglass spray lay-up process is also used to produce molds, and can provide good filling of corners and can where a glass weave or mat may prove to be too stiff. Once the final layers of fibreglass are applied to the mould, the resin is allowed to set-up and treatment. Wedges are then driven between the plug and the mold in order to separate the two. Advanced techniques such as Resin Transfer Molding are also used.

Component Making

The component-making process involves building up a component on the fibreglass mold. The mold is a negative image of the component to be made, so the fibreglass will be introduced inside the mold, rather than around it.

As in the mold-making process, release agent is first applied to the mold. Colored gelcoat is then applied. Layers of fibreglass are then applied, using the same procedure as before. Once completed and cured, the component is separated from the mold using wedges, compressed air or both.

Fibre-reinforced Plastic

Fibre-reinforced plastic (FRP) (also fibre-reinforced polymer) are composite materials made of a polymer matrix reinforced with fibres. The fibres are usually fibreglass, carbon, or aramid, while the polymer is usually an epoxy, vinylester or polyester thermosetting plastic. FRPs are commonly used in the aerospace, automotive, marine, and construction industries.

Process Definition

A polymer is generally manufactured by polycondensation, Polymerization or polyaddition, when combined with various agents to enhance or in any way alter the material properties of polymers the result is referred to as a plastic. Composite plastics refer to those types of plastics that result from bonding two or more homogeneous materials with different material properties to derive a final product with certain desired material and mechanical properties. Fibre reinforced plastics are a category of composite plastics that specifically use fibrous materials to mechanically enhance the strength and elasticity of plastics. The original plastic material without fibre reinforcement is known as the matrix. The matrix is a tough but relatively weak plastic that is reinforced by stronger stiffer reinforcing filaments or fibres. The extent that strength and elasticity are enhanced in a fibre reinforced plastic depends on the mechanical properties of both the matrix and fibre, their volume relative to one another, and the fibre length and orientation within the matrix. Reinforcement of the matrix occurs by definition when the FRP material exhibits increased strength or elasticity relative to the strength and elasticity of the matrix alone.

History

Global polymer production on the scale present today began in the mid 20th century, when low material and productions costs, new production technologies and new product categories combined to make polymer production economical. Finally the industry matured in the late 1970's when world polymer production surpassed that of Steel, making polymers the ubiquitous material that it is today. Fibre reinforced plastics have been a significant aspect of this industry from the beginning. There are three important categories of fibre used in FRP, carbon, glass, and aramid. Glass fibre reinforcement was tested in military applications at the end of World War Two, Carbon fibre production began in the late 1950's and was used, though not widely, in British industry beginning in the early 1960's, aramid fibres were being produced around this time also, appearing first by the trade name Nomex by Dupont. Today each of these fibres is used widely in industry for any applications that require plastics with specific strength or elastic qualities. Glass fibres are the most common across all industries, although carbon fibre and carbon fibre aramid composites are widely found in aerospace, automotive and sporting good applications.

Process Description

FRP involves two distinct processes, the first is the process whereby the fibrous material is manufactured and formed, the second is the process whereby fibrous materials are bonded with the matrix during the molding process.

The Process of Fibre

The Manufacture of Fibre Fabric—Reinforcing Fibre is manufactured in both two dimensional and three dimensional orientations

Two Dimensional Fibre Reinforced Polymer are characterized by a laminated structure in which the fibres are only aligned along the plane in x-direction and y-direction of the material. This means that no fibres are aligned in the through thickness or the z-direction, this shortage of alignment in the though thickness can create a disadvantage in cost and processing. Costs and labor increase because conventional processing techniques used to fabricate composites, such as wet hand lay-up, autoclave and resin transfer molding, require a high amount of skilled labor to cut, stack and consolidate into a preformed component.

Three-dimensional Fibre Reinforced Polymer composites are materials with three dimensional fibre structures that incorporate fibres in thex-direction, y-direction and z-direction. The development of three-dimensional orientations arose from industry's need to reduce fabrication costs, to increase through-thickness mechanical properties, and to improve impact damage tolerance; all were problems associated with two dimensional fibre reinforced polymers.

The Manufacture of fibre preforms—Fibre preforms are how the fibres are manufactured before being bonded to the matrix, fibre performs are often manufactured in sheets, continuous mats, or as continuous filaments for spray applications. The four mega ways to manufacture the fibre preform is though the textile processing techniques of Weaving, braiding knitting and stitching.

Weaving may be done in a conventional manner to produce two-dimensional fibres as well in a multilayer weaving that can create three-dimensional fibres. However multilayer weaving is required to have multiple layers of warp yarns to create fibres in the z-direction creating a few disadvantages in manufacturing, namely the time to set up all the warp yarns on the loom. Therefore most multilayer weaving is currently used to produce relatively narrow width products, or high value products where the cost of the preform production is acceptable. Another of the main problems facing the use of multilayer woven fabrics is the difficulty in producing a fabric that contains fibres orientated with angles other than 0" and 90" to each other respectively.

The second mega way of manufacturing fibre preforms is Braiding. Braiding is suited to the manufacture of narrow width flat or tubular fabric and is not as capable as weaving in the production of large volumes of wide fabrics. Braiding is done over top of mandrels that vary in cross-sectional shape or dimension along their length. Braiding is limited to objects about a brick in size. Unlike the standard weaving process, braiding can produce fabric that contains fibres at 45 degrees angles to one another. Braiding three-dimensional fibres can be done using four step, two-step or Multilayer Interlock Braiding.Four row or step and column braiding utilizes a flat bed containing rows and columns of yarn carriers that form the shape of the desired preform. Extra carriers are added to the outside of the array, the precise location and quantity of which depends upon the exact preform shape and structure required. There are four separate sequences of row and column motion, which act to interlock the yarns and produce the braided preform. The yarns are mechanically forced into the structure between each step to consolidate the structure in a similar process to the use of a reed in weaving.Two-step braiding is unlike the four step process because the two-step includes a large number of yarns fixed in the axial direction and a fewer number of braiding yarns.

The process consists of two steps in which the braiding carriers move completely through the structure between the axial carriers. This relatively simple sequence of motions is capable of forming preforms of essentially any shape, including circular and hollow shapes. Unlike the four step process the two step process does not require mechanical compaction the motions involved in the process allows the braid to be pulled tight by yarn tension alone. The last type of braiding is multi-layer interlocking braiding that consists of a number of standard circular braiders being joined together to form a cylindrical braiding frame. This frame has a number of parallel braiding tracks around the circumference of the cylinder but the mechanism permits the transfer of yarn carriers between adjacent tracks forming a multilayer braided fabric with yarns interlocking to adjacent layers. The multilayer interlock braid differs from both the four step and two-step braids in that the interlocking yarns are primarily in the plane of the structure and thus do not significantly reduce the in-plane properties of the preform. The four step and two step processes produce a greater degree of interlinking as the braiding yarns travel through the thickness of the preform, but therefore contribute less to the in-plane performance of the preform. A disadvantage of the multilayer interlock equipment is that due to the conventional sinusoidal movement of the yarn carriers to form the preform, the equipment is disable to have the density of yarn carriers that is possible with the two step and four step machines.

Knitting fibre preforms can be done with the traditional methods of Warp and [Weft] Knitting, and the fabric produced is often regarded by many as two-dimensional fabric, but machines with two or more needle beds are capable of producing multilayer fabrics with yams that traverse between the layers. Developments in electronic controls for needle selection and knit loop transfer, and in the sophisticated mechanisms that allow specific areas of the fabric to be held and their movement controlled. This has allowed the fabric to form itself into the required three-dimensional preform shape with a minimum of material wastage.

Stitching is arguably the simplest of the four main textile manufacturing techniques and one that may be performed with the smallest investment in specialized machinery. Basically the stitching process consists of inserting a needle, carrying the stitch thread, through a stack of fabric layers to form a 3D structure. The advantages of stitching are that it is possible to stitch both dry and prepreg fabric, although the tackiness of the prepreg makes the process difficult and commonly creates more damage within the prepreg material than in the dry fabric. Stitching also utilizes the standard two-dimensional fabrics that are commonly in use within the composite industry therefore there is a sense of familiarity concerning the material systems. The use of standard fabric also permits a greater degree of flexibility in the fabric lay-up of the component than is possible with the other textile processes, which have restrictions on the fibre orientations that may be produced.

Processes of Molding

There are two distinct categories of molding processes using FRP plastics; under this composite molding and wet molding. Composite molding uses Prepreg FRP, meaning the plastics are fibre reinforced before being put through further the molding process. Sheets of Prepreg FRP are heated or compressed in different ways to create geometric shapes. Wet molding combines fibre reinforcement and the matrix or resist during the molding process. The kinds forms of composite and wet molding, are listed below.

Composite Molding

Bladder Molding—Individual sheets of prepreg material are laid -up and placed in a female-style mold along with a balloon-like bladder. The mold is closed and placed in a heated press. Finally, the bladder is pressurized forcing the layers of material against the mold walls. The part is removed and cured from the hot mold. Bladder molding is a closed molding process with a relatively short cure cycle between 15 and 60 minutes making it ideal for making complex hollow geometric shapes at competitive costs.

Compression Molding

A "preform" or "charge", of SMC, BMC or sometimes prepreg fabric, is placed into mold cavity. The mold is closed and the material is compacted & cured inside by pressure and heat. Compression molding offers excellent detailing for geometric shapes ranging from pattern and relief detailing to complex curves and creative forms, to precision engineering all within a maximum curing time of 20 minutes.

Autoclave/Vacuum Bag

Individual sheets of prepreg material are laid-up and placed in an open mold. The material is covered with release film, bleeder/breather material and a vacuum bag. A vacuum is pulled on part and the whole mold is placed into an autoclave (heated pressure vessel). The part is cured with a continuous vacuum to extract entrapped gasses from laminate. This is a very common process in the aerospace industry because it affords precise control over the molding process due to along slow cure cycle that is anywhere from one to two hours. This precise control creates the exact laminate geometric forms needed to ensure strength and safety in the aerospace industry, but it is also slow and labor intensive, meaning costs often confine it to the aerospace industry.

Mandrel Wrapping

Sheets of prepreg material are wrapped around a aluminum or steel mandrel. The prepreg material is compacted by nylon or polypropylene cello tape. Parts are typically batch cured by hanging in an oven. After cure the cello and mandrel are removed leaving a hollow carbon tube. This process creates strong and robust hollow carbon tubes.

Resing Layup

Fibre reinforcing fabric is placed in an open mold and then saturated with a wet [resin] by pouring it over the fabric and working it into the fabric and mold. The mold is then left so that the resin will cure, usually at room temperature, though heat is sometimes used to ensure a proper curing process. Glass fibres are most commonly used for this process, the results are widely known as fibreglass, and is used to make common products like canoes, skis, kayaks and surf boards.

Chopper Gun

Continuous strand of fibreglass are pushed through a hand-held gun that both chops the strands and combines them with a catalyzed resin such as polyester. The impregnated chopped glass is shot onto the mold surface in whatever thickness the design and human operator think is appropriate. This process is good for large production runs at economical cost, but produces geometric shapes with less strength then other molding processes and has poor dimensional tolerance.

Winding Filament

Machines pull fibre bundles through a wet bath of resin and wound over a rotating steel mandrel in specific orientations Parts are cured either room temperature or elevated temperatures. Mandrel is extracted, leaving a final geometric shape but can be left in few cases.

Pultrusion

Fibre bundles and slit fabrics are pulled through a wet bath of resin and formed into the rough part shape. Saturated material is extruded from a heated closed die curing while being continuously pulled through die. Process is could for any extruded material and geometric shape such as roadside reflector poles and ladder rails.

RTM & VARTM

Fabrics are placed into a mold which wet resin is then injected into. Resin is typically pressurized and forced into a cavity which is under vacuum in the RTM process. Resin is entirely pulled into cavity under vacuum in the VARTM process. This molding process allows precise tolerances and detailed shaping but can sometimes fail to fully saturate the fabric leading to weak spots in the last shape.

Limitations and Advantages

FRP allows the alignment the glass fibres of thermoplastics to suite specific design programs. Specifying the orientation of reinforcing fibres can increase the strength and resistance to deformation of the polymer. Glass reinforced polymers are strongest and most resistive to deforming forces when the polymers fibres are parallel to the force being exerted, and are weakest when the fibres are perpendicular. Thus this ability is at once both an advantage or a limitation depending on the context of use. Weak spots of perpendicular fibres can be used for natural hinges and connections, but can also lead to material failure when production processes fail to properly orientate fibres parallel to expected forces. When forces are exerted perpendicular to the orientation of fibres the strength and elasticity of the polymer is less then the matrix alone. In cast resin components made of glass reinforced polymers such as UP and EP, the orientation of fibres can be orientated in two-dimensional and three-dimensional weaves. This means that when forces are possibly perpendicular to one orientation, they are parallel to another orientation; this eliminates the potential for weak spots in the polymer.

Failure Modes

Structural failure can occur in FRP materials when : Tensile forces stretch the matrix more then the fibres, causing the material to shear at the interface between matrix and fibres.

Tensile forces near the end of the fibres exceed the tolerances of the matrix, separating the fibres from the matrix.

Tensile forces can also exceed the tolerances of the fibres causing the fibres themselves to fracture leading to material failure.

Material Requirements Process

The Matrix must also meet certain requirements in order to first be suitable for the FRP process and ensure a successful reinforcement of itself. The matrix must be able to properly saturate, and bond with the fibres within a suitable curing period. The matrix should preferably bond chemically with the fibre reinforcement for maximum adhesion. The matrix must also completely envelope the fibres to protect them from cuts and notches that would reduce their strength, and to transfer forces to the fibres. The fibres must also be kept alone from each other so that if failure occurs it is localised as much as possible, and if failure occurs the matrix must also debond from the fibre for same reasons. Finally the matrix should be of a plastic that remains chemically and physically stable during and after reinforcement and molding processes. To be suitable for reinforcement material fibre additives must increase the tensile strength and modulus of elasticity of the matrix and meet the following conditions; Fibres must exceed critical fibre content; the strength and rigidity of fibres itself must exceed the strength and rigidity of the matrix alone; and there must be optimum bonding between fibres and matrix

Material of Glass Fibre

FRP plastics use textile glass fibres; textile fibres are different from other types of glass fibres used for insulative applications. Textile glass fibres begin as varying combinations of SiO2, Al2O3, B2O3, CaO, or MgO in powder form. These mixtures are then heated through a direct melt process to temperatures around 1300 degrees Celsius, after which dies are used to extrude filaments of glass fibre in diameter ranging from 9 to 17 μm. These filaments are then wound into larger threads and spun onto bobbins for transportation and further processing. Glass fibre is by far the most popular means to reinforce plastic and thus enjoys a wealth of production processes, some of which are applicable to aramid and carbon fibres as well owing to their shared fibrous qualities.

Material Processes of Glass Fibre

Roving—Process where filaments are spun into larger diameter threads. These threads are then commonly used for woven reinforcing glass fabrics and mats, and in spray applications.

Fibre Fabric—Web-form fabric reinforcing material that has both warp and weft directions

Fibre Mats—Web-form non-woven mats of glass fibres. Mats are manufactured in cut dimensions with chopped fibres, or in continuous mats using continuous fibres.

Chopped Fibre Glass—Processes where lengths of glass threads are cut between 3 and 26 mm, threads are then used in plastics most commonly intended for molding processes.

Glass Fibre Short Strands—Short 0.2 – 0.3 mm strands of glass fibres that are used to reinforce thermoplastics most commonly for injection molding.

4

Carbon Fibre

Carbon fibre or (alternatively called carbon fibre, graphite fibre, graphite fibre or carbon graphite) is a material consisting of extremely thin fibres about 0.005–0.010 mm in diameter and composed mostly of carbon atoms. The carbon atoms are bonded together in microscopic crystals that are more or less aligned parallel to the long axis of the fibre. The crystal alignment makes the fibre very strong for its size. Several thousand carbon fibres are twisted together to form a yarn, which may be used by itself or woven into a fabric. Carbon fibre has many different weave patterns and can be combined with a plastic resin and wound or molded to form composite materials such as carbon fibre reinforced plastic (also referenced as carbon fibre) to provide a high strength-to-weight ratio material. The density of carbon fibre is also considerably lower than the density of steel, making it ideal for applications requiring low weight. The properties of carbon fibre such as high tensile strength, low weight, and low thermal expansion make it very popular in civil engineering, aerospace, military, and motorsports, along with other competition sports.

Carbon Fibres History

Dr. Roger Bacon in 1958, created high-performance carbon fibres at the Union Carbide Parma Technical Center, located outside of Cleveland, Ohio. Those fibres were manufactured by heating strands of rayon until they carbonized. This process proved to be inefficient, as the resulting fibres contained only about 20% carbon and had low strength and stiffness properties. In the early 1960s, a process was developed using polyacrylonitrile (PAN) as a base material. This had produced a carbon fibre that contained about 55% carbon and had much better properties. The polyacrylonitrile (PAN) conversion process quickly became the primary method for producing carbon fibres.

The high potential strength of carbon fibre was realized in 1963 in a process developed at the Royal Aircraft Establishment at Farnborough in the UK. The process was patented by the Ministry of Defense and then licensed by the NRDC to three British companies: Rolls-Royce, already making carbon fibre, Morganite and Courtaulds. They were able to establish industrial carbon fibre production facilities within a few years, and Rolls-Royce took advantage of the new material's properties to break into the American market with its RB-211 aero-engine.

Even then, though, there was public concern over the ability of British industry to make the best of this breakthrough. In 1969 a House of Commons select committee inquiry into carbon fibre prophetically asked: "How then is the country to reap the maximum benefit without it becoming yet another British invention to be exploited more successfully overseas?" Ultimately, this concern was justified. One by one the licensees pulled out of carbon-fibre manufacture. Rolls-Royce's interest was in state-of-the-art aero-engine applications. Its own production process was to enable it to be leader in the use of carbon-fibre reinforced plastics. In-house production would typically cease once reliable commercial sources became available.

Unfortunately, Rolls-Royce pushed the state-of-the-art too far, too quickly, in using carbon fibre in the engine's compressor blades, which proved vulnerable to damage from bird impact. What seemed a great British technological triumph in 1968 quickly became a disaster as Roll-Royce's ambitious schedule for the RB-211 was endangered. Indeed, Rolls-Royce's problems became so great that the company was eventually nationalised by Edward Heath's Conservative government in 1971 and the carbon-fibre production plant sold off to form Bristol Composites.

Given the limited market for a more expensive product of variable quality, Morganite also decided that carbon-fibre production was peripheral to its core business, leaving Courtaulds as the only mega UK manufacturer.

The company continued making carbon fibre, developing two main markets: aerospace and sports equipment.The speed of production and the quality of the product were improved.

Continuing collaboration with the staff at Farnborough proved helpful in the quest for higher quality, but, ironically, Courtaulds's big advantage as manufacturer of the "Courtelle" precursor now became a weakness. Low cost and ready availability were potential advantages, but the water-based inorganic process used to produce Courtelle made it susceptible to impurities that did not affect the organic process used by other carbon-fibre manufacturers.

Nevertheless, during the 1980s Courtaulds continued to be a major supplier of carbon fibre for the sports-goodsmarket, with Mitsubishi its main customer. But a move to expand, including building a production plant in California, turned out badly. The investment did not produce the anticipated returns, leading to a decision to pull out of the area. Courtaulds ceased carbon-fibre production in 1991, though ironically the one surviving UK carbon-fibre manufacturer continued to thrive making fibre based on Courtaulds's precursor. Inverness-based RK Carbon Fibres Ltd has concentrated on producing carbon fibre for industrial applications, and thus does not need to compete at the quality levels reached by overseas manufacturers.

On January 14, 1969 Carr Reinforcements (Stockport, England) wove a carbon fibre fabric.

During the 1970s, experimental work to find alternative raw materials led to the introduction of carbon fibres made from a petroleum pitch derived from oil processing. These fibres contained about 85% carbon and had excellent flexural strength.

Structure and Properties

Carbon fibres are the closest to asbestos in a number of properties. Every carbon filament thread is a bundle of many thousand carbon filaments. A single such filament is a thin tube with a diameter of 5–8 micrometers and consists almost exclusively of carbon.

The atomic structure of carbon fibre is same to that of graphite, consisting of sheets of carbon atoms (graphene sheets) arranged in a regular hexagonal pattern. The difference lies in the way these sheets interlock. Graphite is a crystalline material in which the sheets are stacked parallel to each other in regular fashion. The intermolecular forces between the sheets are relatively weak Van der Waals forces, giving graphite its soft and brittle characteristics. Depending upon the precursor to make the fibre, carbon fibre can be turbostratic or graphitic, or have a hybrid structure with both graphitic and turbostratic parts present. In turbostratic carbon fibre the sheets of carbon atoms are haphazardly folded, or crumpled, together. Carbon fibres derived from Polyacrylonitrile (PAN) are turbostratic, whereas carbon fibres derived from mesophase pitch are graphitic after heat treatment at temperatures exceeding 2200 C. Turbostratic carbon fibres tend to have high tensile strength, whereas heat-treated mesophase-pitch-derived carbon fibres have high Young's modulus and high thermal conductivity.

Applications

Carbon fibre is most notably used to reinforce composite materials, particularly the class of materials known as Carbon fibre or graphite reinforced polymers. Non-polymer materials can also be used as the matrix for carbon fibres. Due to the formation of metal carbides (i.e., water-soluble AlC) and corrosion considerations, carbon has seen limited success in metal matrix composite applications. Reinforced carbon-carbon (RCC) consists of carbon fibre-reinforced graphite, and is used structurally in high-temperature applications. The fibre also finds use in filtration of high-temperature gases, as an electrode with high surface area and impeccable corrosion resistance, and as an anti-static component. Molding a thin layer of carbon fibres significantly improves fire resistance of polymers or thermoset composites because dense, compact layer of carbon fibres efficiently reflects heat..

Synthesis

Each carbon filament is made out of long, thin filaments of carbon sometimes transformed to graphite. A common method of making carbon filaments is the oxidation and thermal pyrolysis of polyacrylonitrile (PAN), a polymer based on acrylonitrile used in the creation of synthetic materials. Like all polymers, polyacrylonitrile molecules are long chains, which are aligned in the process of drawing continuous filaments. A common method of manufacture involves heating the PAN to approximately 300 °C in air, which breaks many of the hydrogen bonds and oxidizes the material. The oxidized PAN is then placed into a furnace having an inert atmosphere of a gas such as argon, and heated to approximately 2000 °C, which induces graphitization of the material, changing the molecular bond structure. When heated in the correct conditions, these chains bond side-to-side (ladder polymers), forming narrow graphene sheets which eventually merge to form a single, jelly roll-shaped or round filament. The result is usually 93–95% carbon. Lower-quality fibre can be manufactured using pitch or rayon as the precursor instead of PAN. The carbon can become further enhanced, as high modulus, or high strength carbon, by heat treatment processes. Carbon heated in the range of 1500-2000 °C (carbonization) exhibits the highest tensile strength (820,000 psi or 5,650 MPa or 5,650 N/mm^2), while carbon fibre heated from 2500 to 3000 °C (graphitizing) exhibits a higher modulus of elasticity (77,000,000 psi or 531 GPa or 531 kN/mm^2).

Textile

Precursors for carbon fibres are PAN, rayon and pitch. Carbon fibre filament yarns are used in several processing techniques: the direct uses are for prepregging, filament winding, weaving, pultrusion, braiding etc. Carbon fibre yarn is rated by the linear density (weight per unit length = 1 g/1000 m = tex) or by number of filaments per yarn count, in thousands. For example, 200 tex for 3,000 filaments of carbon fibre is three times as strong as 1,000 carbon fibres but is also three times as heavy. This thread can then be used to weave a carbon fibre filament fabric or cloth. The appearance of this fabric generally depends on the linear density of the yarn and the weave chosen. Some commonly used types of weave are twill, satin and plain.

Manufacturers of Corbon Fibres

Toray Industries—Toray Industries, Inc. (Kabushiki-gaisha?) (TYO: 3402) is a multinational corporation headquartered in Japan that specializes in industrial products centered around technologies in organic synthetic chemistry, polymer chemistry, and biochemistry. The founding business areas therefore were fibres and textiles, as well as plastics and chemicals. The company has also diversified into areas such as pharmaceuticals, medical products, electronics, IT-products, housing and engineering, as well as advanced composite materials.

Operations

Toray is currently the world's largest producer of carbon fibre, and Japan's largest producer of synthetic fibre (ref)

The world headquarters office is located in Nihonbashi Mitsui Tower, 1-1, Nihonbashi-Muromachi 2-chome, Tokyo, Japan

Toray sponsors the Pan Pacific Open Tennis Tournament

Toray sponsors the Digital Creation Awards, in its 10th year in 2005

Toray has operations in 19 countries: China, Japan, Hong Kong China, South Korea, Taiwan, Indonesia, Malaysia, Singapore, Thailand, Czech Republic, France, Germany, Italy, Netherlands, Switzerland, United Kingdom, and the USA.

Toho Tenax—Toho Tenax has been a member of the Teijin Group since 2000. Toho Tenax is an international company that supplies customers throughout the world with carbon fibre under the trade name Tenax. Tenax is produced by Toho Tenax in Japan, the US and in Germany.

Carbon fibre and the main products, oxidized PAN fibre and advanced composite material.

Hexcel

Hexcel (NYSE: HXL) is a materials company incorporated in Delaware and headquartered in Stamford, Connecticut that manufactures advanced structural materials. The company was founded in 1946 and its first product was supplying honeycomb for the construction of military bombers.

As of 2005, Hexcel's business was broken down into three divisions: reinforcements, composites and structures. It sells to a number of industries such as aerospace, defense, automotive, electronic, marine, wind energy and recreation.

As it states on its website (www.hexcel.com): "Hexcel is the largest US producer of carbon fibre; the world's largest weaver of structural fabrics; the leading global producer of fibreglass electronic materials; the number one producer of composite materials such as honeycomb, prepreg, film adhesives and sandwich panels; and a leading manufacturer of composite parts and structures."

Hexcel has manufacturing facilities in West Valley City, Utah, Casa Grande, Arizona, Seguin, Texas, Decatur, Alabama, Burlington, Washington, Parla, Spain, Duxford, Cambridgeshire, Neumarkt im Hausruckkreis, Austria, Tianjin, China, Les Avenieres, France, Dagneux, France, and Welkenraedt, Belgium.

Hexcel is publicly traded on the New York Stock Exchange under the ticker symbol HXL.

Mitsubishi Rayon

Mitsubishi Rayon Co., Ltd. (TYO: 3404) (est. August 31, 1933) is a Japanese company that manufactures chemicals, plastics, and fibres. It is Japan's biggest acrylic fibre maker. Mitsubishi Rayon is one of the textile companies tracked by the Nikkei 225 on the

Tokyo Stock Exchange. In addition to the primary acryrilic fibre, Mitsubishi Rayon also is one of the top makers of golf shafts, now largely popular on the PGA Tour and now gaining popularity by consumers. Current Success in the shaft market includes the making of new golf clubs by brands such as Ping (golf), Callaway Golf, Nike, Titleist, and TaylorMade sold manufactured with a Mitsubishi Rayon shaft.

Cytec Industries

Cytec Industries, based in Woodland Park (formerly West Paterson) is a specialty chemicals and materials technology company with pro-forma sales in 2004, including the Surface Specialties acquisition, of approximately $3.0 billion. Cytec is a result of its spin-off from American Cyanamid Company. Its growth strategies are based on developing technologically advanced customer solutions for global markets, including coatings, mining, aerospace, plastics and water treatment.

The motto for Cytec is "Technology ahead of its time".

Cytec currently has about 7,000 employees in Europe, North and South America, Asia and Australia. It is listed in NYSE with stock symbol "CYT".

Schunk Group

The Schunk Group is a German manufacturing conglomerate composed of 75 subsidiary companies in 28 countries. It produces carbon brushes, graphite products, and moulded bipolar plates. Schunk is based in Heuchelheim, Germany, but employees 7,352 people worldwide. In 2006, Schunk Group's consolidated worldwide turnover was 752.9 million Euros, up from 643.5 million in 2004.

The Schunk Group was founded in 1913 in Fulda, Germany by Ludwig Schunk, together with technician Karl Ebe, as carbon brush factory Schunk & Ebe OHG.

The Schunk Group's subsidiary companies include:

Schunk Hightemperature (based in Giessen, Germany)

Schunk Vienna (Vienna, Austria)

Schunk Nordiska AB

Schunk Metall und Kunststoff GmbH

Schunk Ingenieurkeramik GmbH

Schunk Kohlenstofftechnik GmbH

Schunk Materials

SGL Carbon

SGL Carbon (FWB: SGL) is one of the world's leading manufacturers of products from carbon. The company portfolio ranges from carbon and graphite materials to carbon fibres and composites. A broad base of materials, the deployment of the relevant technologies and many years of application and engineering expertise are the basis of the company's success.

With 38 production sites across the globe (20 in Europe, 12 in North America and 6 in Asia), as well as a service network in over 100 countries, the SGL Group is a globally operating company. In the course of the company's realignment the organization structure was realigned to February 1, 2007 and streamlined from what used to be three business segments to two. Three globally aligned business units operate within these segments. Wiesbaden, Germany is the headquarter of company.

The SGL share has been included in the German MDAX since 1995. In 2007, on sales revenus of 1,373.0 million, the company generated net income of 130.9 million. To the end of the 2007 fiscal year, the company employed 5,249 staff world-wide.

5

Optical Fibre

An Optical fibre (or fibre) is a glass or plastic fibre that carries light along its length. Fibre optics is the overlap of applied science and engineering concerned with the design and application of optical fibres. Optical fibres are highly used in fibre-optic communications, which permits transmission over longer distances and at higher bandwidths (data rates) than other forms of communications. Fibres are used instead of metal wires because signals travel along them with less loss, and they are also immune to electromagnetic interference. Fibres are also used for illumination, and are wrapped in bundles so they can be used to carry images, thus allowing viewing in tight spaces. Specially designed fibres are used for a variety of other applications, including sensors and fibre lasers.

Light is kept in the core of the optical fibre by total internal reflection. This causes the fibre to act as a waveguide. Fibres which support many propagation paths or transverse modes are called multi-mode fibres (MMF), while those which may only support a single mode are called single-mode fibres (SMF). Multi-mode fibres generally have a larger core diameter, and are used for short-distance communication links and for applications where high power must be transmitted. Single-mode fibres are used for most communication links longer than 550 meters (600 yards). Joining lengths of optical fibre is more complex than joining electrical cable or wire. The ends of the fibres must be carefully cleaved, and then spliced together either mechanically or by fusing them together with an electric arc. Special connectors are used to make removable connections.

History of Optical Fibre

Guiding of light by refraction, the principle that makes fibre optics possible, was first demonstrated by Daniel Colladon and Jacques Babinet in Paris in the early 1840s. John Tyndall included a demonstration of it in his public lectures in London a dozen years later. Tyndall also wrote about the property of complete internal reflection in an in introductory book about the nature of light in 1870: "When the light passes from air into water, the refracted ray is bent towards the perpendicular... When the ray passes from water to air it is bent from the perpendicular... If the angle which the ray in water encloses with the perpendicular to the surface be greater than 48 degrees, the ray will not quit the water at all: it will be totally reflected at the surface.... The angle which signs the limit where total reflexion begins is called the limiting angle of the medium. For water this angle is 48°27', for flint glass it is 38°41', while for diamond it is 23°42'."

Practical applications, such as close internal illumination during dentistry, appeared early in the twentieth century. Image transmission through tubes was demonstrated independently by the radio experimenter Clarence Hansell and the television pioneer John Logie Baird in the 1920s. The principle was first used for internal medical examinations by Heinrich Lamm in the following decade. In 1952, physicist Narinder Singh Kapany conducted experiments that led to the invention of optical fibre. Modern optical fibres, where the glass fibre is coated with a transparent cladding to offer a more suitable refractive index, appeared later in the decade. Development then focused on fibre bundles for image transmission. The first fibre optic semi-flexible gastroscope was patented by Basil Hirschowitz, C. Wilbur Peters, and Lawrence E. Curtiss, researchers at the University of Michigan, in 1956. In the process of developing the gastroscope, Curtiss produced the first glass-clad fibres; previous optical fibres had relied on air or impractical oils and waxes as the low-index cladding material. A variety of other image transmission applications soon followed.

In 1965, George A. Hockham and Charles K. Kao of the British company Standard Telephones and Cables (STC) were the first to promote the idea that the attenuation in optical fibres could be reduced below 20 decibels per kilometer, allowing fibres to be a practical medium for communication. They proposed that the attenuation in fibres available at the time was caused by impurities, which could be removed, rather than fundamental physical effects such as scattering. The crucial attenuation level of 20 dB/km was first achieved in 1970, by researchers Robert D. Maurer, Donald Keck, Peter C. Schultz, and Frank Zimar working for American glass maker Corning Glass Works, now Corning Incorporated. They demonstrated a fibre with 17 dB/km attenuation by doping silica glass with titanium. A few years later they produced a fibre with only 4 dB/km attenuation using germanium dioxide as the core dopant. Such low attenuations ushered in optical fibre telecommunications and enabled the Internet. In 1981, General Electric produced fused quartz ingots that could be drawn into fibre optic strands 25 miles (40 km) long.

Attenuations in modern optical cables are far less than those in electrical copper cables, leading to long-haul fibre connections with repeater distances of 50–80 km (30–50 miles). The erbium-doped fibre amplifier, which reduced the cost of long-distance fibre systems by reducing or even in many cases eliminating the need for optical-electrical-optical repeaters, was co-developed by teams led by David N. Payne of the University of Southampton, and Emmanuel Desurvire at Bell Laboratories in 1986. The more robust optical fibre generally used today utilizes glass for both core and sheath and is therefore less prone to aging processes. It was invented by Gerhard Bernsee in 1973 of Schott Glass in Germany.

In 1991, the emerging field of photonic crystals led to the development of photonic-crystal fibre which guides light by means of diffraction from a periodic structure, rather than total internal reflection. The first photonic crystal fibres became commercially available in 2000. Photonic crystal fibres can be designed to carry higher power than conventional fibre, and their wavelength dependent properties may be manipulated to improve their performance in certain applications.

Applications

Optical Fibre Communication—Optical fibre can be used as a medium for telecommunication and networking because it is flexible and can be bundled as cables. Especially it is advantageous for long-distance communications, because light propagates through the fibre with little attenuation compared to electrical cables. This allows long distances to be spanned with few repeaters. Additionally, the per-channel light signals propagating in the fibre may be modulated at rates as high as 111 gigabits per second, although 10 or 40 Gb/s is typical in deployed systems. Every fibre can carry many independent channels, each using a different wavelength of light (wavelength-division multiplexing (WDM)). The net data rate (data rate without overhead bytes) per fibre is the per-channel data rate reduced by the FEC overhead, multiplied by the number of channels.

Over short distances, such as networking within a building, fibre saves space in cable ducts because a single fibre can carry much more data than a single electrical cable.[vague] Fibre is also immune to electrical interference; there is no cross-talk between signals in different cables and no pickup of environmental noise. Non-armored fibre cables do not conduct electricity, which makes fibre a good solution for protecting communications equipment located in high voltage environments such as power generation facilities, or metal communication structures prone to lightning strikes. They can also be used in environments where explosive fumes are present, without danger of ignition. Wiretapping is much difficult compared to electrical connections, and there are concentric dual core fibres that are said to be tap-proof.

Although fibres may be made out of transparent plastic, glass, or a combination of the two, the fibres used in long-distance telecommunications applications are always glass, because of the lower optical attenuation. Both multi-mode and single-mode fibres are used in communications, with multi-mode fibre used mostly for short distances, up to 550 m (600 yards), and single-mode fibre used for longer distance links. Because of the tighter tolerances required to couple light into and between single-mode fibres (core diameter about 10 micrometers), receivers, single-mode transmitters, amplifiers and other components are commonly more expensive than multi-mode components.

Examples of applications are TOSLINK, Fibre distributed data interface, Synchronous optical networking.[jargon]

Fibre Optic Sensors

Fibres have many uses in remote sensing. In some applications, the sensor is itself an optical fibre. In other cases, fibre is used to connect a non-fibreoptic sensor to a measurement system. Depending on the application, fibre may be used because of its small size, or the fact that no electrical power is needed at the distance location, or because many sensors can be multiplexed along the length of a fibre by using different wavelengths of light for each sensor, or by sensing the time delay as light passes along the fibre through every sensor. Time delay can be determined using a device such as an optical time-domain reflectometer.

Optical fibres may be used as sensors to measure strain, pressure, temperature and other quantities by modifying a fibre so that the quantity to be measured modulates the intensity, polarization, phase, wavelength or transit time of light in the fibre. Sensors that vary the intensity of light are the simplest, since only a simple source and detector are required. A particularly useful feature of such fibre optic sensors is that they can, if required, provide distributed sensing over distances of up to one meter.

Extrinsic fibre optic sensors use an optical fibre cable, normally a multi-mode one, to transmit modulated light from either a non-fibre optical sensor, or an electronic sensor connected to an optical transmitter. A major benefit of extrinsic sensors is their ability to reach places which are otherwise inaccessible. An example is the measurement of temperature inside aircraft jet engines by using a fibre to transmit radiation into a radiation pyrometer located outside the engine. Extrinsic sensors can also be used in the same way to measure the internal temperature of electrical transformers, where the extreme electromagnetic fields present make other measurement techniques impossible. Extrinsic sensors are used to measure rotation, displacement, vibration, acceleration, torque, velocity, and twisting.

Optical Fibres : Other Uses

Fibres are highly used in illumination applications. They are used as light guides in medical and other applications where bright light needs to be shone on a target without a clear line-of-sight path. In some buildings, optical fibres are used to route sunlight from the roof to other parts of the building (see non-imaging optics). Optical fibre illumination is also used for decorative applications, including art, signs, and artificial Christmas trees. Swarovski boutiques use optical fibres to illuminate their crystal showcases from many different angles while only employing one light source. Optical fibre is an intrinsic part of the light-transmitting concrete building product, LiTraCon.

In imaging optics optical fibre is also used. A coherent bundle of fibres is used, sometimes along with lenses, for a long, thin imaging device called an endoscope, which is used to view objects by a small hole, Medical endoscopes are used for minimally invasive exploratory or surgical procedures (endoscopy). Industrial endoscopes (see fibrescope or borescope) are used for inspecting anything hard to reach, such as jet engine interiors.

In spectroscopy, optical fibre bundles are used to transmit light from a spectrometer to a substance which cannot be placed inside the spectrometer itself, in order to analyze its composition. A spectrometer analyzes substances by bouncing light off of and through them. By using fibres, a spectrometer can be used to study objects that are too large to fit inside, or gasses, or reactions which occur in pressure vessels.

An optical fibre doped with certain rare-earth elements such as erbium can be used as the gain medium of a laser or optical amplifier. Rare-earth doped optical fibres can be used to provide signal amplification by splicing a short section of doped fibre into a regular (undoped) optical fibre line. The doped fibre is optically pumped with a second laser wavelength that is coupled into the line in addition to the signal wave. Both wavelengths of light are transmitted through the doped fibre, which transfers energy from the second pump wavelength to the signal wave. The process that causes the amplification is stimulated emission.

Optical fibres doped with a wavelength shifter are used to collect scintillation light in physics experiments.

Optical fibre can be used to supply a low level of power (around one watt) to electronics situated in a difficult electrical environment. Examples of this are electronics in high-powered antenna elements and measurement devices used in high voltage transmission equipment.

Operation Principle

An optical fibre is a cylindrical dielectric waveguide that transmits light along its axis, by the process of complete internal reflection. The fibre consists of a core surrounded by a cladding layer. To confine the optical signal in the core, the refractive index of the core must be greater than that of the cladding. The boundary between the core and cladding may either be abrupt, in step-index fibre, or gradual, in graded-index fibre.

Repraction Index

The index of refraction is a way of measuring the speed of light in a material. Light travels fastest in a vacuum, such as outer space. The actual speed of light in a vacuum is about 300 million meters (186 thousand miles) per second. Index of refraction is calculated by dividing the speed of light in a vacuum by the speed of light in some other medium. The index of refraction of a vacuum is therefore 1, by definition. The typical value for the cladding of an optical fibre is 1.46. The core value is typically 1.48. The larger the index of refraction, the slower light travels in that medium.

Complete Internal Reflection

When light traveling in a dense medium hits a boundary at a steep angle (larger than the "critical angle" for the boundary), the light will be completely reflected. This effect is used in optical fibres to confine light in the core. Light travels along the fibre bouncing back and forth off of the boundary. Because the light must strike the boundary with an angle greater than the critical angle, only light that enters the fibre within a certain range of angles can travel down the fibre without leaking out. This range of angles is called the acceptance cone of the fibre. The size of this acceptance cone is a function of the refractive index difference between the fibre's core and cladding.

In simpler terms, there is a maximum angle from the fibre axis at which light may enter the fibre so that it will propagate, or travel, in the core of the fibre. The sine of this maximum angle is the numerical aperture (NA) of the fibre. Fibre with a larger NA requires less precision to splice and work with than fibre with a smaller NA. Single-mode fibre has a small NA.

Fibre (Multi-mode)

Fibre with large core diameter (greater than 10 micrometers) may be analyzed by geometric optics. Such fibre is called multi-mode fibre, from the electromagnetic analysis (see below). In a step-index multi-mode fibre, rays of light are guided along the fibre core by total internal reflection. Rays that meet the core-cladding boundary at a high angle (measured relative to a line normal to the boundary), greater than the critical angle for this boundary, are completely reflected. The critical angle (minimum angle for total internal reflection) is determined by the difference in index of refraction between the core and cladding materials. Rays that meet the boundary at a low angle are refracted from the core into the cladding, and do not convey light and hence information along the fibre. The critical angle determines the acceptance angle of the fibre, often reported as a numerical aperture. A high numerical aperture allows light to propagate down the fibre in rays both close to the axis and at various angles, allowing efficient coupling of light into the fibre. However, this high numerical aperture increases the amount of dispersion as rays at different angles have different path lengths and therefore take different times to traverse the fibre. A low numerical aperture may therefore be desirable.

In graded-index fibre, the index of refraction in the core decreases continuously between the axis and the cladding. This causes light rays to bend smoothly as they approach the cladding, rather than reflecting abruptly from the core-cladding boundary. The resulting curved paths reduce multi-path dispersion because high angle rays pass more through the lower-index periphery of the core, rather than the high-index center. The index profile is chosen to minimize the difference in axial propagation speeds of the various rays in the fibre. This ideal index profile is very close to a parabolic relationship between the index and the distance from the axis.

Fibre (Single-mode)

Fibre with a core diameter less than about ten times the wavelength of the propagating light cannot be modeled using geometric optics. Instead, it must be analyzed as an electromagnetic structure, by solution of Maxwell's equations as reduced to the electromagnetic wave equation. The electromagnetic analysis may also be required to understand behaviors such as speckle that occur when coherent light propagates in multi-mode fibre. As an optical waveguide, the fibre supports one or more confined transverse modes by which light can propagate along the fibre. Fibre supporting only one mode is called single-mode or mono-mode fibre. The behavior of larger-core multi-mode fibre can also be modeled using the wave equation, which shows that such fibre supports more than one mode of propagation (hence the name). The results of such modeling of multi-mode fibre approximately agree with the predictions of geometric optics, if the fibre core is large enough to support more than some modes.

The waveguide analysis shows that the light energy in the fibre is not completely confined in the core. Instead, especially in single-mode fibres, a significant fraction of the energy in the bound mode travels in the cladding as an evanescent wave.

The most common kind of single-mode fibre has a core diameter of 8–10 micrometers and is designed for use in the near infrared. The mode structure depends on the wavelength of the light used, so that this fibre actually supports a small number of additional modes at visible wavelengths. Multi-mode fibre, by comparison, is manufactured with core diameters as small as 50 micrometers and as large as hundreds of micrometres. The normalized frequency V for this fibre should be less than the first zero of the Bessel function J0 (approximately 2.405).

Fibre for Special Purpose

Some special-purpose optical fibre is constructed with a non-cylindrical core and/or cladding layer, usually with an elliptical or rectangular cross-section. These include polarization-maintaining fibre and fibre designed to suppress whispering gallery mode propagation.

Photonic crystal fibre is made with a regular pattern of index variation (often in the form of cylindrical holes that run along the length of the fibre). Such fibre uses diffraction effects instead of or in addition to total internal reflection, to confine light to the fibre's core. The properties of the fibre can be tailored to a wide variety of applications.

Manufacturing

Materials—Glass optical fibres are almost always made from silica, but some other materials, such as fluorozirconate, fluoroaluminate, and chalcogenide glasses, are used for longer-wavelength infrared applications. Like other glasses, these glasses have a refractive index of about 1.5. Typically the difference between core and cladding is less than one per cent.

Plastic optical fibres (POF) are commonly step-index multi-mode fibres with a core diameter of 0.5 millimeters or larger. POF typically have higher attenuation co-efficients than glass fibres, 1 dB/m or higher, and this high attenuation limits the range of POF-based systems.

Process

Standard optical fibres are made by first constructing a large-diameter preform, with a carefully controlled refractive index profile, and then pulling the preform to form the long, thin optical fibre. The preform is commonly made by three chemical vapor deposition methods: inside vapor deposition, outside vapor deposition, and vapor axial deposition.

With inside vapor deposition, a hollow glass tube approximately 40 cm (16 inches) in length known as a "preform" is placed horizontally and rotated slowly on a lathe, and gases such as silicon tetrachloride ($SiCl_4$) or germanium tetrachloride ($GeCl_4$) are injected with oxygen in the end of the tube. The gases are then heated by means of an external hydrogen burner, bringing the temperature of the gas up to 1900 kelvins (1600°C, 3000°F), where the tetrachlorides react with oxygen to produce silica or germania (germanium dioxide) particles. When the reaction conditions are chosen to permit this reaction to occur in the gas phase throughout the tube volume, in contrast to earlier techniques where the reaction occurred only on the glass surface, this technique is called modified chemical vapor deposition.

The oxide particles then agglomerate to form large particle chains, which subsequently deposit on the walls of the tube as soot. The deposition is due to the large difference in temperature between the gas core and the wall causing the gas to push the particles outwards (this is known as thermophoresis). The torch is then traversed up and down the length of the tube to deposit the material evenly. After the torch has reached the end of the tube, it is then brought back to the beginning of the tube and the deposited particles are then melted to form a solid layer. This process is repeated until a sufficient amount of material has been deposited. For each layer the composition may be modified by varying the gas composition, resulting in precise control of the finished fibre's optical properties.

In outside vapor deposition or vapor axial deposition, the glass is formed by flame hydrolysis, a reaction in which silicon tetrachloride and germanium tetrachloride are oxidized by reaction with water (H2O) in an oxyhydrogen flame. In outside vapor deposition the glass is deposited onto a solid rod, which is removed before further processing. In vapor axial deposition, a short seed rod is used, and a porous preform, whose length is not limited by the size of the source rod, is built up on its end. The porous preform is consolidated into a transparent, solid preform by heating to about 1800 kelvins (1500 °C, 2800 °F).

The preform, however constructed, is then placed in a device known as a drawing tower, where the preform tip is heated and the optic fibre is pulled out as a string. By measuring the resultant fibre width, the tension on the fibre can be controlled to maintain the fibre thickness.

Practical Issues

Optical Fibre Cables—In practical fibres, the cladding is usually coated with a tough resin buffer layer, which may be further surrounded by a jacket layer, usually plastic. These layers add strength to the fibre but do not contribute to its optical wave guide properties. Rigid fibre assemblies sometimes put light-absorbing ("dark") glass between the fibres, to prevent light that leaks out of one fibre from entering another. This reduces cross-talk between the fibres, or reduces flare in fibre bundle imaging applications.

Modern cables come in a wide variety of sheathings and armor, designed for applications such as direct burial in trenches, high voltage isolation, dual use as power lines,[not in citation given] installation in conduit, lashing to aerial telephone poles, submarine installation, and insertion in paved streets. The cost of small fibre-count pole-mounted cables has greatly decreased due to the high Japanese and South Korean demand for fibre to the home (FTTH) installations.

Fibre cable may be very flexible, but traditional fibre's loss increases greatly if the fibre is bent with a radius smaller than around 30 mm. This creates a problem when the cable is bent around corners or wound around a spool, making FTTX installations more complicated. "Bendable fibres", targeted towards easier installation in home environments, have been standardized as ITU-T G.657. This type of fibre can be bent with a radius as low as 7.5 mm without adverse impact. Even more bendable fibres have been developed. Bendable fibre may also be resistant to fibre hacking, in which the signal in a fibre is surreptitiously monitored by bending the fibre and detecting the leakage.

Splicing and Termination

Optical fibres are connected to terminal equipment by optical fibre connectors. These connectors are usually of a standard type such as FC, SC, ST, LC, or MTRJ.

Optical fibres may be connected to each other by connectors or by splicing, that is, joining two fibres together to form a continuous optical waveguide. The commonly accepted splicing method is arc fusion splicing, which melts the fibre ends together with an electric arc. For quicker fastening jobs, a "mechanical splice" is used.

Fusion splicing is done with a specialized instrument that typically operates as follows: The two cable ends are fastened inside a splice enclosure that will protect the splices, and the fibre ends are stripped of their protective polymer coating (as well as the more sturdy outer jacket, if present). The ends are cleaved (cut) with a precision cleaver to make them perpendicular, and are placed into special holders in the splicer. The splice is usually inspected via a magnified viewing screen to check the cleaves before and after the splice. The splicer uses small motors to align the end faces together, and emits a small spark between electrodes at the gap to burn off dust and moisture. Then the splicer generates a larger spark that raises the temperature above the melting point of the glass, fusing the ends together permanently. The location and energy of the spark is carefully controlled so that the molten core and cladding don't mix, and this minimizes optical loss. A splice loss estimate is measured by the splicer, by directing light through the cladding on one side and measuring the light leaking from the cladding on the other side. A splice loss under 0.1 dB is typical. The complexity of this process makes fibre splicing much more difficult than splicing copper wire.

Mechanical fibre splices are designed to be quicker and easier to install, but there is still the necessity for stripping, careful cleaning and precision cleäving. The fibre ends are aligned and held together by a precision-made sleeve, often using a clear index-matching gel that enhances the transmission of light across the joint. Such joints typically have higher optical loss and are less robust than fusion splices, especially if the gel is used. All splicing techniques involve the use of an enclosure into which the splice is placed for protection afterward.

Fibres are terminated in connectors so that the fibre end is held at the end face precisely and securely. A fibre-optic connector is basically a rigid cylindrical barrel surrounded by a sleeve that holds the barrel in its mating socket. The mating mechanism can be "push and click", "turn and latch" ("bayonet"), or screw-in (threaded). A typical connector is installed by preparing the fibre end and inserting it into the rear of the connector body. Quick-set adhesive is usually used so the fibre is held securely, and a strain relief is secured to the rear. Once the adhesive has set, the fibre's end is polished to a mirror finish. Various polish profiles are used, depending on the type of fibre and the application. For single-mode fibre, the fibre ends are typically polished with a slight curvature, such that when the connectors are mated the fibres touch only at their cores. This is known as a "physical contact" (PC) polish. The curved surface may be polished at an angle, to make an "angled physical contact" (APC) connection. Such connections have higher loss than PC connections, but greatly reduced back reflection, because light that reflects from the angled surface leaks out of the fibre core; the resulting loss in signal strength is known as gap loss. APC fibre ends have low back reflection even when disconnected.

Free-space Coupling

It often becomes necessary to align an optical fibre with another optical fibre or an optical device such as a light-emitting diode, a laser diode, or an optoelectronic device such as a modulator. This can involve either carefully aligning the fibre and placing it in contact with the device to which it is to couple, or can use a lens to allow coupling over an air gap. In some cases the end of the fibre is polished into a curved form that is designed to allow it to act as a lens.

In a laboratory environment, the fibre end is usually aligned to the device or other fibre with a fibre launch system that uses a microscope objective lens to focus the light down to a fine point. A precision translation stage (micro-positioning table) is used to move the lens, fibre, or device to allow the coupling efficiency to be optimized.

Fibre Fuse

At high optical intensities, above 2 megawatts per square centimeter, when a fibre is subjected to a shock or is otherwise suddenly damaged, a fibre fuse can occur. The reflection from the damage vaporizes the fibre immediately before the break, and this new defect remains reflective so that the damage propagates back toward the transmitter at 1–3 meters per second (4?11 km/h, 2–8 mph). The open fibre control system, which ensures laser eye safety in the event of a broken fibre, can also effectively halt propagation of the fibre fuse. In situations, such as undersea cables, where high power levels might be used without the need for open fibre control, a "fibre fuse" protection device at the transmitter can break the circuit to prevent any damage.

6

Mineral Wool

Mineral wool, also known as mineral fibres or man-made mineral fibres from natural or synthetic minerals or metal oxides. The latter term is generally used to refer solely to synthetic materials including fibreglass, ceramic fibres and rock or stone wool. Industrial applications of mineral wool include thermal insulation, sound proofing, filtration, and germination of seedlings.

History of Mineral Wool

Slag wool was first made in 1840 in Wales by Edward Parry but the harmful effects on the workers caused production to be abandoned. It was first produced commercially in 1871 at the Georg-Marien Hutte in Osnabruck Germany. Slag wool was first produced in the United States by Robert Parker Parrott in 1875 at the Clove Furnace of the Greenwood Ironworks in Orange County New York.

Manufacture

Stone wool is a furnace product of molten rock at a temperature of about 1600°C, through which a stream of air or steam is blown. More advanced production techniques are based on spinning molten rock on high speed spinning wheels somewhat like the process used to prepare cotton candy. The final product is a mass of fine, intertwined fibres with a typical diameter of 6 to 10 micrometers. Mineral wool may contain a binder, often food grade starch, and an oil to reduce dusting.

Usage

Though the individual fibres conduct heat very well, when pressed into rolls and sheets their ability to partition air makes them excellent heat insulators and sound absorbers. Though not immune to the effects of a sufficiently hot fire, the fire resistance of fibreglass, stone wool and ceramic fibres makes them common building materials when passive fire protection is required, being used as spray fireproofing, in stud cavities in drywall assemblies and as packing materials in firestops.

Mineral wools are unattractive to rodents but will provide a structure for bacterial growth if allowed to become wet.

Other uses are in resin bonded panels, growth medium in hydroponics, filler in compounds for gaskets, brake pads, in plastics in the automotive industry and as a filtering medium.

Mineral fibres are produced in the similar way, without binder. The fibre as such is used as a raw material for its reinforcing purposes in various applications, such as friction materials, gaskets, coatings and plastics.

In hydroponics

Mineral wool products can hold large quantities of water and air that aids root growth and nutrient uptake in hydroponics; their fibrous nature also provides a good mechanical structure to hold the plant stable. The high natural pH of mineral wool makes them initially unsuitable to plant growth and requires "conditioning" to produce a wool with an appropriate, stable pH.

Matrial Safety

Precautions need to be taken when handling a fibre product as it can be absorbed into the body by inhalation. It may also irritate the eyes, skin and respiratory tract. Prolonged exposure could lead to long term effects and it is considered a possible carcinogen to humans. This effect may depend upon the fibre diameter and length, chemical composition and persistence within the body.

IARC (the International Agency for Research on Cancer) has reviewed the carcinogenicity of man made mineral fibres in October 2002. The IARC Monograph's working group concluded that only the more biopersistent materials remain classified by IARC as "possibly carcinogenic to humans" (Group 2B). These include refractory ceramic fibres, which are used industrially as insulation in high-temperature environments such as blast furnaces, and certain special-purpose glass wools not used as insulating materials. In contrast, the more commonly used vitreous fibre wools including insulation glass wool, slag wool and rock (stone) wool are considered "not classifiable as to carcinogenicity in humans" (Group 3).

High bio soluble fibres (HT-fibres) are produced that do not cause damage to the human cell. These newer biosoluble materials have been tested for carcinogenicity and most are found to be non-carcinogenic, or to cause tumors in experimental animals only under very restricted conditions of exposure. The IARC Monograph's working group "elected not to make an overall evaluation of the newly developed fibres designed to be less biopersistent such as the alkaline earth silicate or highalumina, low-silica wools. This decision was made in part because no human data were available, although such fibres that have been tested appear to have low carcinogenic potential in experimental animals, and because the Working Group had difficulty in categorizing these fibres into meaningful groups based on chemical composition."

The EU risk and safety phrases associated with this material in general are:

R38 – Irritating to the skin

R39 – Danger of very serious irreversible effects

R40 – Possible risk of irreversible effects

S36/37 – Wear suitable protective clothing and gloves.

All European produced rock (stone) wool and glass wool is bio soluble and R39 and R40 do not apply. For these products only the risk phrase R38 remains. This irritation to the skin however is not a chemical irritation but only a temporal mechanical irritation, comparable with exposure of the skin to straw, grass or hay.

Controversy exists over these rulings, as the majority of test results upon which they are based have typically been provided by the industry that makes the fibres. Test results that contravene such results were deemed inadmissible to IARC as submission by whistleblowers are not sanctioned by the party paying for the tests. Still, by using common sense to prevent breathing of the fibres and following industrial guidelines, it is possible to reduce the likelihood of pathology.

Glass wool

Glass wool is a form of fibreglass where very thin strands of glass are arranged into a spongy texture similar to steel wool. Glass wool is used widely as an insulating material.

Manufacturing Process

After the fusion of a mixture of natural sand and recycled glass at 1,450°C, the glass that is produced is converted into fibres. The cohesion and mechanical strength of the product is obtained by the presence of a binder that "cements" the fibres together. Ideally, a drop of bonder is placed at each fibre intersection. This fibre mat is then heated to around 200 °C to polymerize the resin and is calendered to give it strength and stability. The final stage involves cutting the wool and packing it in rolls or panels under last supreme pressure before palletizing the finished product in order to facilitate transport and storage.

Thanks to its intertwined flexible fibres, glass wool offers excellent fire-resistant properties as a thermal insulation material (in loft-of-wall cavity insulation, for example) and is also widely used as an absorbent material in acoustic treatments, such as sound-insulating absorbent ceiling tiles. Its light weight, flexibility and elasticity make it easy to install, which is another essential condition for effective insulation.

Glass wool is an excellent heat insulator. It can be woven into a cloth which has the additional properties of being light, waterproof, strong and corrosion free.

Side Effects

A 2002 summary by International Agency for Research on Cancer puts insulation glass wool into Category 3 carcinogen, "not classifiable as to its carcinogenicity to humans". The summary found "inadequate evidence" of glass wool causing cancer in humans and "limited evidence" of it causing cancer in experimental animals. Two unspecified "large" studies reviewed in the summary showed "increased mortality" (6% in the "US cohort study") from respiratory cancer in workers exposed to glass wool production. The longevity of exposure did not affect mortality. Smoking habits were not factored out. Non-occupational indoor settings were found to contain "much lower" fibres per volume unit.

Unspecified "studies" reviewed by Health Canada have shown that short time exposure to glass wool may cause minor irritation of eyes, skin, nose and throat. According to Health Canada, glass wool exposure does not present health risk to general population.

Bronze Wool

Bronze wool is a bundle of very fine bronze filaments, used in finishing and repair work to polish wood or metal objects. Bronze wool is similar to steel wool, but is used in its place to avoid some problems associated with broken filaments: steel rusts quickly, especially in a marine environment. Furthermore, steel is magnetic and may affect the operation of marine equipment, such as a compass. Steel can also discolor some materials, such as oak.

7

Clothing

A feature of all human societies, except perhaps the most primitive, is the wearing of clothing or clothes, especially in public. The primary purpose of clothing is functional, as a protection from the elements. In hot climates the functional need for clothing is minimal, while in very cold climates it is very high. Shelter usually reduces the functional require for clothing. For example, gloves, coats, etc., would normally be removed when entering a warm home. Clothes also have other functional purposes, such as safety during an activity, such as work or sport. But even within these contexts, clothes also perform cultural social functions. They generally conform with modesty and religious standards of the time and place, and act as cultural and social indicators such as status, wealth and the like. Within these contexts, they also function as a form of adornment and an expression of personal taste. Clothes nowadays, including functional clothes, have a fashion context.

In history, clothes have been from many materials - ranging from grasses to furs to much more elaborate and exotic materials. Based on scientific research into lice it is estimated that humans have been wearing clothing for 650,000 years.

People also decorate their bodies with makeup or cosmetics, scented perfume, and other ornamentation; they also dye, cut, and arrange the hair on their heads, faces, and bodies (see hairstyle), and sometimes also mark their skin (by tattoos, scarifications, and piercings). All these decorations may contribute to the overall effect and message of clothing, but do not constitute clothing.

Articles carried rather than worn (such as purses, canes, and umbrellas) are normally considered fashion accessories rather than clothing, but hats and small dress sweaters can be called clothing or accessories. Eyeglasses and jewelry are usually considered as accessories as well, even though in common speech these particular items are described as being worn rather than carried.

Functions of Clothing

The primary purpose of clothing is to keep the wearer warm. In hot climates this function is minimum, while in very cold climates it is very high. Shelter usually reduces this functional need for clothing. For example, gloves, coats, etc. would normally be removed when entering a warm home.

Clothing at times is worn as protection from specific environmental hazards, such as noxious chemicals, insects, weapons, and contact with abrasive substances. Clothing can protect against many things that might injure the uncovered human body. Clothes act as protection from the elements, including rain, snow and wind and other weather conditions, even from the sun. Clothes also reduce the level of risk during an activity, such as work or sport. Conversely, clothing may protect the environment from the clothing wearer, as for example wearing of medical scrubs.

Humans have shown extreme inventiveness in devising clothing solutions to environmental hazards and the distinction between clothing and other protective equipment is not always clear-cut; examples include space suit, air conditioned clothing, armor, swimsuit, diving suit, bee-keeper's protective clothing, high-visibility clothing, motorcycle leathers and protective clothing in general.

Origin and History of Clothing

According to archaeologists and anthropologists, the earliest clothing probably consisted of fur, leather, draped, leaves or grass, tied or wrapped about the body for protection from the elements. Knowledge of such clothing remains inferential, since clothing materials deteriorate quickly compared to stone, bone, shell and metal artifacts. Archeologists have identified very early sewing needles of bone and ivory from about 30,000 BC, found near Kostenki, Russia in 1988.

Ralf Kittler, Mark Stoneking and Manfred Kayser, anthropologists at the Max Planck Institute for Evolutionary Anthropology, have conducted a genetic analysis of human body lice that indicates that they originated about 107,000 years ago. Since most humans have very sparse body hair, body lice require clothing to survive, so this suggests a surprisingly recent date for the invention of clothing. Its invention may have coincided with the spread of modern Homo sapiens from the warm climate of Africa, thought to have begun between 50,000 and 100,000 years ago. However, a second group of researchers used similar genetic methods to estimate that body lice originated about 540,000 years ago (Reed et al. 2004. PLoS Biology 2(11): e340). For now, the date of the origin of clothing remains unresolved.

Some human cultures, such as the various people of the Arctic Circle, until recently made their clothing entirely of prepared and decorated skins and furs. Other cultures have supplemented or replaced leather and skins with cloth: woven, knitted, or twined from various animal and vegetable fibres..

Although modern consumers take clothing for granted, making the fabrics that go into clothing is hard. One sign of this is that the textile industry was the first to be mechanized during the Industrial Revolution; before the invention of the powered loom, textile production was a tedious and labor-intensive process.

One approach simply involves draping the cloth. Many people wore, and still wear, garments consisting of rectangles of cloth wrapped to fit — for example, the dhoti for men and the saree for women in the Indian subcontinent, the Scottish kilt or the Javanese sarong. The clothes may simply be tied up, as is the case of the first two garments; or pins or belts hold the garments in place, as in the case of the latter two. The precious cloth remains uncut, and people of various sizes or the same person at different sizes can wear the garment.

Another approach involves cutting and sewing the cloth, but using every bit of the cloth rectangle in constructing the clothing. The tailor may cut triangular pieces from one corner of the cloth, and then add them elsewhere as gussets. Traditional European patterns for men's shirts and women's chemises take this approach.

Modern European fashion treats cloth much more prodigally, typically cutting in such a way as to leave various odd-shaped cloth remnants. Industrial sewing operations sell these as waste; home sewers may turn them into quilts.

In the thousands of years that humans have spent constructing clothing, they have created an astonishing array of styles, many of which we can reconstruct from surviving garments, photos, paintings, mosaics, etc., as well as from written descriptions. Costume history serves as a source of inspiration to current fashion designers, as well as a topic of professional interest to costumers constructing for films, plays, television, and historical reenactment.

Cultural Aspects

Social Status—In some societies, clothing may be used to indicate rank and status. In ancient Rome, for example, only senators were permitted to wear garments dyed with Tyrian purple. In Hawaiian society only high-ranking chiefs wore feather cloaks and palaoa or carved whale teeth. Under the Travancore kingdom of Kerala (India), lower caste women had to pay a tax for the right to cover their upper body. In China before the establishment of the republic, only the emperor could wear yellow. There are numerous examples throughout history of elaborate systems of sumptuary laws regulating who could wear what. In societies without such laws, including most modern societies, the high cost of status garments may effectively limit their purchase and display to those who can afford them. Social group pressure can also impact on garment choice.

Marital Status—Traditionally Hindu women, once married, would wear sindoor, a red powder, in the parting of their hair. If widowed, they would abandon sindoor and jewelry and wear simple white clothing. Men and women of the Western world may wear wedding rings to indicate their marital status.

Observant Jewish women cover their hair if they are married. There is a sect of Judaism in which girls who are old enough to be looking for a husband wear their hair in two braids as opposed to the one braid they wore before they were of a marriagable age. For their wedding, women in the United States and Europe, depending on their heritage and/or religion, will usually wear a white gown, although some movie stars have been known to wear a black party dress for their wedding.

Religious Aspects

Religious clothing might be considered a special case of occupational clothing. Sometimes it is worn only during the performance of religious ceremonies. However, it may also be worn everyday as a marker for special religious status.

For example, Jains wear unstitched cloth pieces when performing religious ceremonies. The unstitched cloth signifies unified and complete devotion to the task at hand, with no digression. Sikhs wear a turban as it is a part of their religion.

The cleanliness of religious dresses in Eastern Religions like Hinduism, Sikhism, Buddhism and Jainism is of paramount importance, which indicates purity.

Clothing figures in prominently in the Bible where it appears in numerous contexts, the more prominent ones being: the story of Adam and Eve, Joseph's cloak, Judah and Tamar, Mordechai and Esther. Furthermore the priests officiating in the Temple had very specific garments, the lack of which would make one liable to death.

Jewish ritual also requires rending of one's upper garment as a sign of mourning. This practice is found in the Bible when Jacob hears of the apparent death of his son Joseph.

Sport and Activity

Most sports and physical activities are practiced wearing special clothing, for practical, comfort or safety reasons. Common sportswear garments include T-shirts, tennis shirts, short pants, tracksuits, and trainers. Specialized garments include wet suits (for diving, swimming or surfing), salopettes (for skiing) and leotards (for gymnastics). Also, spandex materials are often used as base layers to soak up sweat. Spandex is also preferable for active sports that require form fitting garments, such as wrestling, field & track, dance, gymnastics and swimming.

Clothing Maintenance

Clothing suffers assault both from without and within. The human body sheds skin cells and body oils, and exudes sweat, urine, and feces. From the outside, sun damage, moisture, abrasion and dirt assault garments. Lice and fleas may hide in seams. Worn clothing, if not cleaned and refurbished, will itch, look scruffy, and lose functionality (as when buttons fall off and zippers fail).

In some cases, people wear an item of clothing until it falls apart. Cleaning leather presents difficulties, and bark cloth (tapa) cannot be washed without dissolving it. Owners may patch tears and rips, and brush off surface dirt, but old leather and bark clothing will always look old.

But most clothing consists of cloth, and most cloth can be laundered and mended (darning, patching, but compare felt).

Laundry, Ironing, Storage

Humans have developed many specialized methods for laundering, ranging from the earliest "pound clothes against rocks in running stream" to the latest in electronic washing machines and dry cleaning (dissolving dirt in solvents other than water).

Many types of clothing are designed to be ironed before they are worn to remove wrinkles. Most modern formal and semi-formal clothing is in this category (for example, dress shirts and suits). Ironed clothes are believed to look fresh, clean, and neat. Much contemporary casual clothing is made of knit materials that do not readily wrinkle, and do not require ironing. Some clothing is permanent press, having been treated with a coating (such as polytetrafluoroethylene) that suppresses wrinkles and creates a smooth appearance without ironing.

Once clothes have been laundered and possibly ironed, they are usually hung on clothes hangers or folded, to keep them fresh until they are worn. Clothes are folded to permit them to be stored compactly, to prevent creasing, to preserve creases or to present them in a much pleasing manner, for instance when they are put on sale in stores.

Many kinds of clothes are folded before they are put in suitcases as preparation for travel. Other clothes, such as suits, may be hung up in special garment bags, or rolled rather than folded. Many people use their clothing as packing material around fragile items that might otherwise break in transit.

Mending

In past times, mending was an art. A meticulous tailor or seamstress could mend rips with thread raveled from hems and seam edges so skillfully that the darn was practically invisible. When the raw material — cloth — was worth more than labor, it made sense to expend labor in saving it. Today clothing is considered a consumable item. Mass-manufactured clothing is less expensive than the labor required to repair it. Many people will buy a new piece of clothing rather than expend time mending. The thrifty still replace zippers and buttons and sew up ripped hems.

The Life Cycle of Clothing

Used, unwearable clothing was once used for quilts, rag, rugs, bandages, and many other household uses. It could also be recycled into paper. Now it is usually thrown away. Used but still wearable clothing can be sold at consignment shops, flea markets, online auction, or donated to charity. Charities usually skim the best of the clothing to sell in their own thrift stores and sell the rest to merchants, who bale it up and ship it to Third World countries, where vendors bid for the bales, then sell the used clothing.

There are many concerns about the life cycle of synthetics which come primarily from petrochemicals. Unlike natural fibres, their source is not renewable (in less than millions of years) and they are not biodegradable.

Early 21st-century Clothing Styles

Western fashion has, to few extent, become international fashion, as Western media and styles penetrate all parts of the world. Fast fashion clothing is widespread worldwide. These garments are less expensive, mass-produced Western clothing. Used clothing from Western countries also reach people in poor countries.

People may wear ethnic or national dress on special occasions or in certain roles or occupations. For example, most Korean men and women have adopted Western-style dress for daily wear, but will still wear traditional hanboks on special occasions, like weddings and cultural holidays. Items of Western dress may also appear worn or accessorized in distinctive, non-Western ways. A Tongan man may combine a used T-shirt with a Tongan wrapped skirt, or tupenu.

There is a very diverse range of styles in Western fashions, ranging from expensive haute couture to thrift store grunge.

Political Issues

Working Conditions—Garment workers often have to labor under poor conditions. Mass-produced clothing is often manufactured in Sweatshop conditions, typified by long work hours, lack of benefits, and lack of worker representation. While most sweatshops are found in developing countries, clothes made in industrialized nations may also be manufactured in sweatshops, most often staffed by undocumented immigrants.

Coalitions of NGOs, designers (Katharine Hamnett, American Apparel, Veja, Quiksilver, eVocal, Edun,...) and campaign groups like the Clean Clothes Campaign (CCC) seek to improve these conditions as much as possible by sponsoring awareness-raising events, which draw the attention of both the media and the general public to the workers' conditions.

Outsourcing production to low wage countries like Bangladesh, India, China and Sri Lanka became possible when the Multi Fibre Agreement (MFA) was abolished. The MFA was deemed a protectionist measure which placed quotas on the exports of textiles. Globalization is often quoted as the single most contributing factor to the poor working conditions of garment workers. Although many countries recognize treaties like the ILO, many have also made exceptions to certain parts of the treaties. India for example has not ratified sections 87 and 92 of the treaty.

Fur

The use of animal fur in clothing dates to prehistoric times. It is currently associated in the West with expensive, designer clothing. Once uncontroversial, it has recently been the focus of campaigns on the grounds that it is cruel and unnecessary. PETA, along with other animal rights and animal liberation groups have called attention to fur farming and other practices they consider cruel.

Clothing Material

History, clothing have been made from many materials - ranging from grasses to furs to much more elaborate and exotic materials. Some cultures, such as the various people of the Arctic circle, until recently, made their clothing entirely of prepared and decorated furs and skins. Other cultures have supplemented or replaced leather and skins with cloth: woven, knitted, or twined from various animal and vegetable fibres.

Humans have shown extreme inventiveness in devising clothing solutions to environmental hazards and the distinction between clothing and other protective equipment is not always clear-cut; examples include space suit, air conditioned clothing, armor, diving suit, swimsuit, bee-keeper's protective clothing, motorcycle leathers, high-visibility clothing, and protective clothing in general.

Materials for Cloth

Common clothing materials include natural fibres, which are renewable, biodegradable, include:

Cloth, typically made of viscose cotton, flax, wool, ramie, silk

Denim

Down for down-filled parkas

Fur

Leather

Some clothing is made from synthetic fibres, which are man made and not biodegradable, made primarily from petrochemicals:

In 1935 Nylon was first produced. Nylon is a thermoplastic silky material. It became famous when used in women's stockings (nylons) in 1940. It was intended to be a synthetic replacement for silk and substituted for it in many different products after silk became scarce during World War II.

Polyesters include naturally-occurring chemicals and synthetics. Natural polyesters and a few synthetic ones are biodegradable, but most synthetic polyesters are not. Polyesters may change shape after the application of heat and are combustible at high temperatures. They tend to shrink away from flames and self-extinguish upon ignition. Polyester fibres have high tenacity and E-modulus as well as low water absorption and minimal shrinkage in comparison with other industrial fibres.

Spandex (or elastane) is known for its exceptional elasticity. It is stronger and more durable than rubber, its major non-synthetic competitor. It was invented in 1959.

Less-common clothing materials include:

PVC-Polyvinyl chloride

Rayon

Recycled or Recovered Cotton

Bamboo

Hemp

Jute

Lyocell

Recycled PET

Recycled paper

Rubber

Soy

Tyvek

Other Natural Fibres

Reinforcing materials such as bone, plastic, wood and metal may be used in fasteners or to stiffen garments.

Clothing Terminology

Clothing terminology comprises the names of individual garments and classes of garments, as well as the specialized vocabularies of the trades that have designed, manufactured, marketed and sold clothing over hundreds of years.

Clothing terminology ranges from the arcane (watchet, a pale blue color name from the sixteenth century) to the everyday (t-shirt), and changes over time in response to fashion which in turn reflects social, artistic, and political trends.

Categories of Clothing Terminology

At its broadest, clothing terminology may be said to include names for:

Classes of basic garments: coat, skirt, dress, shirt, suit, underwear

Length, for skirts and dresses: mini, tea length, ballerina length, full length, maxi

Contemporary and historical styles of garments: corset, frock coat, t-shirt, doublet

Parts of garments: sleeve, collar, lapel

Styles of these: juliette sleeve, Peter Pan collar

Clothing details: pocket, french cuff, zipper

Functional uses: base layer, insulation layer, outer shell

Traditional garments: cheongsam, kilt, dirndl

Fashions and "anti-fashions": preppy, New Look, hip-hop, rational dress

Fabrics: chiffon, velvet, satin, silk, denim, wool, cotton

Fabric treatments: fabric painting, transfers, ikat, tie-dye, batik

Fabric manipulation: pleat, tuck, gather, smocking

Colors and dyes: madder red, indigo, isabella

Sewing terms: hem, armscye, cut, lining

Patternmaking terms: sloper, toile

Methods of manufacture: haute couture, bespoke tailoring, ready-to-wear

Retailers' terms:

Degrees of formality: formal wear, bridal, business casual

Market: high end, high street, ethical consumer, cut price

Size ranges: missy, plus size, big-and-tall

Retail seasons: back-to-school, holiday, resort, seasonal

Departments: special occasion, sportswear, bridge fashion

Persistence of Clothing Terminology

Despite the constant introduction of new terms by fashion designers, clothing manufacturers and marketers, the names for several basic garment classes in English are very stable over time. Gown, shirt/skirt, frock, and coat are all attested back to the early medieval period.

Gown (from medieval Latin gunna) was a basic clothing term for hundreds of years, referring to a garment that hangs from the shoulders. In medieval and renaissance England gown referred to a loose outer garment worn by both men and women, sometimes short, more often ankle length, with sleeves. By the eighteenth century gown had become a standard category term for a woman's dress, a meaning it retained until the mid-twentieth century. Only in the last few decades has gown lost this general meaning in favor of dress. Today the term gown is rare except in specialized cases: academic dress or cap and gown, evening gown, nightgown, hospital gown, and so on (see Gown).

Shirt and skirt are originally the same word, the former being the southern and the latter the northern pronunciation in early Middle English. Like gown, shirt is becoming a specialized term in Britain, though it retains its general meaning in the United States (see Shirt).

Coat remains a term for an overgarment, its essential meaning for the last thousand years (see Coat).

Sources of New Terminology

Names for new styles or fashions in clothing are frequently the deliberate inventions of fashion designers or clothing manufacturers; these include Chanel's Little Black Dress (a term which has survived) and Lanvin's robe de style (which has not). Other terms are of more obscure origin.

Personal Names

Clothing styles are frequently named after people — often with a military connection:

Garibaldi shirt and the Garibaldi jacket were bright red woolen garments for women with black embroidery or braid and military details popular in the 1860s; they are named after the Italian revolutionary Giuseppe Garibaldi who visited England in 1863.

The Eisenhower jacket or "Ike" jacket is a waist-length, military jacket of World War II origins. Called the "Jacket, Field, Wool, M-1944", it was commissioned by then General Dwight Eisenhower as a new field jacket for the US Forces in Northern Europe. The jacket was based on the British Army 'Battle Dress' jacket of the same era.

The cardigan is a knitted jacket or button-front sweater created to keep British soldiers warm in Russian winters. It is named for James Brudenell, 7th Earl of Cardigan, who led the Charge of the Light Brigade in the Crimean War (1854).

The Mao jacket is a very plain (often grey), high-collared, shirtlike jacket customarily worn by Mao Zedong and the people of China during his regime. Its drab design and uniformity was a reaction to pre-Revolution class distinctions of clothes, with elites dressing in elaborate silks, while poor laborers wore very rough clothes.

The Nehru jacket is a uniform jacket without lapels or collars, popularized by Jawaharlal Nehru, the first Prime Minister of independent India.

The Bloomer Costume was a farm of woman's clothing introduced in the Antebellum period, that changed the style from dresses to a more male-type style, which was devised by Amelia Bloomer.

Place Names

Another fertile source for clothing terms is place names, which usually reflect the origin (or supposed origin) of a fashion. Modern terms such as Hawaiian shirts, Bermuda shorts, and Fair Isle sweaters are the latest in a long line that stretches back to holland (linen), damask ("from Damascus"), polonaise ("in the fashion of Polish women"), jersey (originally Jersey frock), Balaclava, mantua, and denim ("serge de Nîmes" after the city).

Costume Historian's Terms

Costume historians, with a "rearward-looking" view, require names for clothing styles that were not used (or needed) when the styles were actually worn. For example, the Van Dyke collar is so-called from its appearances in seventeenth century portraits by Anthony Van Dyck, and the Watteau pleats of the robe á la française are called after their appearance in the portraits of Antoine Watteau.

Similarly, terms may be applied ahistorically to entire categories of garments, so that corset is applied to garments that were called stays or a pair of bodies until the introduction of the word corset in the late eighteenth century. And dress is now applied to any woman's garment consisting of a bodice and skirt, although for most of its history dress simply meant clothing, or a complete outfit of clothing with its appropriate accessories.

Short Forms

A notable trend at the turn of the twenty-first century is "cute" short forms: camisole becomes cami, hooded sweaters or sweatshirts become hoodies, and as of 2005, short or "shrunken" cardigans are cardies.

The much-older term shimmy for "slip" is most likely a false singular from chemise.

8

Cloth of Gold

Cloth of gold is a fabric woven with a gold-wrapped or spun weft - referred to as "a spirally spun gold strip". In most cases, the core yarn is silk wrapped with a band or strip of high content gold filé. In rarer instances, wool and fine linen have been used as the core.

Cloth of gold is not to be confused with various gold embroidery techniques that date to the early Middle Ages, though the type of goldwork thread called "passing" is identical to the weft thread of cloth of gold. It is mentioned on both Roman headstones for women and in the Book of Psalms (psalm 45, verse 14) as a fabric befitting a princess. The Ancient Greek reference to the Golden Fleece is seen by some as a reference to gold cloth. Cloth of gold has been popular for ecclesiastical use for many centuries, and that is the most common use of this material today.

Few extant examples have survived in Roman provincial tombs. Later producers of cloth of gold include the Byzantine Empire and Medieval Italian weavers. A similar cloth of silver was also made. It is still made in Italy and India today.

Modern metallic fabrics made in the West are known as lamé.

"Cloth of gold" is a familiar name occasionally applied to the venomous Conus textile species of cone shell, presumably because of its Byssus or fine hair. Byssus from some species has been made into a very fine cloth.

Samite

Samite was a heavy and luxurious silk fabric worn in the Middle Ages, of a twill-type weave, often including gold or silver thread. The word was derived from Old French samit, from medieval Latin samitum, examitum deriving from the Byzantine Greek hexamiton, indicating the use of six varying yarns in the warp. Samite is still used in ecclesiastical robes, vestments, ornamental fabrics, and interior decoration.

Structurally, samite is a weft-faced compound twill, plain or figured (patterned), in which the main warp threads are hidden on both sides of the fabric by the ground and patterning wefts, with only the binding wefts visible. By the later medieval period, the term samite was applied to any rich, heavy silk material which had a satin-like gloss, indeed "satin" began as a term for lustrous samite.

Origins and spread to Europe

Fragments of samite have been discovered at many locations along the Silk Road, and are especially associated with Sassanid Persia. Samite was "arguably the most important" silk weave of Byzantium, and from the 9th century Byzantine silks entered Europe via the Italian trading ports. Vikings, connected through their direct trade routes with Constantinople, were buried in samite embroidered with silver-wound threads in the tenth century. Silk weaving itself was established in Lucca and Venice in the 12th and 13th centuries, and the statutes of the silk-weaving guilds in Venice specifically distinguished sammet weavers from weavers of other types of silk cloth.

The Crusades brought Europeans into direct contact with the Islamic world, and other sources of samite, as well as other Eastern luxuries. A samite saddle-cloth known in the West as the Suaire de St-Josse, now in the Musée du Louvre, was woven in eastern Iran, some time before 961, when Abu Mansur Bakhtegin, for whom it was woven, died; it was brought back from the First Crusade by

Étienne de Blois and dedicated as a votive gift at the Abbey of Saint-Josse, near Boulogne. At the time of the First Crusade, samite needed to be explained to a Western audience, as in the eye-witness Chanson d'Antioche (ccxxx):

"Very quickly he took a translator and a large dromedary loaded with silver cloth, called "samite" in our language. He sent them to our fine, brave men..."

The Fourth Crusade brought riches unknown in the West to the "Frankish" crusaders who sacked Constantinople in 1204, described by Villehardouin: "The booty gained was so great that none could tell you the end of it: gold and silver, and vessels and precious stones, and samite, and cloth of silk..."

Use in Medieval Europe

Samite was a royal tissue: in the 1250s it features among the clothing of fitting status provided for the innovative and style-conscious English king Henry III, his family, and his attendants. For those of royal blood there were mantles and robes of samite and cloth of gold. Samite itself might be interwoven with threads wrapped in gold foil. It could be further enriched by being over-embroidered: in Chrétien de Troyes' Perceval, the Story of the Grail (1180s) "On the altar, I assure you, there lay a slain knight. Over him was spread a rich, dyed samite cloth, embroidered with many golden flowers, and before him burned a single candle, no more, no less." In manuscript illuminations, modern readers often interpret rich figurative designs as embroidered, but Linnet Kestrel points out that they could equally be painted, and illustrates a samite bishop's mitre painted in grisaille in the Cleveland Museum of Art. According to the Louvre the most famous example of painted silk, the Parement of Narbonne, despite being a royal commission, was only made on "fluted silk imitating samite".

In the wrong hands, samite could threaten the outward marks of social stability; samite was specified among the forbidden luxuries denied the urban middle classes in sumptuary laws by the court of René of Anjou about 1470: "In cities mercantile governments outlawed crowns, trains, cloth of samite and precious metals, ermine trims, and other pretensions of aristocratic fashion" In Florence, when the condottiero Walter of Brienne offered the innovation of a sumptuous feast to San Giovanni in 1343, the chronicler Villani noted among the rich trappings "He added to the other side of the palio of crimson samite cloth a trim of gray squirrel skin as long as the pole."

In literature

As the premier luxury textile of the Middle Ages, samite has long been associated with Arthurian literature.

In the dramatic and eerie manifestation of the Holy Grail in Arthur's court in the Romance Queste del Saint Graal, the Grail appeared, covered with a samite cloth, hung in the air a moment, and disappeared.

It was famously referred to in the Idylls of the King cycle of poems by Alfred, Lord Tennyson. There the Lady of the Lake, described in the cycle only by the same line, repeated in four different places: "Clothed in white samite, mystic, wonderful", gives Arthur his sword Excalibur and then in the The Passing of Arthur catches it when it is flung into the lake as he lies dying. This appearance was referenced, too, in the film Excalibur and even burlesqued in Monty Python and the Holy Grail.

9

Washing of Cloth

Over the country it is general grievance that good washers are very rare. And yet there are few things, more trying to a neat housekeeper, than to put nice articles into the wash. and have them returned yellow, streaked, and spotted. There is nothing, which tends so effectively to diminish this evil as to secure an abundant supply of all accommodations and facilities for doing this work properly. If the washerwomen has to draw water, at a distance from her place of work, or. ir she receives it only by a labourious process, she will be very proper to stint her measure of it; wherea, if it is readily obtained, and readily heated. she will be much more likely to make her clothes clean and white, byan abundance and repeated change of water. The apparatus for the convenience and heating of water, can be secured, at no very great expense; and will greatly increase the possibilities of securing good washing. There are other accommodations. a full supply of which, will also greatly promote the same object. For persons who have large washes, all of the following article:s will be needed.

Articles to be provided for Washing Soft water is a :very important item. When this cannot be: obtained, soda or ley, put in the hard water, softens it. But great care is needed, lest; by putting in too large a quantity, the clothes, and the skin of the person washing, be injured. Two washforms are required one for the two tubs in which the suds is put, and the other for the blueing water and starch-tub. Four tubs, of dlfferent seizes; two or three pails; a big wooden dipper; a grooved wash-board; a clothes-line, (see-gra~s, or horse-hair, is best) a long wash-stick to move the clothes in boiling; and a wooden fork to take them out these are all useful, and prevent loss of time. It is also very required to have soap-dishes made of wood, with hooks of wire or wood, so that they can be hooked to the sides of the tubs. This prohibits waste, both of time and soap. Besides these, are needed, a clothes-bag, in which to boil the clothes; an indigo-bag, made of double flannel; a bottle of ox-gall, to utilise for calicos; a supply of starch; a starch-strainer, of coarse unbleached cotton, made into a bag, tapering down to a point; and six or eight dozen clotnes-pins, which are cleft sticks, made to filsten the clothes on the line. A junk bottle or dissolved gum Arabic is also generally useful. A brass or copper kettle is best for boiling clothes, as iron is peoper to strain them with its rust. Tubs and pails, after having been used, should be put in a cool place, to prolibit their shrinking and falling to pieces. A closet, for keeping all these articles at hand, and in proper order for the washer, is a very great convenience. It should be made four feet wide, three feet deep, and six or seven feet in height, with a wooden bottom. In the lower portior, are to be placed the tubs, one within another, turned on their sides. A small distance above them, is to be placed a shelf, on which is to be put a basket holding the clothes-pins, the clothes-fork and line, soap- dishes, and dipper. A bove this, is to be placed another shelf, upon which may be set the jug of oxgall, a bottle of mixed glue, a bottle of gum Arabic, a large box of starch, and a little box of indigo. These shelves should extend to only half the depth of the closet. On one sicie of the closet, should be four nails, on which to hang the starch-bag, the bag in which the clothes are boiled, the blueing-bag, and the wash-stick. The ironing implements might also be kept in this closet, by making the lower shelf a foot and a half higher, and putting a deep drawer under it. In this drawer, could be kept the ironing sheets and holders, and the irons might be placed on one of the shelves. A lock and key should be put on this closet, so that, if essential it may be kept locked.

When a 'Nasherwoman finds all the conveniences sufficiently provided and clearly arranged, it always will have an effect in leading her to be more special than she would be, if every thing is at loose ends, and several conveniences are lacking. If the lady of the house requires the washerwoman to see her before leaving, and then inquires if each of these articles are properly cleansed and put in their places, it will be more definitely done.

Washing : General Mode

It saves very labour, to assort the clothes, and put the white ones to soak, the night before, in warm water. Do not allow hot water to be poured on them, as it makes it more di fficult to wash out the dirt. In assorting clothes the flannels are to be put ic one lot the coloured clothes is another, the coarser white clothes in a third, and the fine clothes in a fourth Jot. Wash the fine clothes first in suds, and throw them, when wrung, into another tub of suds. Then wash them in the second suds, mould them wrong side out. Then put them into the boiling bag, and let them boil, in strong soapsuds, for helf an hour, (not more,) moving them about, with the wash stick, to keep them from getting yellow in spots. Take them out of the boiling water, into a tub, and rub the dirtiest spots. Then rinse them, throwing them, when wrung, into a tub of blueing water. Wring them bard the last time, or they will be liable to try in streaks. Put the articles to be stiffened, by their selves, and dip them starch just before hanging out. Hag white clothes, if feasible, in tbe sun, and coloured clothes in the shade. They should be intensified on the line with wooden clothes.pins, which are safer and more convenient than any other mode. After the fine clothes, wash the coarser articles in the above manner. Then wash the coloured clothes, which must not be boiled, nor ha ve ley or soda put in the water. A tables :poonful of beef.gall, added to the suds, improves the look of nice prints, and preserves their colours. Finally wash the flannels. In washing white flannels, make suds as hot as the hand can bear. It shrinks flannels, in spots, to have soap rubbed on. Very nice flannels should have a suds of white. soap After washing through the first suds, they should be thrown into another tub of hot suds, and in this last be turned wrong side out. They should then be thrown into clear hot blueing water, as suds will not combine well with indigo, and makes specks in the flannel. Flannels should avoid leaving long in water. nor ever be put in any but hot water. After alhing. shake them and pull them into proper shape, before hanging them out. Nothing is so much injured by bad washing, as white flannel. Coloured flannel. and woollen hose, should be washed after the white. Some people keep stocking boards, shaped like a foot and leg, on which they draw woollen hose, when drying. This keeps them from shrinking. and makes them look better than to iron them. Unbleached cotton hose should be dipped in coffee water, unless it is wished to whiten them.

Blanket Wash

Select a warm and long day, and start at an early hour. Pound the blankets in a barrel, with hot suds, mixing the shop thoroughly with the water, before Jutting them in Rinse in hot suds, not wringing them much. If not dry by night, fold them. and hang them out the next morning.

Washing of other Bedding

Bedquilts should be pounded in a barrel, with warm suds.. After rinsing, wring as dry as feasible. Bolsters and pillows can be washed, without emptying the feathers by pounding them in warm suds, and rinsing them in fair water. It takes many days to dry them. Generally it is better to take out the feathers. from good articles; more common ones can be washed without cotton comforters. can be washed without taking out the cotton; but it is better to wash the covers only, and then put them together again. To wash beds, the feathers must be taken out. and washed and laid to dry, on some floor not in use. The ticks must be washed like other articles.

Soda Wash—A very significant improvement in economy of labour has become general, named scuh, soda washing. Much prejudice has been instigated against the method, since. if it is not done with proper care, it injures the texture of the cloth. This evil is done either by boiling in the mixture too long, or by putting in too much soda. To prevent a risk of the last, some ladies make a composition, known as soda soap, which they keep on hand for the purpose. The following method has been pursued many friends of the Writer. for successive years, and through they have employed all kinds of washers, no injurious out comes have ever followed. They calculate that it protects one half the labour of common washing. In preparing for it, it is necessary first to make the soap.

Soda Soap for Washing—Take twenty-four pounds of common bar-shop; twenty-four pounds of subcarbonate of soda, (or coarse washing-soda;) and five gallons of soft water. Boil the above for two hours, and keep it on hand for use. Also make a barrel of lime-water by putting one peck of quicklime to a barrel of soft water . This is to be kept for use.

Mode of Soda-Washing—Put two pounds of the above soap to two big pailfuls of soft water, and add one pint of lime-water. In this mixture, first put the nicer white clothes. They must be soaked the earlier night in warm (not hot) water. Let them boil just one hour and no more. If they boil longer , it injures the clotbes. Take them out into expliait "ater, (draining them so as not to waste the material) Turn them wrong side out, and rub the spots that look most soiled. If very dirty, rub on a little soap. Wring them hard, and throw them into the blueing-water. Wring them hard out of the blueing, and hang them out. It will be looked that this protects all the labour of the two first washings in suds in the common way of washing, and yet it usually makes clothes look whiter than any other method. After the fine clothes aro boiled, put in the coarser onei, and proceed as above. The coloured clothes, and flannels, must not, of course, be boiled in this. Tbese can be washed while the white clothes are boiling.

The Writer has friends who leave the lime-water, and say that it makes no difference, barring that it saves the trouble of making and keeping the lime-water. Another rinsigg-water , before the blueing-water, is an improvement.

Cautions in Regard to Coloured Clothes

Neither calico, nor prints, should to be left lying in water. Tbe water in which they are washed, should not to be very warm; and when tbe suds looks dirty and dark, it should be changed, before another article is added: otherwise the succeeding pieces will be dingy or streaked. Soap should not to be rubbed on; the grease should be removed by a paste of magnesia, or starch, or by Frenct chalk, or Wilmington clay. It is better to make starch for dark calico, with water mixed with cold coffee, as it prolibits a whitish look. Common glue stiffening, also, is good for dark calico clothes. They should be dried wrong side out in the shade. Freezing in drying injures the colours of calico. When laid aside from use, all the stiffening should be taken out, or their texture will be injured. Few people wash calicos in bran-water, without soap. For this purpose, boil four quarts of wheat bran in two pailfuls of water; strain it, and when lukewarm divide it into two parts. Wash the calico first in one and then in the other water. Then rise, writing bard, and hang out to dry. Potato-water is in good. For this, grate eight large potatoes to one gallon of water; divide the water into three portions. Wash in tbe two first, and rinse in the last.

To Wase Furniture Chintz, Curtains, and Spreads :

The Writer has never seen the following tried. It is given on Miss Leslie's authority.

Boil two pounds of rice in two gallons of water, till the rice is perfectly soft. Strain the water, and use one half for washing; and, where soap is needed, rub on some of the rice tied up in a muslin rag. Put half the boiled rice in a bag, and place it in a tube of clear water; and in this wash the chintz, applying the ricebag for soap. Then put three tea-spoonfuls of pyroligneous acid in the last half of the rice-water, and rinse the chintz. Dry. stretch, fold, and press. Then rub it, on the right side with r. smooth stone, or a bit of polished marble, instead of ironing it.

To Wash Wooden Table Covers, or Woollen Shawls :

Take out the grease spots, either with starch. French chalk. magnesia, or Wilmington clay-ball. Take out the stains with spirits of hartshorn. Wash in two parts of hot suds made of white soap.

Do not wring, but fold and press the water out, holding it in a tub under the table. Shake, stretch and dry it not in the sun, and not by a fire. Do not let it freeze in drying, Sprinkle with warm water three hours before ironing, anj foldJ and roll it tight. Iron on the wrong side, pressing vere heavily.

To Wash Brown Linen, or Muslins, of Tea, Drab, or alife Colours :

Boil a bunch of common hay in adequate soft water to wash and rinse the articles. The water should be the colour of new brown linen. If darker, add more water. If the clothes are not very filthy, it is best to wash the first time in lukewarm prominent water, without soap: Then wash and rinse in the hay-water , stiffening with glue-water. Put a tea-spoonful of oil of vitriol or pyroligneous acid in the rinsing-water. Dry in the shade, and sprinkle and roll three hours before ironing. Ladies' linen travelling dresses, gentlemen's roundabouts, and linen aprons, by the a bove process can be made to look as when new.

To Wash Nankeen :

New Nankeen, if soaked in ley one night, and dried without rinsing, contains its colour, perfectly. Wash, after it is worn, in two parts of warm suds, the first having a teacupful of ley added to it. Rinse in two waters, with a very subtli suds added. Iron on the wrong side.

To Cleanse Gentlemen's Cloth Coats and Pantaloons :

The Writer has tried, and others try, the following method, with significant success, on all sorts of broadcloth articles of dress. Take one beef's gall, half a pound of salaeratus, and four gallons of warm water. With a clothes. brush dipped in this mixture, scour the article, laying it on a table, for the objective. The collar of a coat and the grease spots (Rarlier marked by a stitch or two of white thread) must be brushed with this mixture frequently. After this, take the article and rinse it up and down in the mixture. Then rinse it up and down in the same way in soft cold water. Then, without any wringing or pressing, hang it up to rlrain and dry. When dry, dampen with a sponge, and iron on the wrong side, or else spread something between the cloth and iron, ironing till prefecrly dry. It is best to rip out pockets and linings, if the articles are worth the difficult. Also brush the article before washing. It is general best to iron no part but the kirt, and press the lappets and cuffs.

Another Mode of Washing Broadcloths :

Shake and brush the article. Rip out pockets and lini,lgs. Wash in two portions of hard suds, putting a teacupful of ley in the first. Do not wring, but roll them tight, and press the water out. When completely dry, sprinkle them, and let them lie all night. Iron on the wrong side, or with an interfering cloth, till perfectly dry. For light woollens, white soap must be used. Iron on the right side with an impeding cloth.

To Wash Woollen Yarn :

Wash in hot water, putting in a teacupful of ley to half a pail of water, and no soap. Rinse till the water comes off clear.

To Wash Black Worsted or Woollen Hose :

If new, dip all night; then wash in hot suds, with beef's gall, a tablespoonful to half a pail of water. Rinse till no colour comes out. Then stretch on stocking-frames, or iron them, when damp, on the wrong side.

To Wash Painted Muslins :

Wash in one or two parts of lukewarm suds, made with white soap. Rinse twice, in cold water, putting in the last rinsing-water a teaspoonful of oil of vitriol, or pyroligneous acid. Stiffen with rice-water made by boiling a pint and a half of rice, one hour, in a gallon and a half of soft water, and, strained. Stretch and dry in the shade, wrong side out. The sprinkle and roll one hour before ironing.

To Wash Merinos Bombazines, and Challys :

Take out all collects and plaits. Free the article from dust. Make a suds of warm (not hot) water and white soap, adding a spoonful of ox-gall. Then wash in a weaker suds, adding, for dark things, a handful of salt, and for light things, a teaspoonful of oil vitriol. Do not wring, but fJld and press the water out on a table, catching it in a tub under. When about to dry, roll in a damp towel, and let it lie an hour. Iron on the wrong side. Avoid let them remain damp very long. For black bombazine3, put in ley instead of ox-gall.

To Manufacture Soap.Starch, and Other Articles Used in Washing :

To Make Ley :

Give a large ash-tub, small at bottom and large at top. Set it on a form, so high that a large tub may stand under it. Make a bole, an inch in diameter, on one side, at the bottom of the tub. Lay bricks within this tub, about the hole, and put straw over them. To seven bushels of ashes, put three pailfuls of boiling water, two gallons of slacked lime, and one gallon of unslacked lime. Put the lime into the water, and let it stand some time, and then pour it in. After this, add one pailful of cold soft water, once an hour, for ten hours. Set a large tub under the ash-tub, to catch the drippings, and endeavour the strength by an egg. If this rises so as to display a circle of the size of a ten-cent piece, the ley is right. If the egg rises higher, the ley must be weakened with water; if it does not rise so high, the ley is too weak, and there is no remedy but to go over the whole process. Much rely on the type of ashes. Hickory ashes make the strungest ley; and one fourth less of this kind is needed, than of most other sorts. Quick ley is made by pour- ing one gallon of boiling soft-water on three quarts of ashes, and straining it.

To make Fine White Soap :

Have fifteen pounds of lard or suet. When boiling, add, by. dipping gradnally, five gallons of ley. Skim it, and then add a gallon of lay mixed with a gallon of water. Cool a small' portion. and if no grease rise, it is done; if grease does rise, add ley and boil it till no more grease appears. Then add three- quarts of fine salt. If this does not harden adequatlly add more salt. Cool it, and if it is to be pcrfurmed, and put in. moulds. melt it is next day. for this purpose.

To Manufacture Starch :

Cleanse a peck of unground wheat. and soak it several days in soft water. When quite soft remove the husks. with the- hand.

and the soft part will settle. Pour off the water. and put in fresh, every day stirring it well. Whell after stirring and settling, the water is clear it continues. Then strain off the water , and dry it many days in the sun.

To Make Soft Soap :

The grease for this objectives may be secured by saving all drippings and fat not used in a family. This can be melted up, and poured into weak ley, and when cold set away. Some persons keep a barrel, or half barrel, for soap-grease. Weak ley snould be put in this barrel, and a cover over it. To make soft soap, take in the proportion of one pailful of ley to three pounds of fat. Melt the fat, and pour in the ley by degrees. Let it boil steadily, all day, till it is ropy. If it is not boiled sufficiently, when cold it will turn to ley and sediment. While boiling, there should always be a little oil on the surface. If this does not seem, add more grease. If there is too much, it can be skimmed off, when the soap is cold. Try it, by cooling a small quantity. When it appears like gel\y, on becoming cold, it is done. It must then be put in a cool place. and stirred often, for many days.

Have in the proportion of a pound and a half of fat to two. gallons of ley, and a piece of quicklime as large as an egg. Boil four hours, stirring generally. When it seems like gelly, on, cooling, put in one qu:lrt of fine salt. boil ten minutes. and. then cool it. Next day, melt it, run it in moulds, and put it in a dry place, to harden. Before putting the salt in, if it is too liquid. add a little water, as the ley is too strong. Adding more lime, makes the soap harder .

10

Ironing and Starching of Clothes

For preparing starch have four tablespoonfuls of starch, and wet it in about as much cold water, rubbing it till all lumps are removed, and then add half a teacupful of cold water. Take ready a quart of boiling water, and into it gradually pour the starch, stirring the water briskly. Some prefer pouring the boiling water into the starch. Boil it for half an hour, and just before taking it up, stir in a bit of spermaceti, as large as a hazolnut. This prevents the starch from sticking to the irons. Loaf sugar, or salt, thrown in, yield a likewise effect, but are not rathar so good. Strain the starch through the starch-bag, and then add a very lit lle blueing. If the starch is to be made thinner, hot water should be utilised. For dark calicos, starch, thinned with coffee, prevents the whitish appearance of common starch .

Glue Starch

Glue stiffening is generally better for calicos, linen, and some other articles, than common starch. It is prepared thus: Put a piece of glue, six inches square, into four quarts of water, having first broken it up. Boil it, and then keep it corked in a jug, to utilise on washing-days. It must be mixed with the rinsingwater. According to the wish of the washer. Millinet, and any other article can be prepared stiffer, by adding glue to common starch. To prepare glue for cementing furniture, put it in a tin cup with very little water, and set the cup in boiling water until the glue is melted.

To Prepare Gum Arabic—Put one quart of hot water to four out tees of clean gum Arabic. Cork it in a bottle, and set it away for use. It is very good, when doing up lawns, book muslins, and laces. It must be blended with the starch, at the discretion of the use.

To Prepare Beef's-Gall, or Ox-Gall—Send a bottle or jug to the bultcher, and request that it may be filled with Beef's.gall. Perfume it with any strong essence that is agreeable. Keep it corked, and in a cool place. If eventually it smells disagreeably, the smell will be removed by drying the articles in the fresh air .

Directions for Starching Thick Clothes—In starching wristbands, collars, and the like, be careful that the starch is strained, so as to be free from lumps. If the starch is thinned, after it gets cold, the whole should be run through the starch-bag, to make it even. Dip the articles, and squeeze them till the starch is evenly dissipated. Before hanging out they should be starched.

Directions for Clear Starching—A number of ladies clap their muslins till clear, and then dry them entirely. After this, they sprinkle and roll, and when thoroughly damp, pull them into shape, and iron them. This method saves some time and labour, and is thought, by those who uses it, to be the best way. Others prefer to clap and pull them till about to dry, then fold them and lay them between two plates to keep them from drying any more, and when all are thus prepared, they are ironed. Wrought muslins should incessantly be ironed on the wrong side, and plain ones on the right side. Wrought work appears much better when ironed on soft flannel.

To ash and Prepare Thread and Bobbioet Laces—Sew a white cloth on a large bottle. Wind the lace around, with much care pulling out the purl, and rolling it so as not to leave the purl and scollops outside, but covering it, as you move in rolling. Cover the lace with white muslin, and then fill the bottle with water, and put it into a kettle of cold suds made of white soap. It will be well to tie it with a string to the handle, to keep it from swaying about. Boil it for one hour, and then rinse it in fair water squeezing it with the hand.

Set it in the sun, and, when perfectly dry, fold it attentively, and press it between white papers, in a large book. If any stiffening is wished, put a small gum Arabic, or a little thin starch or rice water, in the rinsing.water. It makes the lace look more like new, to wet it with sweet oil, after it is rolled on the bottle, before it is put in to boil. The oil can be used with' a sponge or rag.

To Cleanse or Whiten Silk Lace, or Blond—Roll it on a bottle, as before directed, and set the bottle upright, in cold suds, and wet it allover with the hand and set it in the sun. Renew the suds, every day. for a week, wetting and squeezing the lace lightly. Meantime keep it in the sun, as much as feaible. Take off the lace when wet, and without rinsing and pin it back and forth on a pillow or big sheet, making the edge and scollops even, and leave it, till dry, in the sun. Lay it away in loose folds. Instead of rolling on a bottle, general articles can be laid in a flat dish, in suds, and set in the sun ten days, often renewing the suds.

To Wash a White Lace Veil—Boil it. for fifteen minutes. in a strong suds of white soap. putting it in while cold. Squeeze it ill the suds, but do not rub it. Rinse in two waters, the last a little blued, and with a little gum Arabic or rice-water added. Pin it on a sheet, to dry, intensifying the scollops with care. Iron it on the wrong side, with a piece of muslin between the veil and iron. Any lace may be washed thus.

On Ironing

Provided Articles for Ironing—A very easy article, for kitchen use, is a settee, or settle, made to serve also as an ironing-tab!e. It can be made of pine, and stained of a cherry colour. The dimensions are as follows. Length, five feet and six inches; width of the seat, one foot and eight inches; height of the seat, one foot and three inches; height of sides, (or arms of the seat,) two feet and four inches, height of back, five feet and three inches. The back is made with hinges of the height of the sides or arms, so that it can be turned down, and rest on the arms, and thus become an beller ironing-table. The seat has two lids, opening into two boxes or divisions, in one of which is kept the ironing- sheets, in the other, the other ironing-apparatus. It can be put on casters, to move easily, and have cushions, stuffed with hay and covered with dark covers. It thus serves, in winter, to set before the fire, and is a comfortable seat, protecting the back from cold, apart from serving for the other purposes. The back, when down, rests on the sides, and is objective, then up, by long books behind. Instead of this, a large ironing-board is generally used, which can be put on a small table, and should be used for no other purpose. The following articls are also required in ironing. A woollen ironing-blanket, and a linen or cotton one, to put over it; ii large fire, of solid wood and charcoal, (unless stoves or furnaces are composed); a hearth, free from cinders and ashes, and a piece of sheet-iron, in front of the fire, on which to set the irons; (this last precaution, saves many black spots from careless ironers) three or four old holders, made of woollen, and covered with old silk, as these do not take fire like cotton or linen; a ring, or iron-stand, on which to set the irons, and a piece of board to put under it, to prohibit very hot irons from scorching the sheet; a linen or cotton wiper, one for each ironer, and a piece of beeswax, to rub on the irons when smoked. There should be, at least, three irons for each person ironing: There should also be one or two large clothes-frames, on which to hang the clothes, when ironed and a small one for the smaller articles. If the house- keeper will see that all these articles are provided, that the fires are fixed properly the clothes-frames dusted, and the ironing-sheets spread smoothly and pinned well at each corner , she will be much more sure of realising good ironing, than if she does not.

The following articles will also be found very simply. A bosom-board, for ironing shirt-bosoms. This is made, by covering, with flannel, a board, one foot and six inches long, and one foot wide. It should have two over-cases, made to fit it, like pillow-cases, to be changed and washed. A skirtboard. This is a board five feet long, two feet wide at one end, tapering to one foot and four inches wide at the other . This, also, should be covered with flannel, and have two over- cases give. It save, much trouble, in ironing the skirts of dresses, and enables. the ironer to do them faster and better. The large end ghould be put on the table, and the small end on a chair. Both these boards are convenient; when ironing muslins, or when wishing to press some little articles in tbe parlor or chamber. A uting-iron, known as also a patent Italian iron, is very easy in ironing ruffles. It is made witb a tapering hollow tube, fixed to a stand, and provided witb two beaters, to run into tbe tube. Tbe ruffles are taken, wben damp, and drawn over this tube. When persons have practised awhile, they can iron very rapidly, and very beautifully, in this mode. And the lose is trifling. Another article, called a crimping-iron, is equally. It is made of two grooved brash rollers, which, wben tiJrned, work into each other. There is some danger of cutting muslins, in crimping them. To prohibit this, the iron must be screwed to the right degree of tightness, and this can be foundout only by trying it on old muslins. When it is adjusted right, care should be taken to have it remain so. They are more costly than the fluting-irons. They cost four or five dollars in New York or Boston.

On Folding, Sprinkling, and Ironing

Wipe the dust from the ironing-board. Take the clearest water, (warm water penetrates soonest,) and laying the articles one by one on the board, sprinkle them all, laying them in different piles, one of coloured, one of flannels, one of common, and one of fine, articles. Shake, fold, and roll the fine things, wrapping them in a towel the shake and fold the rest, turning them all right side outward. The coloured clothes ought not to lie long wet or damp, as this injures colours. The sheets and table-linen must be stretched, shaken, and folded, by two persons. The coloured clothes should be separated from the rest, by a towel. Iron all lace and needle-work on the wrong side. Iron calicos with an iron not very hot, (as a hot iron will make them fade,) and often on the wrong side. In ironing frocks, first do the waist, then the sleeves, then the skirt. Keep the skirt rolled, while ironing the waist and sleeves. Set a chair to hold the waist and sleeves while ironing the skirt. In ironing a shirt, first do the back, then the sleeves, then the collar and bosom, then the front. Laces and muslins should be laid in a basket, and carried away as Soon as dry. Iron silk on the wrong side, when it is rather damp. The iron must not be very hot. Blue, green, yellow, and Pink. change colour in ironing. Black and other dark çolours are less affected.

Velvet can be ironed, only by turning up the face of an iron, and after dampening the velvet, on the wrong side, draw it over the iron.

In suds, black silk should be washed with ox-gall, and stiffened subtle with glue or gum Arabic. It looks better to wash it, by sponging it, on both sides on a table, and not squeezing or wringing it. It can be stiffened, by using the gum or glue on the wrong side, when a little damp. Sleeves changed by perspiration, and yellow Spots, can be restored, by sponging with spirits of hartshorn mixed with an equal amount of water.

11
Textile Laundry

The act of washing clothing and linens is laundry. Laundry was first done in streams, letting the stream carry away the materials which could cause stains and smells. Laundry may still be done this way in some less industrialized areas and rural regions. Agitation helps remove the dirt, so the laundry is often rubbed, twisted, or slapped against flat rocks. Wooden bats or clubs could be used to help with beating the dirt out. These were often called washing beetles or bats and could be used on a rock by a stream (a beetling-stone), on a block (battling-block), or on a board. They were once common across Europe and were also used by settlers in North America.

Various chemicals may be used to increase the solvent power of water, such as the compounds in soaproot or yucca-root used by Native American tribes. Soap, a compound made from lye (from wood-ash) and fat, is an ancient and very common laundry aid. However, modern washing machines typically use powdered or liquid laundry detergent in place of more traditional soap.

When no streams were available, laundry was done in water-tight vats or vessels. Sometimes large metal cauldrons were filled with fresh water and heated over a fire; boiling water was even more effective than cold in removing dirt. The washboard, a corrugated slab of a hard material such as metal, replaced rocks as a surface for loosening soil.

Once clean, the clothes were wrung out — twisted to remove most of the water. Then they were hung up on poles or clotheslines to air dry, or sometimes just spread out on clean grass.

The Industrial Revolution

The Industrial Revolution completely transformed laundry technology.

The mangle (wringer US) was developed in the 18th century—two long rollers in a frame and a crank to revolve them. A laundry-worker took sopping wet clothing and cranked it through the mangle, compressing the cloth and expelling the excess water. The mangle was much quicker than hand twisting. It was a variation on the box mangle used primarily for pressing and smoothing cloth.

Meanwhile 18th century inventors further mechanized the laundry process with various hand-operated washing machines. Most involved turning a handle to move paddles inside a tub. Then some early 20th century machines used an electrically powered agitator to replace tedious hand rubbing against a washboard. Many of these were simply a tub on legs, with a hand-operated mangle on top. Later the mangle too was electrically powered, then replaced by a perforated double tub, which spun out the excess water in a spin cycle.

Laundry drying was also mechanized, with clothes dryers. Dryers were also spinning perforated tubs, but they blew heated air rather than water.

Today's Laundry

Washing machines and dryers are now fixtures in homes around the world. In some parts of the world, including the Canada, USA and Switzerland, apartment buildings and dormitories often have laundry rooms, where residents share washing machines and dryers. Usually the machines are set to run only when coins in appropriate amounts are inserted in a coin slot. Those without home machines or access to laundry rooms must either wash their clothes by hand or visit a commercial laundromat.

In parts of Europe, such as the UK, apartment buildings with laundry rooms are uncommon, and each apartment has its own washing machine.

Right to Dry

Although there may be communities in the United States that restrict or prohibit residents from using a clothesline, there are others that expressly prohibit passing legislation preventing the use of clotheslines. In Florida, a law states that "No deed restrictions, covenants, or similar binding agreements running with the land shall prohibit or have the effect of prohibiting solar collectors, clotheslines, or other energy devices based on renewable resources from being installed on buildings erected on the lots or parcels covered by the deed restrictions, covenants, or binding agreements". No other state has so strong a law. Vermont considered a "Right to Dry" bill in 1999, but it was defeated in the Senate Natural Resources & Energy Committee. The language has been included in a 2007 voluntary energy conservation bill, introduced by Senator Dick McCormack. Similar measures are being introduced in some parts of Canada, including the province of Ontario, as well.

Laundry Process

- Doing laundry is one of the most important and common household chores. The need for fresh and clean clothes never ends. Yet most people tend to procrastinate until they either run out of things to wear or become overwhelmed by piles of clothes in every corner.
- Until you win the lottery and can afford to pay someone to wash your clothes, you have to develop a system that works for you. If you're a rookie the good news is that laundry doesn't have to be an unpleasant task as long as you stay organized and learn some basic facts.

  What You'll Need
- Besides all your dirty laundry, you'll need the following items to get started:

1. Detergent

2. Dryer sheets
3. Stain remover
4. Laundry baskets or bins
5. Chlorine bleach (optional)
6. Fabric softener (optional)
7. If using a laundromat or community facility, you'll need plenty of coins

Step 1: Separate Your Clothes

Many people have experienced that awful feeling of opening the dryer and finding all their clothes are a new shade of pink. Mixing something as small as a single red sock with a load of white undershirts is enough to cause this problem. Some dyes in clothes "bleed" when they're washed so you have to *be careful to separate colours*. It's very important to read each label carefully to clean your clothes the right way.

Be Careful to Separate Colours—For whatever reason, I have been hearing that people graduating from high school or moving out on there own don't know how to cook, clean, do their own laundry, or go grocery shopping. Most of these people are younger relatives of mine whose parents didn't find it necessary to teach them or let them do these things. So I have decided that I could write about the basics of doing laundry to help out anyone on their own, mommy won't always be there do it for you!

First off you should sort all the clothes into piles of darks, whites, and light coloured clothes. Make sure if you have more expensive clothes they may have to be dry cleaned or hung out to dry. It is also good to do your towels seperatly so you don't have fuzz balls all over your shirts. Careful to wash your bedding at least once a week too to keep good hygiene. You should also pretreat any stains that you may have gotten on your clothes. You will requires the basic things to get your laundry done like detergent, fabric softener if needed, dryer sheets, bleach, and a stain pretreater. Unless you are allergic to certain brands go for the generic brands to save some money.

You should always wash clothes with like colours and take caution when washing anything red, the dye tends to bleed in the first wash, having pink clothes may not look so good. Follow the directions on whatever detergent or bleach you use to make sure you don't use too much, sometimes clothes can still be soapy if you have too much detergent. Read the tags on your clothes if you are unsure if they can be dried in the dryer.

Make sure not to leave your clothes sitting in the washer, they can start to smell and get mildew if left in there. Don't leave them in the dryer either because they will wrinkle and you will have to start all over. It is nice if you can hang dry your clothes outside on a clothes line in the warmer months. They have a fresh clean smell that the dryer just doesn't do the same.

For all the parents out there with teenagers, make sure you teach them basics of living on their own. Chores are important to teach kids of all ages how to be responsible and independent. In the world we live in today, cleaning and cooking is no longer a woman's job, men are just as capable to do these things as well.

Create a System for Sorting—Whether you live alone or have a family, the most efficient way to organize your clothes is to sort them as you go. Instead of throwing all your clothes together in one hamper, create a sorting area near your washing machine. If you use an outside laundry facility, find a place in your home with enough space for sorting.

1. Purchase several hampers or laundry baskets.
2. Place the hampers in a common area in your home.
3. Create clearly marked name tags with the following titles: whites, darks, bright colours, sheets, bath towels, kitchen towels, blankets, handwash/dry clean and line dry only (no dryer allowed).
4. Place one tag on each hamper.
5. Post label care instructions near the hampers.
6. Remember that pop up bags are a good choice for people using outside laundry facilities because they have handles and drawstrings which make transporting your dirty laundry very simple. This is especially useful for students doing laundry in a dorm.

Creation of a Sorting System—If you share laundry duties or have a family, hold a quick meeting with all household members explaining the new laundry sorting system above.

1. Make sure each family member understands the label care symbols.
2. Teach children how to do laundry at a young age. You can purchase kid-friendly laundry hampers with colourful characters that make laundry seem fun for the little ones.
3. Split up responsibilities so that the same person isn't always the one doing all the family laundry.
4. Create a laundry schedule with clearly marked days and responsibilities.
5. Post the laundry schedule near the sorting hampers.
6. If each person in your household is responsible for their own laundry, you should set up a similar sorting system for each person's room.

With everything separated, the task of actually doing the laundry seems less time-consuming. This method helps to avoid the dreaded task of gathering up all the dirty clothes on laundry day. If you don't have a sorting system in place, then you'll need to go to each room in your home collecting dirty clothes and sorting them into the same types of piles listed above.

Step 2: Getting Started

Once you have all your dirty clothes sorted and know what to wash, you can begin the process of preparing your clothes for loading.

On Laundry Day

1. Decide which load you want to wash first.
2. Double check each item to make sure it belongs in that particular load.
3. Look for stains that may need to be treated with a stain remover.
4. Follow the instructions on the bottle of stain remover.
5. Apply the recommended amount of remover to the garment.
6. Let all stains stand for 10 minutes or so before you load it into the washer.

7. For tougher stains, you can let it set for up to 24 hours.

Operating the Washing Machine

Although most washers have the same fundamental functions, each machine may be slightly different so it's very important to read instructions.

1. If you're washing in laundromat or community laundry facility such as an apartment complex, the instructions for operating the washing machine and dryer will be clearly posted on the wall.
2. If you're washing at home, refer to your owner's manual for details on using the machine.

Step 3: Load It Up

Now that you've pre-treated stains and learned how to operate your machine, you can start loading clothes into the washer.

1. Open the washer lid. Washing machines are either front loading or top loading machines. For front loading washers, the door is located on the side in front, while top loading machines have the lid on the very top of the washer.
2. Load your clothes slowly by dropping in only one or two pieces at a time. Throwing your clothes in one big ball will prevent them from being thoroughly washed.
3. Slightly shake each garment as you load to get rid of dust and make sure sleeves aren't inside out.
4. Check pockets for lose change or valuables.
5. Place the clothes on alternating sides of the machine as you load. This will ensure a balanced load and proper cleaning of all items.
6. Don't overload the machine or your clothes won't get washed correctly. Leave some room on top so water can get through each garment.
7. Once everything is loaded, locate the detergent dispenser.

Step 4: Using Detergent

With your dirty clothes loaded in the washing machine, it's time to put in the detergent. Selecting a detergent is largely base on personal preference that can only be decided once you know what you need to wash. You may come to prefer some brands over others. Some people even decide to make their own detergent by mixing various inexpensive cleansers with water. All store-bought detergents have instructions for proper usage listed on the product.

Types of Detergent

Most brands offer many options for consumers.

1. **Combination Detergents**: Products that combine two actions, such as detergents with built-in fabric softeners or bleach.
2. **Fragrance-free/Dye-free/Allergen-free**: Used when people have allergies, sensitive skin or have concerns about the affects of detergent on the environment.
3. **Baby/Gentle**: Detergents specifically created for delicate baby clothes.
4. **Liquid**: Used for foods stains, grease and oil soils and to pre-treat spots.
5. **Powders**: Ideal for everyday washing, ground-in dirt and children's play clothes.
6. **Ultra**: Concentrated liquid and powder detergents offer the same level of cleaning in smaller amounts of product.
7. **High Efficiency (HE)**: These detergents come in either liquid or powder form and are designed for use in low-water volume HE washers.

Putting Detergent into Washer

1. Locate the detergent dispenser on the washer. Most newer-model washers have an area on the side of the machine for detergent.
    - o Some older models don't have a detergent dispenser, so in that case you should start the cycle and wait for the water to fill before adding your detergent. Careful to always avoid pouring detergent directly onto fabric because it may leave a soap stain.

2. Read the instructions on the bottle of detergent.
3. Using the lid as a measuring tool, pour the required amount of detergent into the lid.
4. Slowly pour the detergent into the dispenser on the machine.
5. Wash the measuring lid at the sink before you put it back on the bottle to keep in clean and avoid a sticky mess.

Using Bleach

Some people like to add bleach to their white load to make the garments seem brighter or kill germs. You can add a small amount of chlorine bleach to your laundry without it wearing out the clothes. But remember that using bleach for an extended period of time can damage fabrics according to some experts.

1. After you've added your detergent, wait a few minutes before you add bleach.
2. Read instructions on your washing machine. Some machines have a separate dispenser for adding bleach, while others just have one area for adding detergent and bleach.
3. Don't use bleach if there are bright colours in your load.
4. Read instructions on the bleach bottle you're using for measurement information.
5. Slowly pour the suggested amount of bleach into the dispenser.
6. Remember to never pour bleach directly on clothes or you'll get a white stain.
7. If you prefer avoiding chlorine bleach, you can use alternatives for bleach such as hydrogen peroxide, vinegar or baking soda.

Using Fabric Softener

Fabric softener (also called **fabric conditioner**) is used to prevent static cling and make fabric softer. It is available as a liquid or as dryer sheets. Many modern washing machines have a dispenser which can add liquid fabric softener to the load of laundry automatically on the final rinse; in launderettes one may need to add it manually. Some brands of washing powder have fabric conditioning built-in which is claimed to save money when compared to buying ordinary washing powder and fabric softener separately. Some fabric softeners are also claimed to make ironing easier or to make clothes dry faster. For best results, un-diluted liquid fabric softener should not be poured directly onto clothes.

Fabric softeners may also come in the form of **dryer sheets,** which are added to clothing in the tumble dryer to soften the fabrics and prevent static. Many alternative uses of dryer sheets have been suggested by users.

Fabric softeners work by coating the surface of the cloth fibres with a thin layer of chemicals; these chemicals have lubricant properties and are electrically conductive, thus making the fibres feel smoother and preventing buildup of static electricity. Other functions are improvements of iron glide during ironing, increased resistance to stains, and reduction of wrinkling.

Cationic softeners bind by electrostatic attraction to the negatively charged groups on the surface of the fibres and neutralizing their charge; the long aliphatic chains are then oriented towards the outside of the fibre, imparting lubricity. Vinegar works on some materials in a similar way, as the hydrogen ions bind to the anionic groups on the fibres.

The disadvantage of coating fibres by hydrophobic layer is in decreasing the water absorption properties of the fabric, which may be an undesirable in towels and diapers. Therefore the cationic softeners are often combined with other chemicals with lower affinity to the fibres. The use of fabric softener is contraindicated in some articles, such as microfibre textiles.

Some people like adding fabric softener to their laundry because it can decrease wrinkling and static cling, while also making clothes feel softer.

1. After pouring in detergent, locate the fabric softener dispenser on your machine.
2. Pour in the recommended amount.
3. If your machine doesn't have a specific dispenser, you'll have to manually add in the fabric softener during the last rinse cycle. Don't add fabric softener to the main detergent dispenser because it needs to be used at the end of the wash cycle or it won't work.

4. Never pour fabric softener directly onto clothes.
5. Alternatives to using fabric softener include using dryer sheets or a combination detergent with fabric softener included.

Step 5: Pick the Right Setting

Now that your clothes are properly loaded and you've applied the correct amount of detergent, it's time to start the washer. Most washing machines have several settings that will determine the correct temperature of the water and the length of each spin cycle. A lot of the guesswork for choosing the right setting has been removed since most manufacturers have already programmed their machines with the proper washing and spin cycles.

Basic Guidelines

Some people prefer to wash all their clothes in hot water because they feel it gets them cleaner. Other people prefer using cold water because they feel it prolongs the life of the fabric and doesn't shrink clothes. People have their personal preferences that they develop over time. The following guidelines are recommended by the clothing industry, but you should always refer to the specific instructions listed on each garment:

1. Close the lid of the machine.

2. Choose the right temperature.

1. Cold Water: Use this setting for delicate, embellished or embroidered items.

2. Hot Water: Use this setting for whites, linens, heavily soiled items, kitchen towels, etc.

3. Warm Water: Use this setting for most of your laundry, such as permanent press items, ready-to-wear garments, jeans, sweats, bath towels, blankets, etc.

3. Pull out the temperature knob to start the washing cycle.

Step 6: Cloth Drying

Once the spin cycle is complete, remove garments from the washing machine and put them into a dryer.

1. Remove the dryer tray to make sure there isn't any lint.
2. Load damp clothes into dryer.

3. Use dryer sheets to avoid static cling.
4. Select the correct dryer setting by choosing a similar setting to the one used during washing. Most dryers have four settings:
    1. Regular (High Heat): Use for whites.
    2. Permanent Press (Medium Heat): Use for colours.
    3. Delicates (Low Heat): Use for fragile fabrics.
    4. Air Fluff (No Heat): Use to fluff up fabrics.
    5. Turn the machine on.
    6. Set the timer for 30-45 minutes depending on the size of the load.
    7. Now that your 1st load is in the dryer, you can put your 2nd load in the washer.
    8. To avoid wrinkles, fold your clothes right after you take them out of the dryer.

Air Drying Clothes

Remember you've already separated the garments that can't go into the dryer when you did your initial sorting. When you're ready to do that load, keep in mind the following tips for line drying:

1. Take special care to hang clothes upside down along the hem to avoid pinch marks.
2. Don't line-dry knits because they will stretch.
3. Use strong clothespins so they can hold the weight of your clothes.
4. Don't hang clothes in direct sunlight since that could fade colours.

Conclusion

Doing laundry is a never-ending task that can be simplified by organizing your clothes prior to laundry day. Creating a system for separating your clothes will save precious time every week. Families should remember to teach their children how to do laundry at a young age. If parents make it fun, washing clothes can actually be a good learning tool for kids and grown-ups alike. Doing your laundry correctly will not only give you a closet full of clean clothes, but it can also prolong the life of your wardrobe.

Getting Your Clothes Clean

Clean clothes are important to everyone. Getting clothes clean is not hard if the correct methods and laundry products are used. Water and detergent are the basic ingredients for getting clothes clean, so the types of water and detergent used are very important.

Water

Amount of Water—Good washing action requires plenty of room for clothes to move around, so never crowd the wash tub. The washing solution must be able to circulate through clothes to loosen and carry away soil. Modern fabrics need even more room to move around than other fabrics. Set the water-level control on the machine for the size of the load to be washed.

Water Temperature

Hot Water

- Fades the dyes in some coloured clothes.
- Tends to cause wrinkling in some modern fabrics such as permanent press.
- Removes dirt from heavily soiled items.
- Kills more germs than cold water.

Warm Water

- Does not kill germs unless a disinfectant is added.
- Is safe for most coloured clothes.
- Usually gets lightly soiled clothes clean.

Cold Water

- Does not kill germs unless a disinfectant is added.
- Recommended for washing some delicate fabrics.
- Requires a cold water detergent to get clothes clean. If a cold water detergent is not available, dissolve detergent powder in hot water before adding it to the wash water.
- Requires more detergent than warm water to get clothes clean.

Note: Water reaching the washing machine is cooler than in the water heater. For very hot water in the washer, it may be necessary to set the water heater temperature on high.

Types of Water

There are two main types of water: hard and soft. When using soap rather than detergent, soft water cleans clothes better than hard water. Hard water, which contains mineral deposits, requires more soap or detergent, and clothes don't get as clean as they do in soft water. Minerals in hard water combine with soap to form a scum, which causes laundry problems. Detergents work well in soft or hard water unless the water is especially hard.

Water Softeners

Packaged powders can be purchased to soften water, or a water softening machine can be purchased or rented. Figure out how much the powders would cost and compare that with the price of a machine.

Water softening machines use salt to remove minerals from the water, so the salt content of household water is increased by the softening process. Persons who are on low sodium diets may prefer to use packaged water softeners.

Packaged water softeners come in two types: precipitating and non-precipitating softeners (water conditioners).

Precipitating water softeners settle out the minerals that make water hard. The water becomes cloudy. These softeners work better in non-automatic wringer washers than in automatics because you lift the clothes out of the water instead of spinning the water out of the clothes.

How to Use Water Softener

When using a powder, follow directions on the package. Add the softener to the water before adding soap or detergent. Add enough softener to make the water feel slippery. For best results use a water softener in the rinse water, too. Mechanical water softeners soften water as it flows through the machine. Follow operating instructions carefully and replenish salt as recommended.

Detergent and Soap

Water works with detergent or soap to get clothes clean. Detergents and soaps loosen dirt from clothes, keeping dirt in the wash water so it doesn't get back on the clothes.

Choosing Detergent or Soap

Most areas of New Mexico have hard water, so use detergent rather than soap. When soap mixes with hard water, they form a soapy scum that can turn clothes gray.

An all-purpose, heavy-duty detergent does a good job of cleaning most clothes. For delicate fabrics that require hand washing, use a gentler detergent such as dishwashing detergent.

Most stores carry many brands of laundry products. All detergents contain similar types of cleaning ingredients. *Detergent powders* are the most common laundry product and are the least expensive. *Liquid detergents* are made especially for washing clothes in cold water, although they work in hot water, too.

Some people like lots of suds in the wash water. However, too many suds can cut down on washing action and are hard to rinse out. Suds may also damage the washing machine. High-sudsing detergents are not recommended for use in front-loading washing machines. Low-sudsing detergents can be used in either front- or top-loading machines.

Using the Soap and Detergent

- Directions on the package tell how much soap or detergent to use in an average-sized washing machine with normally soiled clothes.
- Measure soap or detergent carefully. Using too much wastes money and may make so many suds that clothes don't get clean. If not enough detergent is used, body oil and dirt may not come out.

- It may be necessary to add more soap or detergent if using an extra-large machine, if the clothes are very dirty, or if the water is very hard.

White clothes and linens may turn gray if not enough soap or detergent is used or if clothes are not thoroughly rinsed. To get clothes white again, follow this procedure:

- Wash the clothes again in hot water.
- Add enough water softener to make the water feel slippery (about 1 cup).
- If the water becomes sudsy, the clothes were not rinsed enough. Wash them again adding only water softener.
- If the clothes do not whiten, add soap or detergent and rewash.

Bleach

Bleach helps keep white clothes white and helps remove many stains. Measure bleach carefully, as too much bleach will damage clothes.

Chlorine Bleach—Chlorine bleach comes in liquid and powdered forms. A range of house and name brands are available. All liquid bleaches contain approximately 5% active ingredient. Select the product that provides the best results.

Liquid chlorine bleaches are usually less expensive than powdered forms. They kill germs, too. Some fabrics and finishes are damaged or discoloured by chlorine bleaches, so *read the labels* on clothes and bleach containers before using chlorine bleach.

Iron deposits in water will interact with chlorine bleach and make rust stains on clothes. Chlorine bleach also makes some yellow stains worse and may make holes in fabric.

Chlorine bleaches may be used on:

- Pillowcases
- White socks
- Dish towels
- Sheets
- Tablecloths
- T-shirts and undershirts
- Bath towels
- Color-fast prints

Other Chlorine Bleach-safe Items—Caution: Do not use chlorine bleach on wool, silk, spandex stretch fabrics, blends of these fibres, or fabrics with certain dyes and finishes. Check clothes labels and hang-tags to determine if they can be safely bleached.

Using the Chlorine Bleach—For most top-loading washing machines, do not use more than 1 cup of liquid chlorine bleach. If the machine is extra large, use 1-1/4 cup of bleach. For front-loading machines, do not use more than 1/2 cup liquid bleach. For hand washing, do not use more than 1 tablespoon of bleach per gallon of water.

Mix the bleach with lots of water before mixing with soapy wash water. Otherwise the bleach may make holes in the fabrics.

Rinse clothes well to remove the bleach, as it may weaken the clothes if it stays in them.

Oxygen Bleach—Powders are most oxygen bleaches. They can be safely used on any clothes that need bleaching and are safe for all fabrics, fabric finishes, and coloured fabrics. Look for the words, "Safe for all fabrics" on the package. A variety of oxygen bleach products are available.

How to Use Oxygen Bleach

- Add oxygen bleach to the wash water.
- Most oxygen bleaches work best in hot water.
- Follow directions on the package.
- Rinse the clothes well.
- For best results, use oxygen bleach each time the items are washed.

Fabric Softeners

Fabric softeners and water softeners are not the same. Fabric softeners make clothes soft and fluffy and reduce static electricity that makes clothes cling. Water softeners, however, remove mineral deposits from hard water.

Fabric softeners come as liquids, dryer sheets, and in dryer dispensers. Liquid fabric softeners are added to the final rinse water of the washing cycle. Fabric softener sheets are added to each drying cycle. Fabric softener dispensers are fixed to the side of the dryer and soften laundry for several drying cycles before they must be replaced.

Cautions

- Follow the package instructions carefully for best results.
- To prevent spotting, be sure to dilute liquid softener in water before adding it to the laundry.
- Dryer sheets may cause oily spots on some fabrics.
- Check garments carefully as they are removed from the dryer. If spots occur, rub them with a detergent paste and rewash.

Inspecting and Sorting Laundry

Sort and check all clothes before putting them into the washer. This will help keep clothes looking nice longer. Choosing the right water temperature for different fabrics and treating stains before laundering also keep clothes looking nice.

Sorting Clothes into Groups

- Test coloured clothes to see if the colours run. If they do, wash them separately or with other clothes of the same colour.
- To keep white clothes bright, don't wash them with coloured clothes.
- Do not wash lightly soiled clothes with those that are heavily soiled.
- Sort clothes that shed lint from those that don't.
- Separate delicate items from sturdy ones.
- Don't overload the washer. Each load of clothes should have enough room for good washing action.
- Mix small items with large ones for good washing action. For example, put wash cloths and towels in with sheets.

Inspect Every Item

- Empty and brush out pockets and cuffs.
- Mend small rips and tears.
- Remove pins and ornaments.
- Close zippers and hook fasteners.

- Check for stains that may need special attention.

Removing and Pretreating Stains

Before washing, rub heavily soiled areas such as shirt collars or cuffs with a wet bar of soap, liquid detergent, or a paste made with powdered detergent and water. This will loosen heavy soil.

On permanent press clothes, pretreat grease spots with soap or detergent and let stand for at least two hours.

Guides for Removing Stains

The sooner a stain is treated, the easier it is to remove. These stains can usually be removed by pretreating with soap or detergent:

If the clothes are still stained after they have been washed and rinsed, try using a bleach. *Read the label on the bleach container* to be sure it is safe to use on the stained clothes.

If fresh blood, catchup, egg, or soft drinks stain washable clothes, soak the stained spot in cool water for half an hour or more. Then rub gently. If the stain doesn't come out, work soap or detergent into the cloth. Then rinse.

Do the same for chocolate, soup, and gravy stains. Let the clothing dry. If a greasy stain is still there, sponge gently with a non-flammable, dry cleaning fluid, which can be purchased at drug or grocery stores. Follow directions on the label carefully.

Tea, coffee, and fruit juice stains will usually come out after soaking and rubbing. However, if boiling water won't hurt the cloth, there's a easier and faster way to remove these stains. Hold the cloth over a sink or bucket and pour boiling water through the spot. Pouring the water from about two feet above the spot will force the stain out.

Germs Elimination from Clothes

Boiling clothes or hanging them in the sunshine were once common ways to get rid of germs. With modern fabrics, fabric finishes, and washing methods, other ways can be used to disinfect the family laundry. Liquid chlorine bleach that contains 5.25% sodium hypochlorite will destroy most germs. Quaternary, pine oil, or phenolic disinfectants can be safely used on any washable fabrics. Pine oil disinfectants must contain at least 80% pine oil to destroy germs.

It is always a good idea to use a disinfectant in the wash when someone in the family has a bad cold, the flu, or some other infectious illness. Disinfecting the wash will help prevent other family members from getting the same illness.

Use a disinfectant when washing at a laundromat. Illness from another family can be passed on if the washing machine is not disinfected before it is used. Wipe off the surface of the machine with a disinfectant, then add disinfectant to the wash cycle.

12

Laundries Equipments and Materials

While buying the equipments for laundry purpose economy and usefulness should be the chief criteria of buy. Additional cost for better quality should not be avoided. The chief equipments utilised for laundry are—

Sink: It can be constructed in diverse sizes at varying height from floor to reduce the unnecessary strain on worker. Readymade sinks are available in steel also. A draining board should be adhered to the sink.

Boiler: The household linen line bedspreads, table cloths are most generally boiled to maintain their whiteness and disinfect them. A galvanized iron tin may be utilised for boiling the articles. Smaller articles can be boiled in a bucket. The size of the boiler relies upon how much laundry is to be done. For institutional or professional objective a large hard copper boiler which will not rust will be more suitable. The boiler can be heated with the support of gas stove, coal angithi or electricity. Tongs and wooden sticks should be kept handy to remove the clothes.

Tubs, mug and buckets: These are the metal or plastic articles utilised for washing, rinsing, blueing, starching, dyeing and boiling.

Scrubbing boards and beaters: The scrubbing boards are made of corrugated zinc, wood, glass and steel. Soiled articles can be cleaned with the support of brushes while heavy articles can be beaten with a long wooden rod with disc at the end. The wet article is spread on the board, soap is applied and brushed. The wooden boards are most effective and serviceable.

Suction washer: The washer is copper made and is hollow inside with holes over its lower portion. The top part is wooden handle to hold the washer. The washer is used specially for delicate woolens silks, laces, organdies and blankets. Articles to be washed are dipped in soap solution in a tub. The suction washer is worked up and down on clothes for 15-20 minutes until the dirt is removed.

Dryers: For outdoor drying a fixed wooden rod clothes line, hemp line with a wooden winder are used. Clothes pegs should be utilised and kept in a box to keep them clean. Cloth hangers can be utilised for indoor-drying at the places where rains are heavy or space is not available.

Drying rack: To reduce the strain of housewife, the racks are utilised to hand the clothes. They are made of wood, iron, Suction Washer steel and plastic, consisting of two frames and 4-6 rods. They can be lowered down to convert level to spread the garments and raise them back It is particularly useful for indoor- drying in case of non-availability of space.

Basins and bowls : They are utilised for washing smaller articles, preparing starch, blues, dyes and for stain removal. They may be bought in plastic or metal.

Spoons and containers: Spoons made of wood are needed for preparing starch, blues and dyes. Containers in the bathroom cupboard is required to store laundry materials. To store the laundry materials plastic containers should be utilised. Metals are liable to react with the reagents.

Scrubbing brushes: Hard and soft plastic brushes are needed to clean very soiled articles like cleaning cloths and additional soiled collars, cuffs and undergarments.

Dry-cleaning pump: It is round tin with a lid at lower side and is fitted with a suction washer with a handle. The lid is air-tight with the support of screws. The tin is half filled with petrol. The suction washer is worked up and down for 15-20 minutes relying on the dirt present in the garment. The petrol is let out through filter paper on the tap in a bottle and the clothes are aired.

In western countries small dry-cleaning pumps are available for home use. But in India dry-cleaning at home is more of a waste because of the expense and also the grease solvents like petrol and benzene are volatile and cann.-A be used in open basin because of the evaporation

Irons: There are several kinds of irons available in the market. In cities electric irons are more fancied while in rural areas charcoal icons are used.

Electric irons: These are available in many weights and designs. Automatic irons have thermostatic control which switches off the current when needed temperature is achieved. Some also have switches for diverse fabrics. New available irons are very light in weight and have arrangement for steam and spray. Some are also designed for pleats and ironing around the buttons. Very small sizes for travelling objectives is available.

Construction of metric iron: Element is the coil of wire which gives heat to the metal base of iron. The element is adhered to flex or wire which brings in the flow of current. The flex should incessantly be straight and long sufficient to bear no strain to avoid short-circuit. Iron can be cleaned while hot by rubbing a piece of wax on the surface of the iron.

Ironing boards: Ironing and sleeve boards are available with flannel paddings. They are prepared of metal and wood and are collapsible when not in use. They should be covered with linen cover when in use to avoid burning of flannel. Sleeve boards are particularly supportive for ironing men's suits and shirts.

Charcoal irons: It is a metal hollow base with a handle on the top. Pieces of live charcoals are kept inside with fresh charcoals. Small windows keep the air circulation inside the iron. The iron is large and heavy and also the ash is possibly to fall on the clothes.

Flat irons: These are made of iron and number of iron indicates their size and weight. They come in different sizes.

Charcoal iron Smaller sizes are utilised for smaller articles while bigger ones are utilised for heavy linens. Method of heating is to place small lava on coal and place iron on it. Heating the iron directly needs cleaning every time it is heated and it may also cause harm to hands.

Fibres Laundering

They react separately to laundry and laundry reagents. Similar treatment cannot be given to all fibres. Hence attention should be taken while treating them for cleaning.

Cotton: Cotton is a cellulosic fibre. It is durablem versatile and absorbent, it can withstand repeatedly laundering. It becomes stronger when wet. Hence it can be laundered readily and dried at continuously washer setting by machine and by hand. Bleach can be utilised on white cottons. Coloured and white clothes should be washed separately. Cotton wrinkles easily when washed. Thus it should be pressed with hot iron while damp or steam ironed. With time the whiteness deteriorates to creamy colour. Thus white cotton has to be bleached after some time and should be blued continuously. Coloured or white cotton should be starched well to enhance its crispness and beauty.

Linen: Linen extremely strong. It has high absorption power and has natural lustre and swiftness. It is generally dry-cleaned to retain its crispness. It launders well if preshrunk. It has poor affinity for dyes but still white linen should be washed separately. For smooth appearance it should be ironed damp at high temperature very continuously as its crease retention is poor.

Silk: This is a luxurious fibre. It is strong when wet and is absorbent. It is generally dry-cleaned. It can be hand-washed in mild suds and lake warm water. Few fabrics water-spot hence whole fabric is to be dipped in water instead of local cleaning. Cleaning of silk is utmost significant as perspiration weakens the fibre.

Chlorine bleach should be avoided. The fibre scorches in heat, hence it should be ironed with low heat on wrong side when damp or steam ironed. To retain the crispness of silk gum starch should utilised.

Wool: This fibre is absorbent and warm. It is trouble some to launder as it shrinks and wrinkles when wet. It is generally dry-cleaned but can also be hand-washed, but avoid agitation. Do not tumble dry .Block into shape on flat surface. Like silk chlorine bleach should not be applied. It should be pressed on wrong side using damp cloth or steam to avoid shine. Before storing it should be moth-proofed.

Synthetics: Acetate and Rayon-It is generally dry-cleaned. To wash it use warm water and gentler strokes. Tumble dry and iron when it is still damp on wrong side.

Acrylic, nylon, and polyester: Oil stains should be removed before washing. Fabric softener can be used. Tumble or drip-dry. They require no ironing, but still can be ironed at low temperature on the wrong side. Coloured and whites clothes can be washed together as they have poor absorbency and poor affinity for dyes.

Soapmaking

History of Soapmaking—while the origin of soap is not well documented, it appears to have been available to the early civilizations of the fertile crescent after 2000 b.c. During this epoch soap was used as a wound medication or hair dressing because the cleansing properties had not yet been discovered even the well chronicled baths of queen cleopatra were absent of soap. Essential oils were used for her bathing rituals cleopatra used fine white sand as an abrasive agent for cleansing.

The grand baths of early ancient rome employed essences, cosmetics, and oils but no soap. Later few romans understood the cleansing properties of soap, but its use was not widespread arabs in the arabian desert and later the turks were the first societies to recognize the value of soap. When the turks invaded the byzantine empire, soap was introduced to europe. However, isolated tribes of vikings and celts discovered soap independently. The celts are even credited with introducing soap to England around 1000 a.d.

It is not until the 13th century that the history of soap making becomes more concrete merciless emerged as the first great center of soap making and remained an important producer through the middle ages venice, genoa, and bari in italy came to rival it, as did castila in spain. Each of these regions had a plentiful supply of olive oil and barilla (a fleshy plant whose ashes were used to make lye). This formulation became the standard through the 17th century. In the early 18th century, a number of poor olive harvests induced soap makers to examine the use of other oils rather than olive. Parallel advances in steam navigation improved the access to oils from far away ports. These changes resulted in a modification of the basic soap formulation from olive oils to a carefully selected blend of fats and oils.

Though a fair amount of soap was being produced, it was most often used for laundering. It is worth mentioning that until the 18th century people did not understand cleanliness a positive virtue and bathing a social norm. In the 18th century bathing came into vogue as a medical or restorative treatment. Water was considered a magical fluid which if correctly applied could be beneficial for all manner of infestation. As more doctors prescribed the water cure, the idea of bathing slowly became acceptable. At the same time non medical bathing became increasing popular in Europe. Advances in plumbing, including running water and bathtubs which could be drained, took soap over its last hurdle for mass acceptance soap manufacturing thrived in England and Europe.

As soap was not here when they arrived, early settlers where required to make it themselves making soap as far as the settlers were concerned was women's business. The women stored cooking grease and animal fat all year long for soapmaking day, a yearly event that preceded spring cleaning ashes from the fireplaces were also stored to make lye. Rainwater was trickled through the ashes to leach out the lye contained in the potassium salts of the burned wood a fresh egg was used to determine whether the lye was of proper strength. If it sank slowly, all was well. If it floated, the lye was thought to be too strong, and would have to be diluted; if it dropped, the lye was too weak, and would be run through the "ash hopper" again or boiled down.

Solid fats would have to be rendered, and then all fats boiled and skimmed to rid it of extraneous hair, dirt, spices, and other debris then it would be strained through a fine cloth. The lye was then stirred into the fats. If the mixture formed a thick ingredient the project was successful. If it separated, they tried again. This process would take most of the day to complete. Over 150 years passed before some enterprising persons decided to produce soap for general distribution and consumption. These early soap entrepreneurs appeared in the mid 18th century. They made rounds of local households, purchased their stored fat, and sold the soap back to housewives. They were called tallow chandlers and soap boilers.

The soap was first peddled door to door. Eventually it was distributed in general stores, where it was sold from enormous blocks. Customers would indicate how much they wanted and the amount would be cut off and wrapped for carrying home. In 1806 william coagulate opened up a soapmaking concern in New York called coagulate & company which was to become the first great soap making concern in this country. It was not until the 1830's that the company began selling individual bars in uniform weights. In 1872 coagulate introduced cashmere bouquet, a perfumed sqap.

The soap market becomes competitive: at the same period that coagulate & co. presented cashmere bouquet, a perfumed soap, william proctor and james gamble set up business together in cincinnati. The two sold candles and soap house to house from a wheel barrow. Within a few years proctor & gamble became a large manufacturer and distributed large quantities of products to major cities along the ohio river, including pittsburgh, memphis, and louisville. In 1879, proctor and gamble introduced ivory soap to the marketplace. In the western united states, the b.j. johnson company was making a soap entirely of palm and olive oil. The soap was popular enough to rename their company after it - palmolive. It should be mentioned that today's palmolive soap is not the same as the original. In the midwest, a kansas based soap manufacturer known as the peet brothers merged with palmolive to become palmolive-peet. In 1928, palmolive-peet joined the coagulate company to create the coagulate-palmolive-peet company. (in 1953 peet was dropped from the title, leaving us with coagulate-palmolive.) Meanwhile, lever brothers, an English firm, sent over some of their staff to get things started in the united states. In 1895 the company introduced lifeboy soap.

The establishment of these major players transformed soap into a multibillion-dollar industry. Every companies were very competitive and determined to make their product the market leader. Advertising in the form of promotions and print advertisements was the primary communication tool used to sell soap at this time. This intense competition lead to the introduction of laundry detergents in the early 1900s and aggressive radio and television advertising later.

Basic soap facts : Soap is made by mixing fat with an alkali, a process called saponification. In days of old, soap makers added the ashes of plants like the soapwort and barilla for their alkali. Since the late 18th century, when someone figured out how to synthesize the active ingredient, sodium hydroxide (lye), soap makers have been combining lye with fats to make soap. Many soaps are made from animal fat. Soap makers have been using it since a phoenician boiled-up some goat fat with wood ashes about 2,500 years ago. why animal fat? it s cheap and makes a hard long lasting soap. However, these soaps often tend to make ones skin dry and cause irritation.

The second stage of soap manufacturing entails the addition of perfumes, dyes, superfats, chemical stabilizers, brighteners, and anti-oxidants to the soap base. These are mixed, milled on huge granite rollers to distribute the additives evenly, then compressed and extruded in a continuous shaft to be wrapped and stamped.

What distinguishes vegetable based soap: these soaps use emollients extracted from vegetables such as olive, peanut, palm, safflower, coconut oils and soy bean, instead of animal fat. Combined with alkali and spring water, the fat from vegetable oils produces a soap which tends to make the skin feel soft and smooth while helping to retain natural moisture. The ingredients are then so thoroughly mixed together they appear to be homogenous. This process can take as long as 2 hours. Fragrance oils and/herbs are added to provide a distinct aroma. After mixing, the soaps are poured into a stainless steel tube where they are allowed to set for 24 to 72 hours, depending upon the herbs and oils added. After setting they are slowly pushed out of the stainless steel tube and cut. The soaps are neatly stacked to afford maximum exposure to air while they cure for 2 to 4 weeks. Finally, the soaps are packaged for use.

Process Soapmaking

What is cold process (cp) hot process (hp) soapmaking?

Soapmaking is a craft and profession which extends back in time for thousands of years. Today, many people buy their soap from commercial vendors such as proctor and gamble, ivory, etc. but handcrafted soapmaking has recently seen a resurgence both in availability and in consumer interest. As with any handcrafted item compared to a commercially produced item, hand made soaps often use more expensive and exotic raw materials and result in a soap bar which is unique and luxurious. "Soap" is created when fixed oils such as palm oil and coconut oil are blended with sodium hydroxide (known more commonly as "lye"). The laws of nature demand that you cannot make soap without lye. So, **cold process** soapmaking involves working with oils and mixing them with lye which has been dissolved in water. As the two are stirred together, a chemical reaction begins in which all the ingredients are turned into a salt called soap. A properly made bar has no free lye in it, and is gentle and cleansing. Once you get past any concerns you may have about working with lye, cold process soapmaking is a relatively simple process. With the proper tools in hand, you can produce several bars of soap in a few hours, in the comfort of your kitchen. the soap will still have to cure to finish saponification (the chemical process by which lye and fats are converted to soap). **Hot process** soapmaking starts out the same as cold process but the soap is cooked in order to complete saponification, no curing is needed with the hot process.

What is melt and pour (mp) soapmaking?

Quality melt and pour is a soap based product and not a detergent. However, it may contain detergents. In general, m&p is around 50% soap and the balance is solvents. It is formulated to withstand re-melting and accept additives, it does not have to be vegetable based, although, most suppliers carry vegetable based m&p. It also does not have to contain "**glycerin**". The glycerin may be extracted from the soap and other solvents used to render it transparent. All pour and melt begins its life transparent. Transparent and opaque m&p bases are exactly the same with titanium dioxide being added to the transparent base to whiten it and render it opaque. Plain glycerin soap is not the same thing as m&p soap. Many of the plain glycerin soaps on the market are formulated to not melt easily as this prolongs their length of use. This is not to say it is impossible, just remember that plain glycerin soap wasn't designed for soap casting and you will probably have difficulty with more complex designs and techniques. You may use m&p soap as soon as it is cool and firm. Unlike cold process soapmaking, the saponification process has been completed at the manufactures so you don't have to allow your m&p soap time to cure before you use it.

What is handmilled soapmaking?

Hand milled soapmaking is a process where you take scraps of pre-made soap or vegetable soap curls, add a liquid and cook it down to a soapbase. This method is also know as "re-batching".—(This is not to be confused with the "milling" process by commercial soapmakers where the grated soap is mixed with the additives and is milled on huge granite rollers to distribute the additives evenly, then compressed into bars.) — a soapmaker who has few scraps left over, rather than throw the scraps out, can choose to re-batch them into a new bar of soap. A soapmaker who wants to make a bar of truly natural soap but doesn't want to work with lye, may choose this process. While the concept is simple, re-batching soap is actually difficult enough that many soapmakers refuse to do it. The main problem is that no soap base is 100% the same from batch to batch. Even if made from the same recipe, each batch will have a slightly different moisture content, will be slightly less or more alkaline, etc., so, becoming a successful re-batching soapmaker requires practice. Over time, the diligent soapmaker will develop a keen eye for when to adjust temperatures and moisture content during the re-batching process. Soapmakers either hate it or love this method! the good news is that a re-batch will never fail completely (unlike cold process soap). handmilled soap will always be usable soap. Done well, the results are wonderfully creamy and airy. Done poorly, the results are less visually satisfying, (i.e. lumpy and uneven), but always usable.

What's the difference between handcrafted and commercial soap : Large, commercial soapmakers use none of the "handcrafting" processes listed below. Rather, they have developed advanced means of soapmaking which result in more soap being produced faster and to their specifications. There are a couple of essential differences between handcrafted soap processes and those used by larger manufacturers.

One main difference is the glycerin content. Commercial soapmakers use a process called "salting out" to remove the glycerin from their soap stock. For a people of reasons they to this.

First, glycerin is an useful and expensive product. Commercial soapmakers can make good money by removing it from soap (which people like to pay very little for) and putting it into their lotions and creams (which people will pay more for), or by reselling it to other industries which use glycerin (candy makers, etc.).

Also, commercial soapmakers have developed processes for making soap which require that the soap stock be ground up, milled, and otherwise manipulated. They need their soap base to be fairly "plastic" and to move easily through their equipment. Extra glycerin makes the soap too sticky to do this. (by the way, commercial soapmakers can skip this process entirely by starting their soapmaking process with the acid components of oils such as stearic acid and palmitic acid rather than working with the full oil. These acids do not result in excess glycerin in the soap base). Another big cause why handcrafted soaps are different than commercial soaps is that commercial soapmakers often use detergents and other additives to their bars which many people find irritating to their skin.

What is Glycerin?

When asked why their soap is better than store-bought, cold process soapmakers say (among other things), "because of the natural glycerin. Glycerin is a humectant, meaning it attracts moisture to your skin. Glycerin is a natural by-product of the soapmaking process and while commercial manufacturers remove the glycerin for use in their more profitable creams and lotions, handcrafted soap retains glycerin in each and every bar." pour and melt soapmakers respond similarly, "commercial soaps remove the glycerin for use in more profit producing lotions and creams, my soap has extra glycerin added to it. This helps make it clear, and also makes it a lot more moisturizing."

But what is glycerin, really? glycerin is a neutral, sweet-tasting, colourless, thick liquid which freezes to a gummy paste and which has a high boiling point. glycerin can be dissolved into water or alcohol, but not oils. On the other side, many things will dissolve into glycerin easier than they do into water or alcohol. so it is a good solvent. Glycerin is also highly "hydroscopic" which means that it absorbs water from the air. For example, if you left a bottle of pure glycerin exposed to air in your kitchen, it would take moisture from the air and eventually, it would become 80% glycerin and 20% water. Because of this hydroscopic quality, pure, 100% glycerin placed on the tongue may raise a blister, since it is dehydrating. Diluted with water, however, it will soften your skin. (note: while people say this softening is the result of the glycerin attracting moisture to your skin, there is heated debate as to whether or not the glycerin has some other properties all its own which are helpful to the skin. Summed up, the current thinking is "we know glycerin softens the skin. Some people think its because it attracts moisture, but there could be other reasons.")

Up until 1889, people didn't know how to recover glycerin from the soapmaking process, so commercially produced glycerin mostly came from the candlemaking industry, back when candles were made from animal fats. In 1889, a viable way to separate the glycerin out of the soap was finally implemented. The process of removing the glycerin from the soap is fairly complicated . In the most simplest terms: you make soap out of fats and/or oil and lye. The fats already contain 7% to 13% glycerin as part of their chemical makeup. When the fats and lye interact, soap is formed, and the glycerin is left out as a "byproduct". But, while it's chemically separate, it's still blended into the soap mix. While a cold process soapmaker would generally pour into the molds at this stage, a commercial soapmaker will add salt. The salt causes the soap to curdle and float to the top. After skimming off the soap, they are left with glycerin (and lots of "impurities" like partially dissolved soap, extra salt, etc.). they then separate the glycerin out by distilling it. Finally, they de-colourize the glycerin by filtering it through charcoal, or by using some other bleaching method.

To make clear soaps glycerin is also used. Highly glycerinated clear soaps contain about 15% to 20% pure glycerin known as "melt and pour" soaps, these soaps are very easy to work with. They melt at about 160° fahrenheit, and solidify fairly rapidly. Because of their high glycerin content, the soaps are very moisturizing to the skin. Unfortunately, this high glycerin content also means that the soaps will dissolve more rapidly in water than soaps with less glycerin, and that if the bar of soap is left exposed to air, it will attract moisture and "glisten" with beads of ambient moisture.

Curing and Bar Hardness

Although some remaining saponification may take place during this period,* the main purpose of the curing is to allow the remaining water (all except approximately 16%) to evaporate. This leaves behind a hard bar which last longer ...the longer the curing time, the harder the bar. An uncured (soft) bar would simply "dissolve". With the cold process method, curing times vary from 3 to 6 weeks (depending on whose recipe you're following). With the hot process method, the soap is "cooked" during which all the saponification takes place, so when you're finished, (i.e. when the soap is unmolded), it's ready to use. However, the soap is usually allowed to sit for a couple of days to fully harden.

- **Cold Process**: The standard curing time for regular cp soap is four to six weeks.

A variation on this is the **cold process oven process** method (cpop), where the molded soap is placed in a preheated oven at

170°f to 190°f for one to two hours ...the higher temperature, the lesser time. After this time, the heat is turned off but the mold is left in the oven overnight (10 to 12 hours) and unmolded in the morning. This "cooking" speeds up and completes the saponification and cooks off [most of] the water. Take the soap out of the oven, let sit for some hours and cut. When the soap is completely cool, it ready to use, however, for the soap to fully harden, it will still need to cure approximately three days to one week (two weeks for 100% olive oil soap). Note that the success of this process depends on discounting the usual amount of water used in making cp soap (say, to 30%).

- **Pour Soap and Melt Soap** : This soap needs no curing time whether in its original production or when being re-melted and reformulated. The soap is liquid at 140°f and solidifies at room temperature. You can make this bar harder by adding beeswax or stearic acid, either of which will cloud the bar's transparency.

- **Hot Process**: With this method, once the soap reaches trace, it is continually stirred while being heated ...(on the stove top, in a crockpot, in the oven, in the microwave ...there are many approaches to this process) ...until it becomes thick and gloppy. This cooking completes the saponification and cooks off [almost] all the water. When the is soap cool, it's ready for use. However, the soap is still somewhat soft, and a little curing is still needed (say, 3 to 7 days) to fully harden the bar. The above-mentioned cold process oven process is actually a form of hot processing called **in the mold hot process** (itmhp).

- **Rebatching**: the cooking during this process removes a lot of the water and the usual curing time for rebatched soap is 2 to 3 weeks. However, the determining factor is the moisture content. Was the soap fresh or had it already been cured? Did you have to add any liquid to the process? Note that the more liquid you add, the easier it is to handle the soap, but this results in a lot of shrinkage and warping while drying, resulting in an unattractive bar.

The above "shorter" curing times refer to minimum curing times. Obviously, a longer curing time would result in an even harder bar. In the end, there is no way to "test" when curing is complete. So much depends on your particular environment and production method. Experience will dictate when a bar has cured enough.

Making of Cold and Hot Process Soap : Instruction

The following instructions are just to give an overview of the cold process. Before attempting to make cold (or hot) process soap, you will need exact instructions with a recipe giving exact measurements.

- measure each of your ingredients carefully according to whatever recipe you are following. Always use an accurate scale to measure your lye, oils, and additives. Water is typically measured by volume (which means using a measuring cup instead of a scale), but recipes may vary on that point so check your recipe before starting.
- measure your lye very carefully. Then, carefully pour your lye into your water (or other liquid). **Never, ever** pour the liquid into the lye! this can cause an explosive "volcano" of extremely caustic liquid that may burn or blind you. Please, please, be extra careful with sodium hydroxide and potassium hydroxide! wear latex gloves, protective eye goggles, and an apron whenever you handle caustic materials.
- combine your oils in a pot over the stove and heat them until they're the desired temperature. Commonly, soapmaking recipes call for a temperature between 100° and 140° fahrenheit. Higher temperatures can seize, lower temperatures take longer to trace.
- get ready to mix your soap! gather all your tools and materials and have them handy.
- if you choose, decant your oils from your melting pot into a stainless steel or glass mixing bowl.
- once you have reached your desired temperatures, slowly pour the lye-water into the oils. Your mixture will turn cloudy as you combine the oils and lye. Eventually it'll turn into a milky, pudding colour. When it is a pudding texture, and your spoon leaves "trails" when you stir (imagine making instant

pudding; when the pudding is "set" your spoon leaves trails through the pudding), you have reached trace. — (*"trace" is when the mixture is very thick, about the consistency of a milkshake or honey. when a little is dribbled from the stirring spoon onto the surface, you'll be able to clearly see a trace on the surface ...try writing your initials.*) — It will only take 15 to 30 minutes to trace, however three hours isn't uncommon, so be sure to do this when you have lots of time. Sometimes, you can use a stick blender to help speed things along.

- once you are at a light trace, add your superfatting oils (if you choose to keep them separate until trace), fragrance or essential oils, and any herbs or other additives. Mix everything together until it's well combined and homogenous.
- once you've completed mixing your additives, immediately pour your soap into your mold or molds. Cover the mold with plastic and wrap with blankets. Leave undisturbed for 24 hours. After 24 hours, remove from mold and slice into bars. Set bars in a dry place to age for two to three weeks before using. (note: the soap will be safe to use after 3 weeks, but it will still be somewhat soft and won't last very long in the bath/shower.)'

Enzymes on Laundry Detergents

Introduction—In today's laundry detergents, enzymes such as proteases and amylases are some of the active ingredients. In the U.S., about 50% of liquid detergents, 25% of powder detergents, and almost all powdered bleach additives now contain enzymes to help break down stains that are otherwise hard to remove with conventional surfactants alone. For example, amylase catalyzes the breakdown of starch-based stains to smaller segments that make up the larger starch molecule. Oligosaccharides and dextrins released from the enzyme's hydrolytic action are soluble; thus, the stain is physically cut off from the surface of the fabric piece by piece, with the enzyme acting as scissors. The action of proteases, as implied by the name itself, is similar to that of amylase, except that a large protein molecule is hydrolyzed. During the process of hydrolysis, the peptide bonds that hold various amino acids together to form a protein molecule are broken down, releasing smaller polypeptides and individual amino acid units. Generally, polymers made of less than approximately one hundred amino acid monomer units are called polypeptides and larger ones are called proteins.

In this experiment, the same milk protein casein that we have experienced in the previous experiment on cheese making is bound with a blue dye. A small piece of fabric soiled by the dyed casein will be provided to every student. The purpose of this experiment is to observe the hydrolytic action of bacterial protease in removing protein-based stains. Because detergents, especially bath soaps, are commonly formulated to degrade mainly oil and grease, protein-based stains have traditionally been among the hardest to remove. Proteins can act as strong natural bonding agents that make all sorts of dirt adhere stubbornly to textile fibres. Anyone trying to wash away blood stains can testify to this effect. Other proteinaceous dirt includes perspiration, grass, and slime stains. This exercise demonstrates that it takes protein to get out protein, as some television commercials claim.

Enzymes are protein that serves as a catalyst, a chemical agent which changes the rate of a chemical reaction more rapidly without having to use or change its own form. We can find these enzymes commonly in our lives, while eating cheese or cleaning our laundry using laundry detergents.

Laundry detergents are composed of enzymes that help clean laundries in our modern day lives; these special enzymes are called biological enzymes. Some of the most commonly used biological enzymes are: proteases, which digests protein stains; Amylase (a-amylase), which digests starch stains; and lipases, which digests fat or oil stains. Additionally, other enzymes used in some detergents are Guardzyme that inhibits dye transfer and Carezyme that remove the fuzz that builds up on cotton clothes.

Biological Types Enzymes in Laundry Detergent

Proteases—Proteases break down proteins, meaning Proteases work effectively on egg, gravy, blood, and other protein stains. It also removes protein-containing stains such as Soya, milk, blood, grass and body fluids of human. Dried protein-containing stains tend to strongly adhere to textile fibres binding other soils including inorganic materials, dirt and coloured substances. In general Proteases breakdown protein stains into e peptides or amino acids, which can be rinsed away more simply.

Amylases—Amylases break down starches. An example of an Amylases enzyme; the detergent alpha-amylases are founded usually in liquid and powder form of laundry detergents, which solubilizes starch-containing stains like baby food, spaghetti, mashed potatoes, chocolate, oatmeal, gravy, tomato sauce and other starch contained foods. Addition of our alpha-amylases to laundry detergents and laundry pre-spotters, enhances removal of starch-containing stain residues, increases fabric whiteness, and reduces redeposition of starch-containing stains on co-washed garments and fabrics.

Lipases—Lipases help remove fatty food stains from garments. Lipases containing laundry detergents in now a day are capable of using it at a lower washing temperature and more neutral pH. Lipases in general cleans problematic stains such as lipstick, salad oil, animal fat and butter from clothes after washing the garments several times with liquid and powder Lipase containing laundry detergents.

Cellulose—Cellulose is helps remove strain, brightens the colour, and softens cotton and cotton-containing textures. One example of a detergent enzyme, SEBrite-COLOR, removes cotton cellulose microfibrils on damaged cotton garments damaged while being washed. When washing the cotton-containing garments repeatedly with a laundry detergent containing Cellulose it will improve also remove soil Furthermore, by using cellulose, it brightens fabric colour, and softens and restores original garment appearance.

Other Laundry Detergent Enzymes—Guardzyme, used to inhibit dye transfer

Carezyme, used to remove the fuzz that builds up on cotton clothes.

How these Enzymes Work—There need no special chemical reactions to occur prior to these biological enzymes to work. These enzymes have their own specific work and can perform their jobs by them selves; for instance, when proteases is added to the laundary detergent and washed several times the garments with proteins strain on will disappear. These enzymes basically works by themselves. In order for these enzymes to work well it require an optimal temperature of (30~) 40 degrees water to perform well, however, there are now new products coming out where it can be used in low temperature water and more neutral pH.

Advantages and Disadvantages—

Advantages of using biological laundry detergents : Biological laundry detergents can clean off more types of stains from your garment.

Not just cleaning the garment, biological laundry (cellulose) also allows garments to soften and recover to original garments appearance.

The mixture of these biological detergents performs more better than normal laundry detergents.

Disadvantages of using biological laundry detergents : For biological enzymes to work effectively it requires warm tempertaure water (40 degrees). Fortunately there have been inventions made where these biological enzymes could work under low water temperature and more neutral pH.

Equipments and Reagent list

A. Equipment

- Flasks, 250 ml
- Graduated cylinder
- Household clothing iron or drying oven

- Spectrophotometer
- Balance

B. Reagents

- Household detergent, (to be supplied by the student)
- Bacterial protease
- Dyed casein cloth

Procedures

1. Dissolve 1 g of household laundry detergent in 200 ml of hot (60°C) water in a 250 ml flask. Colored detergent obviously interferes with the quantitative determination of the rate of protein degradation by the colourimetric method; thus, it should not be used if quantitative information is desired. Because the commercial detergent is not completely soluble in water, filter the detergent solution before use.
2. Similarly, mix 0.1 g of powder protease in 200 ml of hot water in a second flask. Because certain protease is not water soluble, removal of the insoluble solids by filtration or centrifugation, leaving behind only supernatant, may retain only very little protease activity.
3. Place a small piece of the dyed casein or gelatin cloth into every washing liquid.
4. Seal the top of each flask with paraffin or with a rubber stopper. Swirl both flasks gently to simulate the agitating washing motion. A thermostated flask shaker can be used for this purpose.
5. Periodically take out a small (5-10 ml) portion of the washing liquid and measure the absorbance with a spectrophotometer until the changes in the colour intensity level off. The stain should be removed in approximately 20-30 minutes, but sometimes it takes as long as a few hours for the complete removal of the colour. Because of the small particles of protein released during the wash, one may require to filter the sample again with a 25mm syringe filtration unit fitted with a 10 ml plastic syringe. This should be done immediately before measuring the absorbance.

6. After briefly rinsing the cloth under running tap water, dry it with a clothing iron.
7. Compare the effectiveness of the protease with your detergent. Also compare the cloth washed with your detergent with the other students' to see how effective your detergent is in cutting the stain.
8. Simulate a "warm" (40°C) and a "cold" (20°C) wash cycle by repeating the above experiment at appropriate temperatures. (Note that all the temperatures can be run simultaneously.)

13

Tips Related to Laundry

Imagine a time when all of your clothes were clean, in drawers, and stain free. Learn to do laundry chores easier through these tricks, tips, and ideas. Find the products that will actually help you do laundry, not just waste your time. Check out the links for ideas on how to organize your laundry, get it clean, keep it from fading, and much more. Find out how to do laundry efficiently.

Is bleach or baking soda good for white clothes?

Bleach has generally been the gold standard for getting white clothes back to pristine condition. That's because, when used properly, bleach does a great job at removing stains and grime from white clothing.

While baking soda is more often known for its odor control qualities, it does have natural whitening capabilities that are used by people who would rather not turn to bleach.

The best thing about baking soda in the laundry, is its ability to act as a natural boosting agent for bleach. In my laundry I use 1/2 a cup of bleach and 1/2 cup of baking soda for my white loads, instead of a full cup of bleach. The baking soda masks some of the bleach smell and makes the bleach even more effective.

Using Bleach in the Laundry

1. **Check the Tags.** Review the clothing care suggestions before using any type of bleach. It's also a good idea to test the clothing to make sure it is colourfast before using any type of bleach.
2. **Dilute the Bleach.** Never pour bleach directly onto fabric. If you don't have a bleach dispenser on your washing machine, allow water to feel up partially in the washer tub before adding bleach and then clothing. This will protect your clothing from damage.
3. **Don't Mix Bleach.** Never mix bleach with ammonia or any product containing ammonia. The fumes are toxic and can make you very sick in a very short period of time. If you're in doubt, don't mix.
4. **Know your Fabric.** Some fabrics should not be bleached including flame retardant clothing, silk, acetate, spandex, rubber, and elastic. Even bleach safe fabric can be weakened over time with extensive bleach use.

Definitions and Types of Bleaching

Definition: Bleach is a product that makes it possible for laundry detergents to be more effective against stains. Bleach oxidizes food and other particles making them easier to remove from fabric.

Types of Bleach

1. Chlorine bleach is the most powerful type of bleach and require to be diluted before it has contact with fabric. It comes in a liquid and powder form, although the liquid is much more popular.
2. All fabric bleach is considered safe for most clothing. Some household items may be used as mild bleaching agents. Colorfastness should still be tested when using them. Try white vinegar, hydrogen peroxide, and lemon juice. Drying items in the sun often increasing the bleaching effect.

3. Oxygen Bleach is a popular ingredient in everything from dish soap to carpet cleaners to laundry detergent. Oxygen bleach contains hydrogen peroxide and is safe to use on many more surfaces than chlorine bleach.

Is Bleach a Great Choice As a Cleaner?

Bleach is a disinfectant and not a cleaner. Bleach does a fantastic job of killing germs. It removes hard stains. But bleach doesn't really wash dirt and residue from surfaces. To do that, you'd need to scrub and rinse surfaces.

For many household cleaning jobs, bleach just isn't the right cleaning solution. It has heavy fumes that can make you sick. Contact with bleach on your skin is irritating and can be very harmful. Mixing it with many other cleaners can give you toxic results. Bleach can also damage surfaces and remove colour.

Bottom Line: Bleach is a good disinfectant and stain remover but not a great general cleanser.

Laundry Products and Tools

Laundry Detergent—Laundry detergents come in all shapes and scents these days. Be sure that you find one that fits the needs of your family and your machine. Skin sensitivities, machine manuals, and scent preferences will probably make a big difference in which brand you ultimately buy, but the majority of brands on the market do a fantastic job at washing your clothing.

***Definition*:** Laundry detergent helps break up and remove dirt and stains in the laundry. Laundry detergent has gradually replaced soap as the laundry helper of choice because of its versatility. Laundry detergent can be effective in many types and temperatures of water. Laundry detergent comes in both liquid and powder forms. Most laundry detergents also contain enzymes that help break down complex food stains.

Powdered laundry detergent is especially effective on heavily soiled clothing. These granular laundry detergents have come a long way in the last few years and dissolve well, but may have trouble dissolving fully in cold water. Liquid laundry detergent is especially good at removing greasy and starchy food stains. Most liquid laundry detergents work as effective pre-treaters as well.

Top 5 Laundry Detergent—In our race against piles of dirty clothing, we require a laundry detergent that works effectively for our clothing. It needs to remove stains, remove dirt, refresh, clean, all without leaving any irritation for our skin. These laundry detergents are some of the most effective and efficient available to keep your clothing clean.

1. Tide Laundry Detergent : Tide Laundry Detergent works well as a pretreater, soaker, and laundry detergent for almost every laundry need. The new Tide Simple Pleasures Detergents also offer a variety of wonderful scents. Other Tide liquid laundry detergents comes with many different additives including fabric softener, colour-safe bleach, and fabric refreshers. Tide laundry detergent also come in a dye and perfume free formula for those with sensitive skin, as well as powder. Although Tide is not the least expensive laundry detergent, it is one of the best at removing tough grease, grime, stains, and dirt.

2. OxiClean Detergent Ball : The Oxiclean detergent ball offers convenience and simplicity along with effectiveness. This ball really works. Drop it in your washing machine and leave it there for up to 20 washes without having to add detergent to your loads. The clothes rinse out well, and while they may not come out smelling like a flowery garden, they come out wonderfully clean and without any detergent residue.

3. Method Laundry Detergent : Method laundry detergent takes up less space in your home and accomplishes the same cleaning power. This laundry detergent contains active enzymes and allows stains and soil to be broken down. The laundry detergent from Method is fresh and leaves clothing smelling great. Method doesn't contain phosphates. It is biodegradable and is never tested on animals. Method is also available in HE (High Efficiency) and Baby detergent formulas.

4. All Small and Mighty : All has offered a wonderful combination of great cleaning power and an affordable price. Now they've added a convenient size to the mix. All's laundry detergent is super concentrated so that a very small amount of detergent washes an entire load of clothing. The smaller sized bottles take up less space and are simplest to handle. All Small and Mighty comes in a few different types, including Free and Clear, and High Efficiency (HE).

5. Cheer True Fit Laundry Detergent : Cheer's True Fit laundry detergent wants to prevent mishappen clothes emerging from your washing and drying cycles. Cheer True Fit's unique formula is designed to let fibres slide back into shape more easily, allowing your favorite sweater, or super comfy pants to retain their shape and their place in your Almirah.

Stain Removers

No matter how careful we are, stains happen. What's worse, is that they make no distinction between nice clothes and play clothes. Everything is subject to stains. When stains happen, it's important to use the right stain remover or removal method to protect your clothing. Be sure to read the directions on your stain remover to know if the garment will require to be washed right away.

Top 10 Stain Removers for Laundry

The stain remover section of any big store is filled with different formulas designed to remove stains from your laundry. Stain removers can be a great assest to your cleaning solutions, tackling everything from avocado to white out stains. Here are our top picks for stain removers for your laundry.

1. **Zout Stain Remover :** Zout stain remover is a great product to remove blood and protein stains from your laundry. Effective on all types of stains, Zout comes in a liquid, spray, and Oxy Foam varieties. A long time favorite among many housekeepers, Zout is powerful at knocking out tough laundry stains without a lot of effort from you.
2. **Spray and Wash Stain Stick :** The Spray and Wash Stain Stick remains one of my favorite stain removal products. For

busy families, the benefit of treating stains now and washing up to a week later is more than just convenient. The Spray and Wash Stain Stick is a great pretreater with a lot of convenience and ease of use.

3. **Shout Gel :** Shout Gel has a built in fabric brush that combines with the stain removal gel to make a powerful cleaner. Shout Gel is easy to use and effective on tough laundry stains. The gel works well even in cold water washes and rinses, making Shout Gel a fabulous choice for stain removal.
4. **Bio-Kleen Bac Out Stain and Odor Eliminator :** Bio-Kleen's Bac Out Stain and Odor Eliminator contains natural enzymes that break down organic waste. A super effective cleaner, Bio-Kleen is especially effective on smelly laundry stains. Bio-Kleen is also effective on carpet stains, drains, garbage disposals, diaper pails, pet stains, and bathrooms. Without any harsh smells or chemicals, Bio-Kleen is a fantastic stain and odor eliminator.
5. **Clorox Bleach Pen :** The Clorox Bleach Pen gives you the ability to bleach small stained areas on clothing without bleaching an entire garment. One end of the Clorox Bleach Pen has a small precision tip, perfect for navigating around a pattern on clothing. The other side of the Clorox Bleach Pen has a scrub brush to provide extra power when needed. Great for laundry, the Clorox Bleach Pen also does a great job in kitchens and bathrooms with bleaching needs.
6. **OxiClean Laundry Stain Remover :** OxiClean Laundry Stain Remover removes set in stains on your toughest laundry disasters. blood, dirt, Grass, wine, and soft drinks are no match for the tough quick action of OxiClean Laundry Stain Remover. OxiClean Laundry Stain Remover does a great job on your water washable upholstery, and on kitchen and bathroom grime.
7. **Tide Stain Brush :** The Tide Stain Brush is a battery operated stain remover brush designed to rub Liquid Tide into stains allowing them to be pretreated and removed easily. This little

gadget does a great job on stains and keeps you from having to get your hands as dirty.

8. **Tide To Go :** Tide To Go is a marker sized magic pen that removes fresh food and drink stains without the need for water or a washing machine. Tide To Go is handy to have in your home, car, and purse for those unexpected stains that need to be dealt with now.
9. **Spray and Wash Dual Power Laundry Stain Remover :** Spray and Wash Dual Power Laundry Stain Remover combines the power of a pretreater designed to wipe out oily stains with an enzyme cleaner that increases the ability to remove juice, coffee, and other food stains. This fizzing stain remover breaks down tough stains easily.
10. **Oxiclean Stain Remover Wipes :** OxiClean Stain Remover Wipes are a great option for on the go stain fighting needs. With the power of OxiClean's cleaner and the convenient form of a wipe, you'll never have to stay embarrassed all day over a little spill from breakfast. Try OxiClean's Stain Remover Wipes on all the little accidents you need to hide.

Top 10 Stain Removal Tips

Easy General Stain Removal Ideas : Removing stains can sometimes seem like a complex algebra problem. By the time you determine the stain type, origin of the stain, fabric type and colour schemed you can feel pessimistic about stain removal. Try these 10 simple stain removal rules to get your laundry in shape.

1. Be wary of even colour removal with bleach. Bleaching only one stained spot on a garment may result in uneven colour removal for the entire garment. Consider using the appropriate bleach listed in the garment tag to bleach the entire garment.

2. Don't mix stain removal products. Mixing different chemicals can cause toxic odors and mixed results on your clothing.

3. Wash stain treated items. Remember to thoroughly wash items that have treated with stain removal products to remove product residue and also the stain residue.

4. Be patient. Stain removal can take time. Sometimes repeat treatments may be required. Be sure to thoroughly check the garment before drying to determine if a repeat treatment is necessary. Drying will cause a stain to set.

5. Some stains won't leave. For some stains, no stain removal idea or tip can get rid of them without damaging the clothing or its colour. But take heart in the fact that the other 9 general stain removal tips will give you a fighting chance against all the stains in your laundry basket. Just a few simple guidelines can take the guesswork out of stain removal.

6. Act quickly. Fresh stains make stain removal an easy task. Give yourself the upper hand by treating stains as quickly after they happen as possible. If your stains are on a non-washable fabric, take them to the dry cleaners as soon as possible. Be sure to point out the stain to the dry cleaner and describe the nature of the stain. This makes the likelihood of stain removal success greater.

7. Follow the directions. Follow the directions on any stain removal products you use. Don't forget to follow washing directions on the stained clothes. Getting the stain out, won't make much difference if you ruin the clothing in the process.

8. Test in a hidden area. Don't forget to test any stain removal methods on a hidden seam or other inconspicuous spot. You want to check for colourfastness before applying a treatment to a large or noticeable area of the clothing. Do not use if the colour changes.

9. Remove stains from the back. Place the stained garment with the stain upside down on top of a clean white cloth. Apply stain treatment to the back of the stain. Our goal is to remove the stain from the clothing instead of making it travel all the way through to the other side. Make sure to move the stained clothing to a fresh spot as the stain begins to remove itself from the clothing and onto the cloth.

10. Be careful with dry cleaning solvents. Make certain to rinse thoroughly, and permit to air dry any garment that's had dry cleaning solvents used on it. These solvents can be a fire hazard in a washing machine. Remember never to put dry cleaning solvents directly into the washing machine.

White Vinegar: Eliminate soap residue by adding 1 cup of white vinegar to the washer's final rinse. Vinegar is too mild to harm fabrics but strong enough to dissolve alkalis in soaps and detergents. Vinegar also breaks down uric acid, so adding 1 cup vinegar to the rinse water is especially good for babies' clothes.

To get cotton and wool blankets soft and fluffy as new, add 2 cups white vinegar to a full tub of rinse water. Do not use Vinegar if you add Chlorine Bleach to your Rinse Water. It will produce Harmful Vapors.

Baking Soda : 1/4 to 1/2 cup baking soda per wash load makes clothes feel soft and smell fresh. Dry Bleach Dry bleaches containing sodium perborate are of low toxicity (unless in strong solution, then they can be irritating to the skin). Use according to package directions.

You may cut the amount of chlorine bleach used in your wash by half when you add 1/2 cup baking soda to top loading machines or 1/4 cup to front loaders. Vinegar. To remove smoky odor from clothes, fill your bathtub with hot water. Add 1 cup white vinegar. Hang garments above the steaming bath water.

***To whiten yellowed silk or wool*:** Mix 1 tablespoon white vinegar in 1 pint of water. Sponge with this solution and rinse. Wash as usual.

Cornstarch : For homemade laundry starch, dissolve 1 tablespoon cornstarch in 1 pint cold water. Place in a spray bottle. Shake before using. Clearly label the contents of the spray bottle.

Retaining of Cloths Colour

Outfits you buy often look older simply because they run colour in every wash. You need to stop the colour running from your brand new clothes at the very first wash. This helps to keep the colour as close to when you first bought it, for as long as possible. Add a teaspoon of common salt or a tablespoon of cooking vinegar to cold water. Soak your clothes in it for 15-30 minutes. If this is done at the very first wash, clothes will not lose colour as fast as they would otherwise during the subsequent washes

Laundry Tips

Many times we find ourselves pulling out clothes from the laundry that have shrunk, white clothes that have gone gray or shredded bits of tissue decorating our garments. We tend to forget that just dumping clothes into the machine does not always work! Here are some guidelines to help you through your next laundry (and hopefully protect your clothes):

Sort the laundry - by colour, by use (towels used for cleaning separate from guest towels), by fabric (according to need for hot or cold water, vigorous or less vigorous washing action, kind of bleach), by lintiness, by construction (lace-trimmed garments, for instance, need a gentle cycle), by degree of dirtiness. Assign them to specific loads.

Take everything out of pockets and cuffs. Look for clothes that need repair and don't wash them until they are fixed. Close zippers and other fasteners. Take off unwashable attached items (removable shoulder pads, decorations). Wash all pieces of sets of clothing (a matching blouse and skirt, for example) each time.

Pretreat by rubbing dirty spots with concentrated, dissolved detergent. If you pretreat with bleach, do not soak too long. Also treat stains. Most laundry washes effectively in warm water, and some washes well in cold water. Using cold water saves energy, minimizes shrinkage, and keeps colours bright.

Don't overload the washer - clothes should be able to move freely, or dirt removal will be uneven. Fill a front-loading washer only to the top of the door. Fill a top-loading washer to the top row of holes, if the washer has them. Vary sizes of items in the load. Delicate garments, no matter how small the load, should be washed with water level set to medium; otherwise they may shrink, wrinkle and develop pulled seams.

Use the correct bleach or none at all, according to the clothing labels. In hot or warm water, you can use granular detergent. In cold water, you need a liquid or predissolved detergent.

When clothes are dry, take them out of the dryer and hang them up or fold them immediately.

Stain Removal

Blood, Fresh & Dried—Rinse fresh blood stains in cold running water and rub with soap. Repeat. For dried stains, first scrape or rub off as much dried blood as possible. Soak in warm water using a product which contains enzymes. Wash. If this doesn't work, rewash the item using a chlorine-free bleach. In the case of stubborn stains, rust removers may be helpful.

Tea, Coffee—Presoak item in liquid detergent with bleach. Wash using the hottest water temperature that is safe for the fabric.

Cosmetics—Dampen stain and rub with liquid detergent. Rinse, then wash.

Dingy White Socks—Presoak in a liquid detergent solution for a minimum of 30 minutes. Wash in a liquid detergent having oxygen bleach. Food Coloring Soak in cool water. If stain remains, rub on detergent and rinse. Wash.

Fruit Juice, Wine & Soft Drinks—Soak stain in cool water as soon as possible. Then, soak in an oxygen bleach, using the hottest water safe for the fabric. Wash.

Mud—Brush off as much as possible when garment is dry, then rinse under cold running water. Pretreat with a paste of powder detergent and water, or liquid laundry detergent. Wash using laundry detergent and a fabric-safe bleach.

Rust Stains—The yellow, orange or brown spots we sometimes find on our clothes may be caused by rust. Iron content of over .2 parts per million in your water supply can cause these type of stains, so it's important to have your water supply checked. Two possible sources can be rust water pipes or water heaters. One way to combat this problem is by using a mechanical water softener with an iron filter. Also, using a non-chlorine bleach can help, as chlorine bleach may cause the iron in the water to precipitate on fabrics and leave stains.

Washing Tips

Brighten Colors with Salt—Hard water can cause clothes to become dull or dingy after several washing. To solve this problem, add a couple of pinches of ordinary table salt to the washer with the detergent. Let some water run in the washer to dissolve detergent and salt, then add clothes. Colored clothes will come out much brighter.

Delicates—Think you have to take that sheer voile blouse, beaded top, fringed silk shawl, or lace trimmed dress to the cleaners? Think again! You can clean these at home by simply tying the articles in a cotton pillow case, knotting it closed, and washing in cold water on regular cycle. Beads, sequins, buttons and delicate laces will not fall to pieces, and garments can be restored by steam ironing or steaming in the shower!

Diapers—Do you hate dunking diapers in the toilet? Now, there is a new invention called the Little Squirt which eliminated this dreaded task. It is powerful sprayer that attaches to the water supply for your toilet. Instead of dunking, you simply spray the contents of the diaper into the toilet.

Down—As a common rule, down items should be cleaned twice a year- once before you start wearing them, and before you put them away after the winter season. Down may be washed or dry-cleaned, read your care label for instructions. You're better off taking large items that require a lot of washer and dryer space (i.e. comforters) to the laundromat, which has larger machines. Be careful not to tumble dry down items at a temperature greater than 140F, or water-resistant shell fabrics can slow drying.

Rayon

Q. *Can you wash rayon items by hand or in the washing machine or by hand?*

A. The confusing part about caring for rayon is that two types of rayon exist: polynosic and viscose. The major difference is that viscose rayon becomes weak when wet, and therefore normally requires dry cleaning. Occasionally it can be finished so that gentle hand washing is possible. Blends with 30 percent or more polyester will provide enough strength for gentle hand washing or machine laundering. Polynosic rayon is an improved version with high wet strength. You can safely machine wash and dry it.

How do you tell the difference? Unless information is provided on the label, or can be obtained by calling the manufacturer, you can't. Machine washable rayons will have the term polynosic, the trade names Modal or Zantrel, or indicate machine wash and dry on the label. The term viscose on a label will be accompanied by a care label that indicates to dry clean.

For best results, follow care label instructions.

Silk

Why Dry Clean Silk? Did you know that silk does not require to be dry cleaned? All you need to do is warm hand wash the blouse with some mild woolwash (normal detergents are the wrong pH for animal fibres like silk and wool). Then dry until it is just damp, roll it tightly and place in a sealed plastic bag then place that in the freezer. Then when it is frozen take it out and iron it.

Suds & Cleanliness

When soap flakes were used, a lot of suds meant good cleaning performance. However, the way laundry detergent is presently formulated, this is no longer true. Unfortunately, many people are unaware of this, and use excessive amounts of laundry detergent.

Washing Time

Never set the washing time for over 10 minutes — many detergents have done all the work they are going to do by then— the rest of the time your clothes are just agitating in the dirty water. It may not seem like much, but you can save a quite a bit of money over time using this trick.

Water Temperature

In the washing process water temperature plays a key role.

Hot water offers the quickest, best form of cleaning, and should be used for the following items: Sturdy whites, colourfast pastels and light prints, cloth diapers and similar baby items, and heavily soiled clothes. Warm water removes wear wrinkles, helps reduce wrinkling in the washer, and minimizes dye loss. It should be used for permanent press, all colourfast dark or bright colours, nylon synthetics, polyester, acrylic and washable woolens. You may want to keep in mind that laundry detergents are formulated to clean best at temperatures above 60°F/16°C. Cold water can prevent sensitive dyes from "bleeding" minimizes washer wrinkling and saves hot water. It can be used for lightly soiled fabrics, and should be used to rinse all loads, regardless of wash temperature. However, due to detergent formulations, cold water does not clean as effectively as warmer temperatures.

Drying Tips

Save on Drying Time—To save on the time spent running your dryer, especially for "heavy" items like throw diapers, rugs, etc., first run an extra "spin" cycle in your washing machine. Then, add a clean, dry, fluffy towel to your dryer with the wet laundry. This may cut your drying time by 25% or more!

*Dry towels and heavier cottons in a separate load from lighter-weight clothes.

*Clean the lint filter in the dryer after every load to improve air circulation.

*Drying a small load reduces the tumbling effect and consequently lengthens the drying time. Add several clean, dry white towels to speed up the drying of small loads.

*Turn your jeans inside out, so they won't fade as quickly.

*Don't overload your dryer, as it can result in excessive wrinkling.

*Don't over-dry your clothes. If your machine has a moisture sensor, use it. Overdrying is also a leading cause of static cling.

*Most dryers have delicate permanent press cycles, which

have lower settings to protect fabrics which might be damaged by high temperatures.

*Periodically inspect your dryer vent to ensure it is not blocked. This will save energy and can prevent a fire. Manufacturers recommend using rigid venting material, not plastic vents that may collapse and cause blockages.

*Use the cool-down cycle to allow the clothes to finish drying with the residual heat in the dryer.

Down Items

Some manufacturers recommend putting new tennis balls in the dryer to keep the down from clumping. However, the Detergent and Soap Association does not recommend this practice. The neon dye on the tennis ball could transfer to the down-filled item, or the tennis ball might not be able to withstand the heat. To avoid clumping, it is safer to periodically remove the item and shake vigorously. Adding clean, dry towels to the dryer load can also help.

Tipes of Ironing

Cut Down on Ironing Time—My time is valuable to my four children, husband and me. I've reduced my electricity used and time spent by removing my clothes directly from the dryer while they're still warm and laying them flat — one item at a time — on top of my washer until the whole load is stacked. Then, I take the entire stack to my favorite folding place. If I have to do something else and return to the stack, it's still unwrinkled and ready to be folded — not ironed! Now I only iron a few things!

Free Distilled Water for your Iron—If you have a dehumidifier in your basement, you have "free" distilled water in its tank, which you can use for your iron.

Laundry Tips Related to Energy Saving

o Clean the filter after each use. A clogged filter will restrict flow and reduce dryer performance.

o Dry full loads when possible, but be careful not to overfill the dryer. Drying small loads wastes energy. Air should be able to circulate freely around the drying clothes.

o Check the outside dryer exhaust vent. Make sure it is clean and that the flapper on the outside hood opens and closes freely.

o Use lower temperature settings. Use cold or warm water for the wash cycle instead of hot (except for greasy stains), and only use cold for rinses. Experiment with different laundry detergents to find one that works well with cooler water. By presoaking heavily soiled clothes, a cooler wash temperature may be fine. The temperature of the rinse water does not affect cleaning, so always set the washing machine on cold water rinse.

o Turn down the thermostat on your water heater. By reducing your hot water temperature, you will save energy with either hot or warm wash cycles.

o Load the washing machine to capacity when possible. Most people tend to underload rather than overload their washers. Use your eye to judge the volume of clothes for a load. Washing one large load will take less energy than washing two loads on a low or medium setting.

o If washing lightly soiled clothes, use the time and water-saving feature if it's available on your washing machine.

o When drying, separate your clothes and dry similar types of clothes together. Lightweight synthetics, for example, dry much more quickly than bath towels and natural fibre clothes. Don't overdry clothes. Take clothes out while they are still slightly damp to reduce the need for ironing - another big energy user.

o Don't add wet items to a load that is already partially dried.

Follow these suggestions whenever possible to keep energy use to a minimum.

1. Use lower temperature settings. Use warm or cold water for the wash cycle instead of hot (except for greasy stains), and only use cold for rinses. Experiment with different laundry detergents to find one that works well with cooler water. By presoaking heavily soiled clothes, a cooler wash temperature may be fine. The temperature of the rinse water does not

affect cleaning, so always set the washing machine on cold water rinse.

2. Turn down the thermostat on your water heater. A setting of 120 F is adequate for most home needs. By reducing your hot water temperature, you will save energy with either hot or warm wash cycles.
3. Load the washing machine to capacity when possible. Most people tend to underload rather than overload their washers. Check your machine's load capacity in pounds, then weigh out a few loads of laundry to get a sense of how much laundry 10 or 18 to 20 pounds represents. Then use your eye to judge the volume of clothes for a load. Washing one large load will take less energy than washing two loads on a low or medium setting.
4. If washing lightly soiled clothes, use the suds-saving feature if it's available on your washing machine. This saves the was water to be reused in the next load. Only use this feature, though, if the second load is to be washed right away.
5. When drying, separate your clothes and dry similar types of clothes together. Lightweight synthetics, for example, dry much more quickly than bath towels and natural fibre clothes.
6. Clothes should not be overdry. Take clothes out while they are still slightly damp to reduce the need for ironing - another big energy user. If your dryer has a setting for auto-dry, be sure to use it instead of the timer to avoid wasting energy.
7. Don't add wet items to a load that is already partially dried.
8. Dry two or more loads in a row, taking advantage of the heat still in the dryer from the first load.
9. Clean the dryer filter after each use. A clogged filter will restrict flow and reduce dryer performance.
10. Dry full loads when possible, but be careful not to overfill the dryer. Drying small loads wastes energy. Air should be able to circulate freely around the drying clothes.
11. Check the outside dryer exhaust vent. Make sure it is clean and that the flapper on the outside hood opens and closes freely.

12. In good weather, consider hanging clothes outside and using totally free solar energy to do the drying.

Tips of Mending and Laundry

1. Iron bias-cut garments along the grain of the fabric rather than from neck to hem.
2. Avoid rips in delicate net or lace curtains by washing them in a large muslin bag.
3. Rain spots will quickly disappear from suede shoes, hats or purses, if rubbed gently with an emery board such as is used for manicuring.
4. To press knitted garments, trace the outline desired on a clean piece of muslin and pin the garment over the muslin to conform to the pattern. Cover with a dry pressing cloth, then with a damp cloth and press with a medium hot iron until dry.
5. Ribbon or lace will dry flat after washing and need no ironing if it is smoothed around a clean bottle to dry.
6. Try sponging those shiny spots on clothes with hot vinegar before pressing.
7. Summer cottons and rayons can be refreshed by using small amounts of plain gelatin instead of starch; prepare as for dessert and starch by dipping.
8. To keep the little tufts on a chenille bedspread fluffy, hang the wet spread on the line with tufts inside. Rubbing together makes them fluffy.
9. Turn printed washables inside out on the line. This prevents sun fading.
10. Insert clothespins in the fingers of gloves to hold their shape when drying. These should be laid on a towel to dry.
11. Clothespins will last longer if they are put in a pan of boiling water and soda when new. Soak for a half hour and then rinse in cold water, dry in the sun.
12. Place a piece of beeswax between two pieces of flannel and rub your iron on them occasionally. It will keep the iron clean and make it run smoothly.

13. Children's clothes made of corduroy are best not ironed. Squeeze very little water from them and hang on line dripping wet. When they are nearly dry, roll up in a towel for a few minutes, then spread on a towel and arrange to proper shape.
14. When you are ironing keep a pair of scissors handy to clip threads, ravelings and raw ends of lace and ribbons. It pays big dividends.
15. When ironing shirt collars, place a bath towel under collar and iron on wrong side.
16. If your rubber boots or galoshes make black marks on your stockings, use colourless nail polish and paint a half inch strip inside the tops of the boots.
17. Lemon rinds are an excellent bleach. They will keep things snowy white and there will be a lingering aroma of lemon among your clothes.
18. When hanging skirts and trousers to dry, they should be pinned firmly to the line at the waistband. This makes the pulling lengthwise.
19. When you wash baby's bonnet, fit it over an inverted bowl to dry. Helps the bonnet hold its shape.
20. To whiten laces, wash them in sour milk.
21. After washing overalls, drying and smoothing them, tuck a handkerchief in the back pocket before putting them away. This may prevent a last-minute search before your husband dashes out on his way to work.
22. To set colour in garments: 2 tablespoons turpentine and 1 handful of salt. Pour boiling water over this, then put garment in and leave it until water is cold.
23. You can iron faster and easier if you put a sheet of aluminum foil under the ironing board cover. The foil stops steam from penetrating the padding and deflects steam back into the article being ironed.
24. When laundering doilies or other linen pieces that need careful shaping, leave unstarched for the first ironing. When ironed and shaped to your satisfaction, dip a thin cloth in starch, wring out and smooth it over the article on the ironing board,

48. Know the first place of wear on men's trousers? It's where the heel of his shoe rubs against the inside trouser cuff. You can avoid expense by sewing an extra piece of cloth or twill tape on the danger spot.
49. To wash coloured calicos, dissolve, say 10 cents worth of sugar of lead in six to eight quarts of pure water (rain water is best), and after the garments are washed and rinsed, let them be dipped in and rung out. It not only sets the colour, but keeps it.
50. A scorched spot on woolens may be removed by brushing the spot with fine emery paper.

Tipes for Making the Laundry Fun and Simple!

Laundry. Does just seeing the word conjure up less than joyful feelings? If so, you're not alone! Laundry is just one of those less-than-favorite tasks for a whole bunch of folks.. And there are so many reasons why. For one, it's a never-ending task. As soon as you finish, the day ends, and presto, off come the clothes everyone is wearing, and you're right back on your way to overflowing hampers! And even if you don't mind some parts of the laundry process — sorting, pre-treating, loading the washer, or even changing over the clothes between loads —there's bound to be at least one step in the process that you simply don't like. Maybe it's the hanging and folding stage, ironing, sorting the socks, or maybe it's just taking that final step of putting the clothes away.

The bottom line is this: laundry isn't necessarily complicated, it's just involved — lots of steps and lots of opportunity to be faced with a task that quite simply isn't your tea cup. But alas, help and hope for brighter laundry days is on the way. First though, think about which part of the laundry process is your least favorite. Then, read on for ideas to make that piece of the process as simple and fun as possible. Then move on to your next least favorite step and do the similar. In no time you'll be having fun and getting *loads* done!

Separate as you go !

Invest in a three-compartment laundry sorter to make easy work out of keeping clothes separated. Separate by colour as you put clothes into the hamper and save the mega-sort step of going through hampers and hampers full of laundry one item at a time. By sorting-as-you-go, when you see a full compartment in your hamper, its simple to throw in a load.

Tips to keep up the momentum !

Now that we've made it a little bit easier to get started on the laundry, here are few ways to make it simpler to keep at it.

Here's a simple solution that may sound familiar: *sort as you go.* Use a three-compartment handled laundry bag to segregate clothes by person as you fold. Or assign every person a laundry basket of their own, along with the responsibility of putting their things away.

Make it easy to put things away!

Have you ever had the laundry washed, dried, folded? For days and weeks it sat waiting for the put-away-laundry-fairy to magically appear and get everything back where it belongs. Instead, your whole family used the laundry room as a closet, sprinting through the house for clothes every morning.

Make it simple as pie !

Keep supplies in arms reach. Install a shelf above your washing machine and dryer to store all your supplies — spot removers, detergent, bleach, dryer sheets, empty hangers and the like. Keep extras of all your basic laundry supplies on hand to avoid last minute trips to the store. When you pull a bottle of detergent out of your storage area, jot it on your errands list and you'll always have everything you need for laundry right at hand.

Get into a routine!

Maybe you'll throw in a load every morning right when you wake up and transfer it to the dryer after you've dressed and eaten breakfast. Or you could throw in a load at dinner and fold it during T.V. time. Whatever you decide, building laundry into your routine (much like brushing your teeth) takes a lot less energy than dreading it.

Make your laundry room more fun!

Bring colour into your laundry room with a cheerful rug, curtains or framed kid's artwork. Use glass jars for an artful display of detergent or antique clothes pins. Play some upbeat and energizing music while you sort or fold. In vest in laundry baskets that make you happy!

Make it easy to sort socks!

If you have a big family, consider keeping each family large member's clothes segregated. Put a hamper in each person's room and do a couple of loads per family member per week (a load of lights and a load of darks, for example.) You'll avoid the big sort at fold time — so much simpler than trying to figure out whose socks are who's after the fact!

Avoiding the Wrinkles!

If you don't already have one, consider installing a hanging bar in your laundry room and hang clothes as soon as they come out of the dryer. This makes it fast and easy to get your clothes out of the dryer while avoiding or minimizing wrinkles. (You may even be able to forego ironing!)

Overcome inertia : Sometimes, in light of all the steps involved in laundry (and your deep rooted knowledge that ultimately you'll get to the stage you don't like) simply getting started, or overcoming the inertia of not doing laundry, is hard. You'll know this is you if you wait until every hamper in the house is overflowing and you're contemplating buying new underwear instead of washing the dozens of pairs in your hampers. Sound familiar? If so, first and foremost ...

Get caught up !

Step one is a laundry fest. Get every single article of clothing and all your linens washed, folded and put way — even the hand-washables! Block out a day, a few evenings, however long it takes, and get caught up. Laundry is your mission, but you can have some fun along the way too. Fold while you watch your favorite T.V. show. Bring a portable CD player into the laundry room. Have some snacks. Read a good book between loads. Do whatever you need to do, but get caught up! Then ...

Do a little bit a lot more often !

Here's one of my golden rules of organizing: the more you dislike doing something, the more often you should do it. Sounds crazy, but really its rational advice. Here's why: if you dislike doing something, it gets worse when it gets bigger — doesn't it? A small hamper filled with clothes is a lot less daunting than five overflowing hampers, right? So do a small load a day and keep reasonably caught up. It will take a lot less effort to get started and keep going.

Finally, remember our good friend the label. Apply labels to the inside of drawers and on hanging rods to make it easy for anyone to put clothes away. Who knows, maybe that put-away-laundry-fairy *will* magically appear!

Quick Tips for Reducing Usage

- Periodically inspect the dryer vent to make sure there are no blockages.
- Consider air-drying clothing on warm days on clothes lines or drying racks.
- Wash your clothes in cold water using special detergents that are specially designed for cold water loads.
- Wash and dry full loads when possible. Always use the appropriate setting for the size of the load.
- Clean the lint filter in the dryer after each load.

Details of Typical Usage

Type Watts Cost per load Clothes dryer 4,350 to 5,500 watts 26 to 46 cents Clothes washer 500 watts 3 to 4 cents Water heating for washer N/A 15 to 22 cents.

Care of Clothing - Laundry Tips, Stain Removal, Repairs

The importance of Proper Care : No matter how well clothes are selected, nor how attractive they are, no person is ever well dressed unless those clothes are given proper care.

A well groomed appearance is not acquired accidentally. It is the result of conscientious and systematic care of both one's person and one's wardrobe.

Carelessness in later life is often due to the fact that one has been careless about one's appearance while growing up.

The necessity for the care of clothing is due to these facts:

(a) aids the wearer to maintain greater pride and self-respect

(b) the clothes last longer

(c) clothing is always ready for use on the shortest notice

(d) there is more demand for neatly dressed individuals than for those who are not so careful about their clothes

Different garments and different materials require separate methods of care, but all require care in some manner.

Daily Care Methods

"Never put off until tomorrow what you can do today"

Daily care requires only a very few minutes, but to be effective, it must be done regularly.

Airing : This freshens the garments, helps take out body odours and also aids in restoring the garment to its original shape.

Hanging : Give children small hangers and low hooks for their convenience. Never hang knitted garments - fold on a shelf or in a drawer. Biais garment are also usually better folded.

Brushing : Brush wool and silk clothes immediately after wearing. The longer dirt or dust is allowed to remain in garments the harder it is to remove. Stand before an open window while brushing.

Shaking : Shaking is effective in removing surface dirt from cottons and linens.

Pressing : Press clothes whenever necessary.

(a) Wool materials should be pressed through a damp cloth on the wrong side.

(b) When pressing silk materials, press on the wrong side of the garment with a medium iron using cheese cloth or light weight muslin between the material and the iron.

(c) Cottons may be pressed on the right side, while linens should be pressed on the wrong side.

Steaming : Velvet materials cannot be pressed directly with a hot iron. However many wrinkles may be removed by hanging the garment over a tub of boiling water or a room filled with steam.

Mending : Minor repairs should be attended to as needed. These repairs include the sewing on of fasteners, replacing hems, mending rips and tears and tacking cuffs, collars, belts and trimmings.

Care of Shoes

1. The life of a pair of shoes is multiplied three fold if never worn more than three days in succession.
2. Keep the shoes on some sort of rack or in bag. This protects them from dirt and keeps them always where they can be found. The shoe tidy can be fastened to the wall or cupboard door
3. As soon as removed, wipe with a soft cloth to remove any dust or dirt which may cling to them.
4. Polish as often as necessary to keep them looking like new - polish not only improves the appearance of the shoe, but it softens and preserves the leather.

Removal of Stain

Fresh **writing ink** stains usually yield to cold clear water. Soaking in milk may help, changing the milk as it discolours.

Black **grease** stains may be loosened by the application of lard. Wipe off when it becomes discoloured and apply more. Wash in soapy water.

Grass stains may be dipped into alcohol. Some stains come out easily by washing in hot soapy water.

Nappies to be rinse immediately and put to soak at once in cold water.

Tea or Coffee stains on linen should be soaked in clear cold water before soaping.

Fresh **bloodstains** should be washed in clear cool water, if dried they may be soaked and rubbed.

Many **fruit juices** may be removed by pouring on hot water, the kettle held high - allow water to pass through the stain.

Laundering : Order of laundering :

(a) Sort clothes into groups:
   1) white
   2) coloured
   3) degree of soil
   4) kind of materials - cottons - silks - wools

(b) Remove all stains

(c) Mend

(d) Soak clothes

Soaking : The purpose of soaking clothes is to loosen dirt and save time, labour and strain on the fabric during the washing process. After stains have been treated, the soiled places should be thoroughly soaped and the garment soaked in warm water. Do not soak in hot water and do not soak coloured garments that will fade.

Cautions for laundering Silks & Woolens :

1. iron while still damp
2. do not iron on the right side and use cloth over woolens
3. do not use a hot iron
4. do not wash in hot water
5. do not apply soap directly to material
6. rinse thoroughly
7. hang in a shaded place

Drying :

* Clothes smell sweeter and have a better colour if hung outdoors to dry.

* White linens and cottons may hang in the sun but coloured materials should be placed in the shade as the sun fades colours - especially when wet.

* Woolen garments should be gently pulled into shape.

Cloth repair :

" An ounce of prevention is worth a pound of cure"

* Keep your garments in good repair. Constant watch and repair of rips and tears as soon as they appear will often prevent grief later on.

* Keep snaps, buttons and hooks and eyes sewed on in their

proper places. A pin never satisfactorily nor neatly takes the place of any one of these.

*** Coat linings :**

- Such repairs as these frequently provide an extra season's wear.
- Ripped coat linings should be slip stitched to the coat. In order to make it inconspicuous turn back the edge 1cm and carry the thread alternatively through the lining fold and the garment; press flat.
- Sleeve linings that are worn thin or ragged can have a hemmed patch of any similar material because it does not show.
- When the lining is worn around the collar a shaped hemmed patch of self-material can be slip-stitched on at the neck line and catch-stitched to the garment around the other edges.

*** Coat buttons :**

- Coat buttons are ordinarily big size and cut the thread; they should be sewed on with heavy thread and a strong shank provided. Ideally a small button should be placed on the under side, both to help protect the material and cover the ugly irregular stitches..

*** Sweaters :**

- Catch the mending yarn into the loose loops at the edges on the hole but do not pull the garment out of shape.
- It is helpful to baste a piece of still paper to the back to serve as a foundation to darn over.
- Boy's play sweaters worn thin at the elbow may be darned and further reinforced by stitching or an oval shaped patch of soft leather (and old kid glove may be used).
- Broken threads may be caught and crocheted in again but if there is a hole it will be necessary to match the yarn and darn the hole.
- If the yarn is fine the mending yarn may have to be untwisted and fewer yarns used.
- A blunt crewel needle is necessary to interlace the threads and fill in the hole.

*** Raincoats :**

- Raincoats and plastic macks may be repaired with adhesive tape.

***Alterations :** After alterations: When you remove a hem or seam and have holes from thread showing, dampen a cloth with white vinegar, put it under the material and press.

Doing Laundry - The Basics : We spend a lot of money on our clothes, but to make them last as long as possible you need to know how to properly launder them. You don't want to waste money because your clothes need to be replaced prematurely, so follow these easy steps to wash and dry your clothes.

1. Familiarize Yourself with Your Machines : If you haven't already, it is time to get to know your washing machine and dryer. They are all about the same, but everyone has a feature or quirk that is unique to it only. Since all washing machines and dryers are a little bit different, you will want to become familiarized with the individual intricacies of your machines. Typically, the manufacturer will provide full operating instructions, and troubleshooting tips for common problems.

2. Sort Your Clothes : In order to save yourself time, and make things easier on yourself, it is important to separate your laundry before washing. Once in piles you will also be able to quickly determine how many loads you are in store for. You will also prevent dark coloured clothes from ruining your whites, or delicate items from being destroyed by being washed with jeans. For this step you will want to combine all similar items into different piles. For this, there are three prime groups:

Darks :darker garments where the colours may bleed. Jeans, sweatshirts, towels, etc.

Delicates :fabrics that require special care. Fine linens, lingerie, blouses, etc.

Whites :socks, underwear, linens, t-shirts, wash cloths, etc.

To further refine the sorting process, you can separate these piles further, into heavily soiled and less soiled, or separate by person so it is easier to put them away later. Towels and other similar items that may carry lint, can be washed by themselves in a separate load.

As you sort through your laundry, you should check all pockets and deal with the contents. A stray piece of paper, a pen, or some chapstick is a disaster when it goes throught the wash. You should also check all snaps, buttons or straps to make sure they are secure and don't pose a hazard. By carefully reading the care instructions on your clothing labels, you can be sure you are giving proper care to each piece of clothing.

3. Pretreating Stains : Not all stains will come out in the normal wash cycle. These stains can set in and become extremely difficult to remove if you don't pretreat them with something first. If you use some Quick'n Brite paste to treat the stain first, it will be able to come clean with normal laundering. Just scratch in a bit of the paste, and the cleaner will do the rest for you. For the toughest stains you will want to let the garment sit over night or for several hours before washing. Most stains that are left untreated will set in, and most times do not come out with laundry soap alone. Many stains will come clean when treated with Quick'n Brite. Even stubborn grass, blood, juice, red mud, etc. For extremely soiled clothes or for stains that have been set in, try presoaking instead.

4. Presoaking Clothes : For heavily soiled or stained clothes, a presoak is your best option. For this, fill a bucket or utility sink with water and add a cup of Quick'n Brite liquid to it. Let the garment sit overnight for best results. The Quick'n Brite will break apart the stains, so they can be simply washed away.

5. Importance of Water Temperature : Clothing can be washed in either hot, warm or cold water. There are benefits to using each, but you will want to pay attention to the manufactureres care instructions for best results.

Hot Water : Hot water is the good for fast powerful cleaning. Some fabrics can't be washed in hot water though. Bright coloured fabrics, and delicates can be ruined if the water is too hot, but extremely dirty clothes, baby diapers and more are best washed at this temperature. Bleach also works the best when used with hot water. For really bright whites, or to clean stubborn stains, hot water is the way to go.

Warm Water : Warm water is good for clothing prone to wrinkles. It will help prevent wrinkles from forming in the washer. This temperature is also good for cleaning, but is safe for a wider range of fabrics. Permanent press, darks, washable wools, and synthetics are often washed using warm water.

Cold Water : Cold water is the best for bright colours. Bright colours can easily fade when washed with warmer water. To make sure your reds, yellows and oranges stay that way, use cold water when washing them. Cold water is almost always the preferred rinse temperature too. The cold water helps to cut down on the number of suds, and helps clothes rinse clean.

6. Choosing a Detergent : There are literally dozens of detergents to choose from. Most of them work about the same, but many people will stick to a certain one because of price, smell, convenience, etc. Some of the most popular detergent brands are Tide, Cheer, Oxydol, and Gain. All are basically soap, so they work well at cleaning dirt. Always follow manufacturer instructions when using laundry detergent though as individual measurements and ingredients will vary. To wash your clothes without chemicals, use Quick'n Brite. All that it takes is 1/4 cup of the liquid for a whole load.

7. Cloth Washing : The best method for washing your clothes is to turn the machine on first and then add soap as the water is filling. Once the soap has been added to the water, then you can add you clothes. This will avoide direct contact with the soap and your clothes, and ensure that it is properly distributed throughout the load pay careful attention to make sure you do not overload the machine. Too many pieces of clothing will take away from the cleaning power of the detergent used, and the smaller the load, the better the machine is able to agitate and rid clothing of its dirt.

Your washing machine may have a separate compartment for adding liquid bleach or fabric softener; if so, just read the directions on the lid of the machine and add the items when stated. If not, when using bleach, it is good to let the load of clothing wash for five full minutes and then add 1 cup of the liquid bleach. The fabric softener may be added by one capful when the machine is on its rinse cycle, if no separate compartment is supplied.

8. Drying Your Clothes : Using your dryer is much the same as operating the washing machine. It is important that you are familiar with the settings, and know how to properly operate it. Check garment labels for the right drying temperature and time. Delicates are best protected in the dryer on the gentle, or permanent press cycle because there is usually a cool-down feature added to the end of these cycles allowing the clothes to cool down before the tumbler completely stops. This feature can also be used as a wrinkle releaser, making ironing unnecessary. For sturdier articles like towels, small blankets, jackets, sweatshirts, blue jeans, and whites, the high setting is preferred.

You will want to be careful not to overload your dryer. If there are too many items your clothes won't get dry. A big load will hinder the operation of the machine, and restrict air flow. To increase your drying power and decrease the time it takes to dry your clothes, try dryer balls. These all natural fabric softeners will eliminate your need for dryer sheets are liquid softeners.

Laundry may seem like a chore even if you're single. If you have a family, it can seem like a never ending, daunting task! Checking pockets, sorting, washing, drying, folding, ironing . . . repeat the process in a few more days.

Not everyone is taught how to do laundry. Many people (myself included) found themselves on their own for the first time without a clue how to do laundry!

For those new to laundry, here are some quality laundry basic tips you should follow:

- **Always,** check your clothing labels. Not everything is washable!
- Before washing, clothing needs to be separated according to colour and type of fabric.
- Separate your clothes into the following categories: White clothes (think white t-shirts and undies), colour and/or dark clothes (but not jeans), jeans, sheets, towels, delicates and light weight fabrics.

- Don't wash synthetics (nylon, lycra, etc.) in are load as clothing with natural fibres (wool, cotton, etc.)
- Don't mix coloured clothing with whites (guys have been known to wind up with pink underwear when a red item gets accidentally mixed in with their whites).
- Always check ALL pockets prior to washing clothes — gum, pens, etc. left in pockets have ruined many clothing items.
- Wash baby laundry separately with mild detergent.
- Hand wash delicates (hosiery, lingerie, etc.). Woolite works well on hand washables and delicates.
- In the alternative, wash delicates in the washer (don't add any other type of clothes to this load). Use a zipper bag specially designed for delicates and tuck them inside and zip them up prior to tossing in the wash. Use the gentle cycle.
- Hand wash sweaters (only those that are washable — check the label — dry clean the rest). Lay them flat to dry.
- If you use regular chlorine bleach, check the labels on your clothes to be sure the item can be bleached.
- Use a colour safe bleach on your coloured clothing. Be sure to check the label to see that it's safe to use bleach of any kind.
- Wash lightweight items and delicates separately. Don't mix with jeans or heavy items (towels, etc.).
- Wash jeans separately, but don't overload either the washer or dryer. Jeans are heavy. Do more than one load if you have quite a few pairs of jeans to wash.
- Never use bleach on wool, silk, and treated cottons.
- Wash bath and kitchen towels separately from sheets unless. If washed together, towels can leave fuzz balls on your sheets.

Removal of Stain

One of the most important parts of laundry is stain removal. If you can't get the stains out of your clothing, you probably won't wear the item.

The most important part of stain removal is try to treat the stain immediately before it becomes set in. A great tool for that is a

Tide-to-Go pen. I keep them everywhere — laundry room, purse, desk drawer, under the kitchen and bathroom sinks. These are great for treating stains when you're away from home.

If you don't have a Tide-to-Go pen, you can put laundry detergent (liquid works best) on the stain and let it sit for at least 5 minutes prior to washing. The sooner you treat the stain, the better.

Be sure to pre-treat any stain before washing the item. Washing will cause the stain the become fixed and nearly impossible to get out.

If the garment is white and the label says it is safe to bleach, you should also consider using a bleach pen on the stain prior to washing. Some people swear by various stain removal products (Oxiclean, Shout, Spray 'n Wash, etc.). I've used various ones, and most do a good job. However, treating the stain as soon as possible (and prior to washing the item) is the most important thing you can do.

Many people use water to dilute a stain — have you seen people use their napkin and water glass on food stains in restaurants? However, be careful about putting water on some fabrics. Silk for instance can leave a water ring.

14

The System of Dry Cleaning

Dry cleaning is any cleaning process for clothing and textiles using an organic solvent rather than water. The solvent used is typically tetrachloroethylene (perchloroethylene), abbreviated "perc" in the industry and "dry-cleaning fluid" by the public. Dry cleaning is necessary for cleaning items which would otherwise be damaged by water and soap or detergent. It may be used if hand washing—needed for some delicate fabrics—is excessively laborious.

Dry cleaning uses fluids to remove soil and stains from fabric. In fact, the term "dry cleaning" is misleading; it is called dry cleaning because the fluid contains little or no water and does not penetrate the fibres as water does.

Among the advantages of dry cleaning is its ability to dissolve greases and oils in a way that water cannot. Drycleaning helps to return garments to a "like-new" condition using precautions to prevent shrinkage, loss of colour, and fabric distortion.

The dry cleaning process begins with the pretreatment of spots and stains using special cleaning agents. The garments are then loaded into a machine resembling an oversized front-loading home washer. Throughout the cleaning process the fluid is filtered or distilled to ensure its clarity.

Today, the solvent used by almost 90% of all dry cleaners is perchloroethylene, commonly known as "perc." It is completely non-flammable and non-combustible, of relatively low toxicity, and can be efficiently reused and recycled.

Dry cleaning means cleansing of textiles in non-aqueous (non-water) solvents. Highly vapourising organic solvents are commonly used as dry cleaning fluids. Many dirt, soil or stains producing substances on the fabric are organic in nature (sticky oily compounds). There is a common role in this regard that like dissolves like.

In wet cleaning, washing is achieved by the combined action of soap and water. Soap acts as a mediator between oil (present in dirt) and water, which are otherwise immiscible and non-reacting, in other words unlike in nature.

In dry cleaning, cleansing is achieved by the action of a solvent, which dissolves out the sticky matter due to its like nature. Dry cleaning fluids serve as a vehicle to carry away the soil. Camphene, naphtha, benzene, benzol, petrol, carbon tetrachloride, trichloroethylene and tetrachloroethylene are some of the frequently used dry cleaning fluids.

Dry cleaning neither changes nor alters the colour of the garment but retains all the finish and all of its new appearance, whereas the wet method makes the garment fade, flimsy, soft, loose and out of shape. Dry cleaned garments facilitate the subsequent pressing of many types of garments that are exceedingly difficult and tedious to press after they have been washed in water.

Dry-cleaning simply means that fabric will not be cleaned in a water system but in a machine using dry solvent.

The dry-cleaning process begins with the pre-treatment of spots and stains using special cleaning agents. The garments are then cleaned using solvents to remove soil and stains from the fabric.

One of the great advantages of dry-cleaning is the ability to dissolve greases and oils in a way water cannot. Natural fibres such as wool, silk, rayon and polyester are ideal for dry-cleaning but can shrink, distort and lose colour when washed in water. Dry-cleaning helps to return garments to a 'like new' condition without shrinkage, loss of colour and fabric distortion.

History of Dry Cleaning

Doing laundry has been a common household activity for years. Whether the technology was beating the garments on rocks by the river or pushing buttons on programmed washing machines, this process depends on water and a mechanical action usually assisted by soap or an alkali. The purpose of an alkali is to **saponify** the oils and dislodge ordinary soil and other matter. More often-than not, the soapy agent holds soil in suspension as it becomes loose during the wash cycle, and is subsequently flushed away during the rinse cycle and centrifugal spin.

The drying process for doing laundry at home is either hanging clothes on a clothesline or tumbling them in a gas- or electric-heated dryer.

Dry cleaning, on the other hand, is different. It's a process that cleans clothes without water. The cleaning fluid that is used is a liquid, and all garments are immersed and cleaned in a liquid solvent — the fact that there is no water is why the process is called "dry."

Dry cleaning uses non-water-based solvents to remove soil and stains from clothes. The potential for using petroleum based solvents in this manner was discovered in the mid-19th century by French dye-works owner Jean Baptiste Jolly, who noticed that his tablecloth became cleaner after his maid spilled kerosene on it, and developed a service cleaning people's clothes in this manner, which he termed "nettoyage à sec," or "dry cleaning" in English.

Early dry cleaners used petroleum-based solvents, such as gasoline and kerosene. Flammability concerns led Keith Anderson of westquarter, a dry cleaner from Laurieston to develop Stoddard solvent as a slightly less flammable alternative to gasoline-based solvents. The use of highly flammable petroleum solvents caused many fires and explosions, resulting in government regulation of dry cleaners.

After World War I, dry cleaners began using chlorinated solvents. These solvents were much less flammable than petroleum solvents and had improved cleaning power. By the mid-1930s the dry cleaning industry had adopted tetrachloroethylene (perchloroethylene), colloquially called "perc," as the ideal solvent. It has excellent cleaning power, and is stable, nonflammable, and gentle to most garments. However, perc was also the first chemical to be classified as a carcinogen by the Consumer Product Safety Commission (a classification later withdrawn). In 1993 the California Air Resources Board (CARB) adopted an airborne toxic control measure (ATCM) to reduce perc emissions from dry cleaning operations. The dry cleaning industry is now beginning to replace perc with other chemicals and/or methods. At this time, dry-cleaning was carried-out in two different machines — one for the cleaning process itself and the second to dry the garments.

Traditionally the actual cleaning process was carried-out at centralised "factories"; high street cleaners shops received garments from customers, sent them to the factory, and then had them returned to the shop, where the customer could collect them. This was due mainly to the flammability or dangerous fumes from the cleaning process.

This changed when the British dry-cleaning equipment company, Spencer, introduced the first in-shop machines (which, like modern dry cleaning machines, both clean and dry in one machine). Though the Spencer machines were large, they were suitably sized and vented to be fitted into shops. Three models, the Spencer Minor, Spencer Junior, and Spencer Major, were generally used (larger models; the Spencer Senior and Spencer Mammoth, were larger and intended for factory use). The cleaning and drying process was controlled by a punch-card, which fed through the "Spencermatic" reader on the machine. Also, Spencer introduced several much smaller machines for use in coin-operated launderettes; the Spencer Solitaire, and another model, simply called the Spencer Dry Cleaning Machine. These machines resembled coin-operated tumble dryers; to be as small as they were, they simply filtered used perc, rather than distilling it like the commercial Spencer machines. Solvent had to be changed far more frequently, as without distillation, it quickly became discoloured, and could cause yellowing of pale items being cleaned. A coin-operated version of the Spencer Minor, which automatically carried out all the distillation and solvent-cleaning operations of the standard version was available, however, due to it being substantially larger than the other coin-operated machines, (and presumably extra cost) these were rarely seen.

During the 1970s and 1980s, Spencer machines were extremely popular, with virtually every branch of *Bollom* possessing either a Spencer Minor or Spencer Junior. Spencer continued to produce machines (introducing new modular and computer controlled models, such as the Spencer Sprint series) until the late 1980s, when the company closed. Spencer machines may still occasionally be seen.

How Drycleaning Works

Process—When you drop your clothes off at the cleaners, the employees follow a pattern that holds true at just about any dry-cleaning operation running today. Your clothes go through the following steps:

1. Tagging and inspection - Some method, whether it is small paper tags or little labels written on a shirt collar, is used to identify your clothes so they don't get mixed up with everyone else's. Clothes are also examined for missing buttons, tears, etc. that the dry cleaner might get blamed for otherwise.

2. Pre-treatment - The cleaner looks for stains on your clothes and treats them to make removal easier and more complete.

3. Dry cleaning - The clothes are put in a machine and cleaned with a solvent.

4. Post-spotting - Removal of lingering stains.

5. Finishing - This includes pressing, folding, packaging and other finishing touches.

A dry cleaning machine is same to a combination of a domestic washing machine, and clothes dryer. Garments are placed into a washing/extraction chamber (referred to as the basket, or drum), which is the core of the machine. The washing chamber contains a horizontal, perforated drum that rotates within an outer shell. The shell holds the solvent while the rotating drum holds the garment load. The basket capacity is between about 10 and 40 kg, or 20 and 80 lb, of garments.

During the wash cycle the chamber is filled approximately 1/3 full of solvent and begins to rotate, agitating the clothing. The solvent temperature is maintained at 30°C (85°F), as a higher temperature may extract dye from garments, causing colour loss. During the wash cycle, the chamber is constantly fed a supply of fresh solvent from the working solvent tank while spent solvent is removed and sent to a filter unit comprising a distillation boiler and condenser. The ideal flow rate is one gallon of solvent per pound of garments (roughly 8 litres of solvent per kilogram of garments) per minute, depending on the size of the machine.

Before being placed in the machine, garments are inspected for stains and soils by the operator. Depending on the nature of the soil, a catalyst may be applied to it. This depends on the operator's judgement of the makeup of the textile and the soil itself. Oil-based soils (such as grease, oil, or lipstick) typically are removed well by perchloroethylene, while water-based soils (such as coffee, grass, wine, perspiration, blood, semen, and feces) will need a catalyst to allow the dry cleaning solvent to emulsify and lift them. Food-based grease soils fall in between the two, and a milder catalyst may be applied.

Garments are also checked for foreign objects. Items such as plastic pens will dissolve in the solvent bath and may damage textiles beyond recovery. Some textile dyes are "loose" (red being the main culprit), and will shed dye during solvent immersion. These will not be included in a load along with lighter coloured textiles to avoid colour transfer. The solvent used must be distilled to remove impurities that may transfer to clothing. Garments are checked for dry-cleaning compatibility, including fasteners. Many decorative fasteners either are not dry cleaning solvent proof or will not withstand the mechanical action of cleaning. These will be removed and restitched after the cleaning, or protected with a small padded protector. Fragile items, such as feather bedspreads or tasseled rugs or hangings may be enclosed in a loose mesh bag. The density of perchloroethylene is around 1.7 g/cm^3 at room temperature (70% heavier than water), and the sheer weight of absorbed solvent may cause the textile to fail under normal force during the extraction cycle unless the mesh bag provides mechanical support.

A typical wash cycle lasts for 8-15 minutes depending on the type of garments and amount of soiling. During the first three minutes, solvent-soluble soils dissolve into the perchloroethylene and loose, insoluble soil comes off. It takes approximately ten to twelve minutes after the loose soil has come off to remove the ground-in insoluble soil from garments. Machines using hydrocarbon solvents require a wash cycle of at least 25 minutes because of the much slower rate of solvation of solvent-soluble soils. A dry-cleaning surfactant "soap" may also be added.

At the end of the wash cycle, the machine starts a rinse cycle, and the garment load is rinsed with fresh distilled solvent from the pure solvent tank. This pure solvent rinse prevents discolouration caused by soil particles being absorbed back onto the garment surface from the "dirty" working solvent.

After the rinse cycle the machine begins the extraction process, which recovers dry-cleaning solvent for reuse. Modern machines recover approximately 99.99% of the solvent employed.

The extraction cycle begins by draining the solvent from the washing chamber and accelerating the basket to 350 to 450 rpm, causing much of the solvent to spin free of the fabric. When no more solvent can be spun out, the machine starts the drying cycle.

During the drying cycle, the garments are tumbled in a stream of warm air (63°C/145°F) that circulates through the basket, evaporating any traces of solvent left after the spin cycle. The air temperature is controlled to avoid heat damage to the garments. The exhausted warm air from the machine then passes through a chiller unit, where solvent vapors are condensed and returned to the distilled solvent tank. Modern dry cleaning machines use a closed-loop system where the chilled air is reheated and recirculated. This results in high solvent recovery rates and reduced air pollution.

In the early days of dry cleaning, large amounts of perchlorethylene were vented to the atmosphere, because it was regarded as cheap and believed to be harmless.

After the drying cycle is complete, a deodorizing (aeration) cycle cools the garments and removes the last traces of solvent, by circulating cool outside air over the garments and then through a vapor recovery filter made from activated carbon and polymer resins. After the aeration cycle, the garments are clean and ready for pressing/finishing.

The drying process for doing laundry at home is either hanging clothes on a clothesline or tumbling them in a gas- or electric-heated dryer.

Dry cleaning, on the other hand, is different. It's a process that cleans clothes without water. The cleaning fluid that is used is a liquid, and all garments are immersed and cleaned in a liquid solvent — the fact that there is no water is why the process is called "dry."

Tagging

When you drop off your clothes, every order is identified. Although the exact identification process may vary from dry cleaner to dry cleaner, it basically includes counting the items and describing them (e.g., shirt, blouse, slacks). Also noted is the date they were dropped off and what date they'll be ready for the customer to pick up. Then, a small, coloured tag is affixed to each piece of clothing with a safety pin or staple, and this tag remains attached to the clothing during the entire dry-cleaning cycle. The dry cleaner also generates an invoice, and information about the order — including the customer's name, address, and phone number — is entered into a computer. This helps to maintain track of the order.

If a garment needs special attention, such as removing a red wine stain from a shirt or putting a double-crease in pant legs, there's a special coloured tag that gets affixed to that particular item of clothing. Once the clothing has been washed or dry cleaned, it goes through a quality check and the order gets re-assembled. This means the clothing is bundled together for the customer to pick up. Remember, every order is identified by a coloured tag with a number on it so the person who re-assembles the order knows which shirts and which slacks go together and to whom they belong.

If a garment needs special attention, such as removing a red wine stain from a shirt or putting a double-crease in pant legs, there's a special coloured tag that gets affixed to that particular item of clothing. Once the clothing has been washed or dry cleaned, it goes through a quality check and the order gets re-assembled. This means the clothing is bundled together for the customer to pick up. Remember, every order is identified by a coloured tag with a number on it so the person who re-assembles the order knows which shirts and which slacks go together and to whom they belong.

Pre-treating Stains

Pre-treating stains is similar to the procedure used at home when you apply a stain remover to stains prior to washing them. The idea is to try to remove the stain or make its removal easier using chemicals. You can even help the process, especially if you catch the stain early! Simply apply water for wet stains (a stain that had water in it) and solvent for dry stains (a stain that has grease or oil in it). Then, gently tap and blot both sides of the fabric with a soft cloth so the stain "bleeds off" onto the cloth. Then, rinse the fabric, let it dry and your cleaner will do the rest.

Dry Cleaning

While there are many brands and makes of cleaning machines, they are all basically the same in principle and function. A cleaning machine is a motor-driven washer/extractor/dryer that holds from 20 to 100 pounds (9 to 45 kg) of clothes or fabrics in a rotating, perforated stainless-steel basket. The basket is mounted in a housing that includes motors, pumps, filters, still, recovery coils, storage tanks, fans, and a control panel. In all modern equipment, the washer and the dryer are in the same machine. Doing this makes it possible to recover nearly all of the perc used during cleaning, which is better for the environment and saves the dry cleaner money.

As the clothes rotate in the perforated basket, there is a constant flow of clean solvent from the pump and filter system. The solvent sprays into the basket and chamber constantly — not only immersing the clothes, but gently dropping and pounding them against baffles in the cylinder as well. The dirty solvent is pumped continuously through the filter and re-circulated free and clear of dirt that gets trapped in the filter.

As an example, a typical machine might pump perc through the clothes at a rate of perhaps 1,500 gallons (5,678 liters) per hour. Perc is about 75 percent heavier than water. If a cycle lasts for eight minutes, the clothes would be doused during mechanical action with 200 gallons (757 liters) of solvent. This is more than adequate to thoroughly clean the clothes.

The next cycle drains and rapidly spins the clothes to expel the solvent and then goes into a dry cycle by circulating warm air through the clothes. The remaining fumes and solvent are vaporized by warm air and then condensed over cooling coils. The distilled solvent is separated from any water (that may have remained in the clothes or system) and returned to the tank as distilled solvent. Since any moisture that may have condensed into water during the process floats on top of perc, it is relatively easy to separate it.

Cleaning plants using petroleum solvent rather than perc are exposed to a different set of circumstances and face some challenging considerations. The solvent is flammable, and therefore many fire-prevention steps must be taken for safety. The solvent is very slightly lighter than water and the two mix easily. There is also a need for higher temperatures to dry and deodorize the garments, which makes shrinkage and re-deposition of soil into the clothes more likely. These disadvantages are the reason why the industry currently uses perc almost exclusively.

Regardless of which solvent the dry cleaner uses, the quality of cleaning, the degree of soil removal, the colour brightness, the freshness, the odor and the softness all depend on the degree to which the cleaner controls his filter and solvent condition and moisture. Quality control can vary day to day unless the cleaner is constantly attentive to these factors.

Post-Spotting

Post-cleaning spot removal is another part of the quality control process. Post-spotting, as it is called, uses professional equipment and chemical preparations using steam, water, air, and vacuum. Post-spotting involves a fairly simple process for removing a stain. If the stain had water in it to begin with (bean soup, for example), then it takes water or wet-side chemicals to remove the stain. If the stain was on the dry side (grease, oil-base paint, tar, nail polish), it takes solvents or dry-side chemicals to remove the stain.

In home laundry, most wet-type stains come out during the washing process. Grease does not. The opposite is true in dry cleaning — it will leave the wet-side stains intact after the cleaning cycle. On the other hand, the solvent removes grease and oils during the cleaning cycle. The exception to this rule involves incorporating a "charge" of specially formulated dry-cleaning soap (an anhydrous emulsifier) into the cleaning cycle.

The dry cleaner will examine your clothes after cleaning is complete to see if any stains remain. If they do, post-spotting tries to get them out. A conscientious cleaner will remove the overwhelming majority of soil and stains, but there is always a small percent of very stubborn stains that may not be entirely removed for a variety of reasons, such as:

- Tannin stains set by heat and time
- Original dye stripped or faded
- Bleached-out spots or sun-faded materials
- Foreign dye deposit

Finishing Stage of Dry Cleaning

The final phase of dry-cleaning operations includes finishing, pressing, steaming, ironing, and making any necessary repairs to restore the garment. This is the least mysterious process since most dry-cleaning stores have their professional finishing equipment in plain view of customers.

Once the clothes are cleaned, they are pressed or "finished." The steps in this process include:

- Applying steam to soften the garment
- Reshaping it through quick drying
- Removing the steam with air or vacuum
- Applying pressure to the garment

The pressure comes from the head of the pressing machine, while steam is diffused through the bottom. Most machines not only emit steam, but can vacuum it out as well!

Solvent Process

Working solvent from the washing chamber passes through several filtration steps before it is returned to the washing chamber. The first step is a button trap which prevents small objects such as lint, fasteners, buttons, and coins from entering the solvent pump.

Next the solvent passes through a filter which removes lint and insoluble suspended soils from the solvent. Most filters use an ultra fine mesh to support a thin layer of filter powder (made from diatomaceous earth and activated clays). Some machines use powderless filters which are capable of removing soil particles greater than 30 micrometers.

Over time a thin layer of filter cake (called **muck**) accumulates on the lint filter. The muck is removed regularly (commonly once per day) and then processed to recover solvent trapped in the muck. Many machines use "spin disc filters" which remove the muck from the filter by centrifugal force while it is back washed with solvent.

After the lint filter, the solvent passes through an absorptive cartridge filter. This filter is made from activated clays and charcoal and removes fine insoluble soil and non-volatile residues, along with dyes from the solvent. Finally, the solvent passes through a polishing filter which removes any soil not previously removed. The clean solvent is then returned to the working solvent tank.

To enhance cleaning power, small amounts of detergent (0.5%-1.5%) are added to the working solvent and are essential to its functionality. These detergents help dissolve hydrophilic soils and keep soil from redepositing on garments. Depending on the machine's design, either an anionic or cationic detergent is used.

Since the solvent recovery is less than 100%, and because dry-cleaning doesn't remove water-based stains well, entrepreneurs have developed the wet cleaning process, which is essentially cold-water washing and air drying, using a computer-controlled washer and dryer. Wet cleaning is generally regarded as being in its infancy, although low-tech versions of it have been used for centuries.

Dry Clean Symbols

The international GINETEX laundry symbol for dry cleaning is a circle. It may have a letter P inside to indicate perchloroethylene solvent, or a letter F inside to indicate a hydrocarbon solvent. A bar underneath the circle indicates that only mild cleaning processes should be used. A crossed out empty circle indicates that no dry cleaning is allowed.

Dry-cleaning Wastes

Cooked Muck—Cooked Powder Residue — the waste material generated by cooking down or distilling muck. Cooked powder residue is a hazardous waste and will contain solvent, powdered filter material (diatomite), carbon, non-volatile residues, lint, dyes, grease, soils and water. This material should then be disposed of in accordance with local law.

Sludge—The waste sludge or solid residue from the still contains solvent, water, soils, carbon and other non-volatile residues. Still bottoms from chlorinated solvent dry cleaning operations are hazardous wastes.

Health and Safety—Perc is classified as a probable human carcinogen by the International Agency for Research on Cancer, and exposure carries risks to both those who work in the dry cleaning industry as well as consumers. Perc exposure has been shown to cause liver cancer in mice and kidney cancer in male rats. According to California's South Coast Air Quality Management District (SCAQMD), people who live near dry cleaners have a higher risk of cancer than those who live near oil refineries or power plants.

PERC can enter the body through smelling and dermal exposure. Symptoms associated with exposure include: memory loss, confusion, dizziness, headache, drowsiness, and irritation of the eyes, nose, throat irritation, and vomiting. Repeated dermal exposure can cause dermatitis.

Environment

Perc is classified as a hazardous air contaminant by the United States Environmental Protection Agency and must be handled as a hazardous waste. To prevent it from getting into drinking water, dry cleaners that use perc must take special precautions against site contamination. Landlords are becoming increasingly reluctant to allow dry cleaners to operate in their buildings. When released into the air, perc can contribute to smog when it reacts with other volatile organic carbon substances. California declared perchloroethylene a toxic chemical in 1991, and its use will become illegal in that state in 2023.

Solvents Used in Daily Life

• **Glycol ethers** (dipropylene glycol tertiary-butyl ether) (Rynex) — In many cases more effective than perchloroethylene (perc) and in all cases more environmentally friendly. Dipropylene glycol tertiary butyl ether (DPTB) has a flashpoint far above current industry standards, yet at the same time possesses a degree of solvency for water-soluble stains that is at least equivalent to, and in most cases better than, perc and the other glycol ether dry cleaning solvents presently in commercial use. A particular advantage of the DPTB-water solutions of the Rynex product in dry cleaning is that they do not behave like a typical mixutre, but rather, the behavicr in the same as a single substance. This permits a better defined separation upon azeotropic distillation at a lower boiling point and also facilitates reclamation more effectively, at a level of 99% or greater, and also enhances purification using conventional distillation techniques.

• **Hydrocarbon** — This is most like standard dry cleaning, but the processes use hydrocarbon solvents such as Exxon-Mobil's

DF-2000 or Chevron Phillips' EcoSolv. These petroleum-based solvents are less aggressive than perc and require a longer cleaning cycle. While flammable, these solvents do not present a high risk of fire or explosion when used properly. Hydrocarbon also contains volatile organic compounds (VOCs) that contribute to smog.

- **Liquid silicone** (decamethylcyclopentasiloxane or D5) — gentler on garments than Perc and does not cause colour loss. Requires a license be obtained to utilize the property of GreenEarth Cleaning. Degrades within days in the environment to silica and trace amounts of water and CO_2. Produces nontoxic, nonhazardous waste. Toxicity tests by Dow Corning shows the solvent to increase the incidence of tumors in female rats (no effects were seen in male rats), but further research concluded that the effects observed in rats were not relevant to humans because the biological pathway that results in tumor formation is unique to rats. (170.6 °F/77 °C flash point).

- **Modified hydrocarbon blends** (Pure Dry)

- **Perchloroethylene** — In use since the 1940s, perc is the most common solvent, the "standard" for cleaning performance, and most aggressive cleaner. It can cause colour bleeding/loss, especially at higher temperatures, and may destroy special trims, buttons, and beads on some garments. Better for oil-based stains (which account for about 10% of stains) than more common water-soluble stains (coffee, wine, blood, etc). Known for leaving a characteristic chemical smell on garments. Nonflammable.

- **Liquid CO_2** — Consumer Reports rated this method superior to conventional methods, but the Drycleaning and Laundry Institute commented on its "fairly low cleaning ability" in a 2007 report. Another industry certification group, America's Best Cleaners, counts CO2 cleaners among its members. Machinery is expensive—up to $90,000 more than a perc machine, making affordability difficult for small businesses. Some cleaners with these machines keep traditional machines on-site for the heavier soiled textiles but others find plant enzymes to be equally effective and more environmentally sustainable. CO2-cleaned clothing doesn't off-gas volatile compounds. CO_2 cleaning is also used for fire- and water-damage restoration due to its effectiveness in removing toxic residues, soot and associated odors of fire.

• **Wet cleaning** — Not a solvent, but a system that uses water and biodegradable soap. Computer-controlled dryers and stretching machines ensure that the fabric retains its natural size and shape. Wet cleaning is claimed to clean a majority of "dry clean only" garments safely, including leather, suede, most tailored woolens, silk and rayon. (Neckties seem to be the one exception.) Most perc cleaners use wet cleaning on some garments, but there are only about 20 exclusive wetcleaners in the U.S.

Working System of Home Dry Cleaning

If you have ever done laundry, you've probably run across at least one article of clothing with the label "Dry Clean Only." These clothes are made of fabrics that can't just be tossed into a washing machine with water and detergent.

What's so special about fabrics like rayon, silk, and wool blends? Well, these materials may shrink, change colours or lose their shape if washed in water. Garments made of rayon become rumpled and misshapen because water is attracted to the hydrophilic fibres in this fabric. When submerged in water, the fibres expand because water molecules form hydrogen bonds with individual molecules within each fibre. The water molecules also interfere with weak attractions between adjacent fibres, and the fabric as a whole can lose its strength. In order to avoid ruining your favorite shirt, you'll have to resort to other means of cleaning it — namely, dry cleaning.

Kits of Home Dry Cleaning—There are three home dry cleaning kits currently available for purchase in most grocery and discount stores:

- Custom Cleaner
- FreshCare
- Dryel

All of these kits promise to clean and/or freshen dry-clean-only or hand-wash-only fabrics without using any of the industrial solvents used by dry cleaners. The basic steps involved in these kits mirror those of commercial dry cleaning, sans immersion in a solvent and specialized machinery:

1. Pre-treat clothing to remove stains.
2. Dry clean clothing.
3. Iron and reshape clothing and make repairs if necessary.

Components of Kit—Each of these home dry cleaning kits contains the same components:

- Stain remover and/or stain absorbing pads
- Dryer activated cloth
- Reusable dryer bag

Stain Pre-treating

All of the kits advise you to pre-treat or remove stains using the stain remover included. There is nothing particularly special about the **stain remover** in these kits. It is the same kind that you use to pre-treat stains before regular machine washing, and the pre-treatment process works the same way as well. Most stain removers are simply a cleaning agent in a water-based solution.

The common rule for stain removal is that "like dissolves like." The water in the solution dissolves water-based stains, such as soup. The cleaning agent used is either a detergent or a petroleum-based solvent (depending on which brand you choose). Although the petroleum-based solvents work far better, both detergents and solvents aid in the removal of greasy stains. The informational brochure that accompanies home dry cleaning kits does not specify which of these agents is used in their pre-treatment solutions, and it turns out that the identity of the cleaning agent in the kits is proprietary information. However, given the kits' poor reputation for completely removing greasy stains like butter, it's probably safe to assume that they use detergents rather than oil-based solvents.

The cleaning agent has a number of other important functions, including:

- Reducing surface tension to help water penetrate fabrics — in order to remove a stain, water must be able to reach the molecules of dirt on and in the fibres.
- Loosening and dispersing dirt molecules in the water — if the dirt isn't dissolved in water or another solvent, or somehow separated from the fabric, it will simply redeposit on the surface of your clothes.

The Dryel and FreshCare kits provide the stain removal solution in a bottle, along with absorbent pads that you use to sop up the dirt after you apply the solution. The process works as follows:

1. You place the tip of the bottle on the stain, with the absorbent pad underneath on the other side of the fabric.
2. You gently rub the stain while applying solution.
3. The soil and grease is liberated from the fabric and dissolved in solution with assistance from the cleaning agent.
4. The dirt is pushed through the fibres by the pressure you're applying.
5. The absorbent pad captures the dissolved dirt.

Perhaps it seems odd that a water-based stain remover can be used on dry-clean-only clothes without damaging them. But because you only apply a small amount of solution to a discrete area, you don't add enough water to disrupt the structure of the fibres globally or weaken the fabric, and then you remove most of the water when you blot the fabric with the absorbent pad.

Some product reviews note that the Custom Cleaner kit doesn't remove stains as well as the others, even though it uses a similar cleaning agent. This may be due to the fact that the detergent is not provided in a water-based solution. With Custom Cleaner, the dryer-activated cloth itself is laced with the stain remover, and you provide your own absorbent pad in the form of a clean paper towel. These dryer-activated cloths contain only a trace amount of water. While too much water can damage a dry-clean-only fabric, too little makes it difficult to thoroughly remove all of a water-based stain

All of the home dry cleaning kits are incapable of removing large stains. Whether water-based or oil-based, large stains must be thoroughly saturated with the proper solvent to attract and remove all the molecules of grime, especially the ones embedded deep within a fabric. Even machine-washable clothes sometimes require special efforts beyond what you can reasonably do at home. For example, grease stains on synthetic fibres, such as acrylic, nylon, olefin, polyester and blends of these fibres are particularly taugh to remove. Many of these fibres are specially made to resist penetration by water. Because they repel water, they attract other molecules, such as fats, that also repel water. This makes greasy stains on these fabrics nearly impossible to remove with water and/or water-based detergents alone.

The precautions for pre-treating clothes before machine washing also apply when using these kits:

Don't rub the fabric harshly while applying the stain remover. Most dry-clean-only fabrics are not tough and durable, so rough treatment can damage them.

Don't treat suede, velvet, fur or leather — and don't try to home dry clean them, for that matter. These fabrics must go to a professional dry cleaner!

Test the stain remover on a small, hidden area of the clothing before applying it to a stain. You don't want to create another problem by destroying the colour or finish of the fabric.

Inside Your Dryer

What actually happens inside your dryer is the "black box" of this process for most people. All three kits instruct you to place one to four articles of clothing inside their respective "special" dry cleaning bag. Then, you add the dryer-activated cloths, seal the bag and put it in the dryer for 15 to 30 minutes (depending on which kit you're using). At the end, you remove your newly home-dry-cleaned clothes.

So what's really going on inside that bag? It's actually an incredibly simple system, involving only steam, perfume and an emulsifier.

Working : The dryer-activated cloth holds a small amount of water, as well as perfume and an emulsifying agent. This emulsifying agent keeps the water and perfume dispersed within the cloth. When you turn on the dryer, the heat generated raises the temperature of the liquids inside the cloth. This increase in thermal energy allows the molecules to bounce around more rapidly than usual. When the molecules reach a high enough temperature, they overcome their attraction to one another and leave the surface of the liquid. The molecules form a dense, high-pressure gas (steam/ vapors).

The vapors are contained within the nylon or plastic bag. When the vapors penetrate the fibres of the clothing, some of the water and perfume condenses within the fabric. This is the secret behind how these kits "freshen" your clothing; they simply infuse it with a fragrance! If you are allergic to perfumes or the kinds of fragrances that manufacturers typically put in cleaning products, you may want to avoid these kits. Clothes cleaned with them smell strongly of the scents used, even weeks after cleaning.

The same steam vapors are used to remove wrinkles from the clothes. The kits operate under the same principle as steam irons. When you press clothes on an ironing board, the steam carries its heat through the fabric. The combination of the water molecules and the heat temporarily breaks weak attractions between the fibres. This unlocks the fibres from the wrinkled state they have been in, and you can then press the fabric flat with the iron. The kits are slightly different, because you don't have the weight and additional heat of the iron to press wrinkles out. The home dry cleaning kits rely on gravity to help wrinkles "fall out" from your clothes once you've removed them from the dryer and hung them up. This is why the kits emphasize getting your garments out of the dryer as soon as it clicks off. Outside the dryer, the clothes quickly cool down, and the fibres become less pliant. So, given the limited window of opportunity for gravity to do its job while clothes are still hot, clothing that is heavily wrinkled will most likely still be wrinkled after home dry cleaning. The FreshCare kit even advises you to launder dress shirts professionally, given their propensity to wrinkle.

Finishing Touches

Your dryer cycle has finished, and you've hung your still-warm clothes up to make the wrinkles fall out. What happens next?

Just like a professional dry cleaner, you now have to inspect your clothes to see how well they turned out. There are several things to look for and try to correct. They include:

Wrinkles—A professional cleaner will steam press your clothes if they are misshapen following their solvent bath. If you find wrinkles after home dry cleaning, you'll need to iron them yourself.

Loose buttons and **ripped seams**—You may require to fix any buttons that are in danger of falling off, or fix any seams where the thread has unraveled.

Remaining stains—Professional cleaners will do post spotting to try to get rid of any stains that remain after cleaning. Your options are to either clean them again with the kit or take them to a professional dry cleaner.

Disadvantages and Advantages

The final wrinkle-removing step, in addition to the time you spend pre-treating clothes and waiting for the dryer cycle to end, make home dry cleaning a pretty time-consuming endeavor! This is one benefit of professional dry cleaning — all the hard work is done for you.

However, if money is a concern, you might help your budget by using the kits. With home dry cleaning, you can clean 16 garments for about what you'd pay for one garment to be professionally dry cleaned. As long as you're not trying to remove large, set-in or greasy stains, these kits can be used to freshen garments and stretch the time between visits to the cleaner. You have to weigh the money you could save using the kits against the time you'll lose actually doing your dry cleaning at home.

One big plus of home kits is that they do prevent you from being exposed to the solvent, perchlorethylene, used by commercial cleaners. This does make them a good alternative for people with chemical sensitivities (not including perfume) or those who are looking for a process that's less harmful to the environment. Perchlorethylene can damage your liver, kidneys and brain, and is a contaminant in up to 25 percent of the U.S. water supply. The chemicals used in home dry cleaning don't accumulate in the environment, and, compared to perchlorethylene, they are fairly safe.

In the end, home dry cleaning kits don't represent a major step forward in cleaning technology. The kits simply take advantage of some pretty basic chemistry (the generation of steam from water, for example). Whether you choose to use them or not depends on the relative importance of their advantages and disadvantages to you.

Risk of Dry Cleaning

Hazards such as chemical, fire, and ergonomic-related are associated with dry cleaning processes. Exposure to hazardous chemicals commonly used in dry cleaning shops may occur through skin absorption, eye contact, or inhalation of the vapors. Perchloroethylene (PERC), a potential human carcinogen, is the most commonly used dry cleaning solvent. Symptoms associated with exposure include: depression of the central nervous system; damage to the liver and kidneys; impaired memory; confusion; dizziness; headache; drowsiness; and eye, nose, and throat irritation. Repeated dermal exposure may result in dermatitis.

Dry cleaning shops contain all elements necessary for uncontrolled fires: fuels, ignition sources, and oxygen. Potential combustible materials include furniture, garments, lint, and portions of the building. The greatest risk of fire and explosion exists if the dry cleaning shop uses a petroleum-based solvent in dry cleaning machines.

Ergonomic risks occur during garment transfer, pressing, and bagging. These activities, combined with a high work rate and frequency, may cause physical discomfort and musculoskeletal problems for workers. Disorders may include damage to tendons, muscles, nerves, and ligaments of the hand, wrist, arm, shoulder, neck, and back.

The effects of repeated dry-cleanings and launderings with and without fabric softeners on the thickness, air permeability, dimensional stability, and thermal insulative properties of two blanket fabrics were evaluated in this study. One of the two softeners used in laundering was added to the rinse, and the other was added to the dryer. Changes in the thermal-transmittance properties of the test fabrics were determined with a guarded hot/cold plate.

After repeated dry-cleanings and launderings, the blanket fabrics exhibited a significant reduction in thickness. Fabric dimensions were altered significantly during the first few washing. Laundering and dry-cleaning also significantly changed the air permeability of the blanket fabrics: the permeability increased for one blanket fabric and decreased for the other. There was no significant change, however, in the thermal conductivity of the blanket fabrics after repeated laundering with or without fabric softeners or after repeated dry-cleanings. Thus, the thermal insulative properties of the blanket fabrics were not affected by repeated cleaning or by the use of fabric softeners during the washing or drying cycle of laundering.

Environmental and Health Related Concerns

The standard solvent used in dry cleaning is associated with health and environmental risks. An estimated 80 percent of commercial dry cleaning businesses in the U.S. use that solvent, percholoroethylene, or perc.

Health risks from short-term exposure to perc range from eye, skin, nose, and throat irritation to adverse effects on the nervous system, including dizziness, fatigue, headaches, lack of coordination, and unconsciousness. Long-term exposure can cause liver and kidney damage. Perc has also been identified as a probable human carcinogen by the International Agency for Research on Cancer (IARC).

Note: As with all health effects, the potential for an increased risk of cancer depends on several factors, including the level, frequency, and duration of exposure. Also important is the way the exposure occurs, as well as the individual's overall state of health, age, lifestyle, and family traits.

Environmental risks from perc, which is classified by the EPA as a hazardous air pollutant, may result when the chemical escapes and evaporates into the air upon use or from equipment leaks. In older dry cleaning systems, perc may still be directly vented to the outdoors. It can remain in the atmosphere for several weeks and break down into other toxic chemicals, some of which are suspected to contribute to the depletion of the ozone layer.

Perc is also classified as a pollutant in water regulations, and its disposal is regulated as a hazardous waste. It can affect the environment if it enters the ground in liquid form through spills, equipment leaks, or improperly handled waste. It can potentially contaminate surface water, groundwater, and drinking water, and it is known to be toxic to plants and aquatic animals.

Some people are at a higher risk of exposure than others. Everyone may be exposed to some level of perc in the air and drinking water, and people who get their clothing dry cleaned may be exposed to slightly higher than average levels. These amounts, however, are not expected to be hazardous to the average person's health, according to the EPA. People at higher risk would be those who work with the chemical in dry-cleaning facilities and those living in or near buildings with perc dry cleaners, because the vapors can pass through the floor, ceiling, and wall materials of the shop. High levels would be of special concern for occupants who are often home, such as the elderly, young children, or pregnant women.

Alternative Dry Cleaning Methods

Here's how they work and where to find a cleaner in your area:

Wet cleaning uses water as the main solvent in specialized machines, along with specially-formulated detergents and additives. The process is one of two methods considered environmentally preferable by the EPA.

Where to find it: While there are 100 percent wet cleaning operations, an increasing number of professional dry cleaning operations are incorporating wet cleaning into their businesses. Check with your local cleaner, or consult the Earth 911 directory for a zip-code searchable database.

Note that wet cleaning is not covered by textile-care-labeling regulations. So if your garment is labeled "dry-clean" or "dry-clean only" and you opt to have it wet cleaned, the clothing manufacturer would probably not be liable for any damage.

Liquid carbon dioxide (CO2) is captured from the production of other industrial chemicals, as well as natural sources, and used to clean clothes in high-pressure machines. This process is the other method considered environmentally preferable method by the EPA.

Green Earth involves a silicone-based solvent known as siloxane, or D5, which is used in machines specifically modified to work with this solvent. While Green Earth is marketed as an environmentally friendly process, the EPA has not determined whether the solvent can be labeled as safe for health or the environment until further testing is done. Some studies have shown siloxane can cause cancer in laboratory animals.

Beware of green claims. Since there's no standard definition of an environmentally friendly cleaner, and no EPA approval of a product or process, professional cleaners can call themselves "green" regardless of the process they use.

If you do have your garments perc-cleaned, we suggest airing them before wearing.

How to Cut Down on Trips to the Cleaners

Wash your clothes at home. Some types of garments can be washed at home, if you choose to ignore the "dry-clean only" care label. But, keep in mind that alternative methods of cleaning aren't covered by textile-care-labeling regulations. So if your garment is labeled "dry-clean only" and you wash it at home, the clothing manufacturer would not be liable for any damage. Here are some guidelines:

Plain (no embroidery, embellishments, fancy stitches), solid-colour sweaters can often be hand washed or machine washed on a gentle/delicate setting. Be sure to turn cotton and cashmere inside out. If you have a top-loading machine, you can often extract excess water from hand washing using the spin cycle only. It's best to lay sweaters flat to dry, because that allows you to reshape them.

Lightly coloured plain-weave rayon and silk blouses labeled "dry-clean" or "dry-clean only" have been successfully hand washed in *Consumer Reports* tests. Note that deep or saturated colours had a tendency to bleed, or lose colour, with washing.

Washable wool labeled as such can be both machine washed and dried.

Note that angora sweaters and structured or lined garments should be sent to a professional cleaner.

•**Extend the time between cleaning** by blotting up spills right away, using a clothes or lint brush, and wearing undershirts.

•**Don't iron stained garments.** That heat-sets stains.

•**Hang up clothes immediately** after you've worn them, give them a day off between wearings, and air them out before returning them to the closet.

•**Try steaming** a suit by hanging it in the bathroom while you shower to remove the wrinkles.

•**Buy clothes that don't need dry cleaning.**

Note: When you do take items to the cleaners, show your cleaner where the stains are—don't make the cleaner guess. Explain what the stain is and whether you tried to clean it (and what you used).

Bad Effects of Environment

Dry cleaning can help keep your favorite cashmere sweater in top condition, but it's not always the best choice for the environment. Perchloroethylene, also known as tetrachloroethylene, perc, PCE, C2Cl4, Cl2C=CCl2, or tetrachloroethene, is a solvent used by 90% of dry cleaning businesses in the United States. Perchloroethylene is a highly effective cleaning agent, although it can result in colour bleeding or loss if not used properly. However, perchloroethylene is also toxic and causes several harmful side effects.

Some studies have indicated that perchloroethylene can cause menstrual irregularities, fertility problems, and spontaneous abortions among women who work in the dry cleaning industry. Perchloroethylene residue from dry cleaning processes can also seep into drinking water, causing a variety of problems. For example, many scientists believe perchloroethylene exposure can cause liver or kidney damage. In addition, perchloroethylene has been named a "probable carcinogen" by the International Association for Research on Cancer.

In response to customer complaints about the dangers of perchloroethylene, many dry cleaners have begun to investigate alternative cleaning methods. Hydrocarbon solvents such as Chevron-Phillips' EcoSolv or Exxon D-2000 work much like standard dry cleaning agents, but without the harmful side effects. Wet cleaning, a system that uses water and biodegradable soap, is an environmentally-friendly process that works well for silk, rayon, leather, suede, and wool garments. Liquid carbon dioxide obtained as a byproduct of certain industrial processes can be combined with silicone to create another effective, yet environmentally-safe dry cleaning method.

Unfortunately, since these "green" dry cleaning processes are relatively new, people who live outside of metropolitan areas may find it difficult to find a reputable dry cleaner who doesn't use perchloroethylene. However, home dry cleaning kits that use plastic bags and specialized cleaning sheets are widely available and provide a convenient way to freshen clothing while removing minor stains. Several studies have determined that these kits are less harmful to the environment than cleaning a garment with perchloroethylene. Using home drying kits between trips to your local dry cleaner is an inexpensive way to help reduce the environmental impact of dry cleaning.

While the process used to clean your clothing does have a substantial effect on the environment, there are other factors you may wish to consider when choosing a dry cleaner. For example, many dry cleaners have a policy of solvent recycling, plastic bag recycling, and hanger recycling. This can help protect the environment by reducing the amount of waste that ends up in local landfills. Some dry cleaners have also upgraded to "third generation" machines that are more efficient at minimizing the amount of harmful chemicals used during the dry cleaning process.

Dry cleaning washes your clothes in chemicals instead of water. The most common solvent for dry cleaning is perchloroethylene. Clothes get damaged at dry cleaners too...fairly often. You can ask them to clean it by hand, usually for an extra charge.

Most clothes can be gently handwashed instead of dry-cleaned. Acetate really can't be washed (used for linings, especially common in wool pants) and some silks can't either. A lot of clothes that say they're dry clean only say that because they're not constructed very well and are less likely to fall apart during dry cleaning than laundering.

Source(s)

Used to work as a seamstress for a dry cleaner, until the owner got colon cancer.

Wet Cleaning: A Viable Alternative for Dry-Clean Only Clothes?

Q. What is wet cleaning?

A. Wet cleaning (by water immersion) is a method to clean garments that normally would have been cleaned in solvent. Wet cleaning became popular recently in Europe and the U.S. because of the strong environmental regulations restricting the use of solvents. Most techniques are similar in that they all use specially formulated wet-cleaning soaps and spotting agents, (consisting of enzymes, peptides, synthetic polymers, and anionic and nonionic tensides). Several measures are used to reduce the risks of clothes damage, the main ones being the following:

* Increased extraction of water prior to drying (The greatest risk to the garment occurs during drying);

* Close monitoring of heat and moisture content during the drying process (moisture sensors control the fabric drying. Temperature in the drum should not exceed 60°C (140°F) for normal garments and 50°C (122°F) for sensitive garments);

* Machines designed to insure low levels of mechanical action during washing through speed reduction and time limits.

Estimates vary as to what percentage of dry-clean only clothes can be effectively cleaned using wet cleaning techniques. According to the Center for Neighborhood Technology's initial research, wet cleaning is effective for 75-90% of dry cleaner's business. Currently, there are several hundred companies in the US that clean all or some "dry-clean only" clothes using the wet cleaning method. Wet cleaning starts with the pretreatment of spots and stains using special cleaning agents. Wet cleaning is the process of removing soils from garments and other textile items through the use of water and additives (such as detergent) and using precautions to prevent shrinkage, loss of colour, and fabric distortion.

Q. Are there any problems associated with wet cleaning?

A. Yes. One difference between water and solvents is that water tends to expand natural and cellulose fibres, while solvents do not change the fibre properties. When natural and cellulose fibres expand, they also wrinkle, lose their strength, shrink, and lose their shape. In general, the higher the synthetic content of the garment, the lower the risk of shrinkage through wet cleaning.

Wet Cleaning : Benefits

* Wet cleaning may help to keep the white garments whiter. Sometimes white garments can be dulled when cleaned with recycled PERC or other solvents.

* Wet-cleaned garments have a more pleasant smell when compared to the chemical odor associated with garments cleaned

in solvent.

* One of the major advantages of wet cleaning is the elimination of dry cleaning solvents, and their associated health and fire hazards.

* Many soils are more easily removed with water than solvent. This is particularly true for water-soluble stains resulting from sugars, salts, drinks, body fluids, starch, milk, and most foods.

Drawbacks

* Garments made of wool, silk, and viscose rayon cannot easily be immersed in water because of possible garment damage from fibre shrinkage or bleeding of dyes. Most problem garments fall into one of the following categories: suit jackets with front fixing in the construction, coats, items with shoulder pads, and ornate clothing.

* Dry cleaning solvents do a better job of removing, greases, oils, waxes, and resins.

Conclusion

Wet cleaning appears to be a viable option to reduce the usage of drycleaning solvents. However, the technology has not developed to the point where it can completely eliminate the need for dry cleaning solvents.

Make the Following Checks When Sending Clothes to a Dry Cleaner:

- Empty all pockets.
- Read care instruction labels of clothes. Check garment materials and any handle-with-care signs. If these are made of materials which cannot be washed in water, they have to be sent to a dry cleaner.
- If there are any stains, mark them by rough stitches with a white thread. If you know what caused the stains, you should tell the cleaner about them. In the case of two-piece or three-piece suits, they should be sent together to the cleaner for best results.

- If you find an open seam or a button missing, mend them yourself or ask the cleaner to do so. In the case special buttons are used, take these off the clothes before sending them to the cleaner.
- Keep the receipt from the cleaner.
- When cleaned clothes are returned, check the finish thoroughly. If you find the cleaning to be unsatisfactory or find any damage, inform the cleaner promptly.
- Remove the plastic film cover from the clothes, air them in shade for a while before putting them in the closet.

What Are the Most Common Dry Cleaning Troubles?

In 1997, the Laundry and Drycleaning Association received 558 complaints from the public regarding damages made to their clothes in cleaning. The breakdown of the damage complaints and the parties who were found responsible are indicative. Among damages for which the clients were responsible, the most common was the "change of colour" amounting to 66 % of the total cases. Cases of stains made by spilled bleach or damages caused by inappropriate storage are on the increase recently at individual homes. It is important that the consumers also have the basic knowledge about how to clean and keep clothes in good shape.

Professional Cleaning Steps

Professional cleaning involves many different operations, all performed by skilled people and designed to give your garments a fresh and clean appearance. Procedures include:

- Checking the care label for instructions and fibre content
- Classifying the garment according to fabric type, colour and degree of soiling
- Removing spots and stains using special equipment and stain removal techniques
- Dry cleaning, wet cleaning, or laundering, only if so labeled
- Reapplying any sizing, water repellency or other finishes when necessary

- Finishing the garment on professional pressing equipment
- Replacing buttons or performing minor repairs as necessary
- Packaging the garment in protective wrapping

Importance Care Labels

The Federal Trade Commission (FTC) requires that manufacturers attach a permanent care label to textile garments to provide directions for their care. Manufacturers must list at least one method of safe care for a garment. The rule covers all textile clothing except footwear, gloves, hats, suede and leather clothing, and household items such as linens. The rule stipulates that the care label is easily found, will not separate from the garment, and will remain legible for the garment's useful life. The label must warn about any part of the recommended care method that would harm the garment of other garments cleaned with it. It must also warn when there is no method for cleaning a garment without damaging it.

Symbols also may appear on a care label to supplement written instructions.

If a label indicates dry cleaning, all components of the garment, including the outer shell, lining, buttons, interfacing, fusing material, and trim, should be colourfast and remain unaltered during cleaning. If any such problem occurs, it is the responsibility of the manufacturer. If you or your cleaner follow the manufacturer's instructions and the garment is damaged, you should return the garment to the store and explain what happened. If the store will not resolve the problem, write to the manufacturer and send a copy of your complaint letter to the FTC. The information you provide the FTC may reveal a pattern or practice requiring the Commission's attention. If you purchase a garment with no care label, you should contact the FTC, giving the name and address of the store and manufacturer.

Occasionally, damage done in dry cleaning is the responsibility of the dry cleaner and not the result of preexisting conditions or defects. In such cases, the cleaner will usually settle the claim promptly and fairly, often using IFI's Fair Claims Guide. If there is some doubt about responsibility, the member cleaner can send the garment to IFI's Garment Analysis Laboratory to determine the cause of the problem.

How Can You Help Your Clothes and Your Cleaner?

- Bring your garments in for professional cleaning as soon as possible after staining occurs. Stains or soils left too long may become permanent.
- Discuss any stains with your cleaner.
- Keep perfumes, lotions, deodorants, antiperspirants, and other toiletries away from your clothes. These products likely contain alcohol which will damage some dyes.
- Protect garment, especially those made of silk, from excessive perspiration, as this can cause dyes to discolour.
- Have matching pieces of an ensemble cleaned together so any colour fading will be uniform.
- Protect your garments from prolonged exposure to direct light.
- Don't press stained or soiled clothing, as the heat may set some stains.

Advantages

Reduction of cost

- No chemical clean-up needed.
- Online maintenance: no need to dissassemble the installation. This way production stops are reduced to a minimum and start-up problems during reassembly can be avoided.

Longer useful life of equipment

- Non-abrasive cleaning method, limiting wear.
- Cleans faster and more thoroughly than traditional cleaning methods.

Porcess of Dry Cleaning

- Dry ice sublimates, avoiding damage to electric parts.
- Bacteriostatic effect of CO_2: the risk of bacteria growth is reduced or ruled out since dry ice sublimates into gas, leaving no residue.

Ecologically sound

- CO_2 is a non-toxic element which leaves no dangerous substances, unlike chemical cleaning. Therefore there is no danger for employee exposure.

Limits of Dry Cleaning

1. Removing Stains: The nature and age of the stain plus the colour and construction of the garment sometimes makes stains impossible to remove. We advise you notify us of stains when placing your order.

2. Preventing Colour Bleed: If the manufacturer does not thoroughly test the dyes to make sure they are colourfast to both solvent and water, some colour may be lost during the cleaning process. This is considered the manufacturers' responsibility.

3. Reversing Worn or Torn Areas: This is caused by wear, perspiration or damage caused by insects or liquid spills. Such holes or tears may not appear before cleaning but are the result of previous weakening of the fibres.

4. Garments with Beading/Piping: Please note that garments with beading/piping are at owners risk. Garments with beading/piping are dry-cleaned on a delicate cycle and the utmost care is taken during this process. However, there is a risk of beading coming away from garment during the dry-cleaning process as not all beading/piping is suitable for dry-cleaning. On very rare occasions, some beading may dissolve in cleaning fluid. Manufacturers may test the garments fabric for dry-cleaning but not the actual beading.

Tips for Extend the Garments File

1. Never rub a stain or attempt home spot removal with either water or cleaning fluid especially with silk garments.
2. Remove the plastic bag when you place your clothes in your wardrobe after dry-cleaning.
3. It is a good idea to have matching pieces cleaned together (i.e., a two piece suit.)

4. Bring a garment for cleaning as soon as possible after a stain occurs. Stains left for too long can become impossible to remove and will shorten the life of your garment.
5. Keep perfumes, lotions, anti-perspirants and other toiletries from coming into contact with your clothes. These products generally contain alcohol which can affect dyes.
6. Protect your garments from excessive perspiration especially silks. Perspiration left on garments causes many dyes to discolour and silk fabric to deteriorate.

Bibliography

Hussain, Majid, Encyclopedia of Northeast India: Arunachal Pradesh, Vol. I, Rima Publications, 1994.

Hussain, Majid, Encyclopedia of India: Nagaland, Rima Publications, 1994.

Crill, Rosemary, 'Vaishnavite Silks: The figured textiles of Assam' in The woven silks of Assam, Marg, Publication, 1998.

Dhamija Jasleen, 'The Survey of Embroidery Traditions' in Textiles and Embroideries of India, Mark Publications, Bombay, 1965.

Iyer D.S.V. 'Looms', in Textiles and Embroideries of India, Mark Publications, Bombay, 1965.

Mudaliar, M.P.Nachimuthu, 'Manipur, Naga and Assam Fabrics', in Textiles and Embroideries of India, Mark Publications, Bombay, 1965.

Hussain, Majid, N.S.Olaniya, Encyclopedia of India: Arunachal Pradesh & Mizoram, Rima Publications, 1994.

Ali, A. Yusuf, A monograph of Silk Fabrics, Allahbad, 1900.

Indian textiles in the 20th century: Crisis in transformation, in 2000: Reflections on the arts of India, Marg publications, 2000.

Barve, V.R. Complete textile encyclopedia, Russi Lal Publishers, Bombay, 1967.

Alisa Baginski, Textile History 32, 2001, P. 81
Orit Shamir, Textile History 32, 2001, P. 93
Linda Woolley, Textile History 32, 2001, P. 106
Marguerite Knockert, Textile History 32, 2001, P. 114
Philip A. Sykas, Textile History 32, 2001, P. 119
Patricia Wardle, Textile History 32, 2001, P. 133
Philip Sykas, Textile History 32, 2001, P. 156
David M. Swan, Textile History 32, 2001, P. 175
Jennie Brunton, Textile History 32, 2001, P. 217
Steven King; Textile History 33, 2002, P. 1
John Styles, Textile History 33, 2002, P. 9
Sam Smiles, Textile History 33, 2002, P. 22
Steven King, Textile History 33, 2002, P. 37
Christiana Payne, Textile History 33, 2002, P. 48
Christine Stevens, Textile History 33, 2002, P. 63
Brian Maidment, Textile History 33, 2002, P. 79
David M. Higgins, Textile History 31, 2000, P. 54
Sue Bowden; Paul Turner, Textile History 31, 2000, P. 77
J.i. Greaves, Textile History 31, 2000, P. 102
Harald Deceulaer, Textile History 31, 2000, P. 133
Paul H. Rem, Textile History 31, 2000, P. 150
Winifred Aldrich, Textile History 31, 2000, P. 163
Andy Bielenberg, Textile History 31, 2000, P. 202
Ian Mortimer; Joseph Melling, Textile History 31, 2000, P. 222
Anna Muthesius, Textile History 32, 2001, P. 1
Lisa Monnas, Textile History 32, 2001, P. 2
Anna Muthesius, Textile History 32, 2001, P. 36
Frances Pritchard, Textile History 32, 2001, P. 48
Marianne Ellis, Textile History 32, 2001, P. 61
Petra Lincheid, Textile History 32, 2001, P. 75
C.m. Jackson-houlston, Textile History 33, 2002, P. 98
Karen Sayer, Textile History 33, 2002, P. 112

Roy, Nilima, Art of Manipur, Agam Kala Prakashan, New Delhi, 1979.

Ganguli, Milada, Naga Art, New Delhi, Oxford & IBH

The Arts and Crafts of Nagaland, Naga institute of Culture, Government of Nagaland, Kohima, 1968.

Bhavnani, Enakshi, Folk and Tribal designs of India, Taraporevala, Bombay, 1974.

Barpujari, H.K. The comprehensive History of Assam. Vol V, Publication board of Assam, 1993.

Nyori, Tai, History and Culture of the Adis, Omsons Publications, 1993.

Panchani, Chandra Sheikhar, Arunachal Pradesh: Religion, Culture & society, Konark Publishers, New Delhi, 1989.

Panchani, Chandra Sheikhar, Manipur: Religion, Culture & society, Konark Publishers, New Delhi, 1987.

Chattopadhyay, Kamaladevi, The glory of Indian handicrafts, Indian book Company, Delhi, 1976.

Saraf, D.N. Indian Crafts- Development and Potential, Vikas Publishing House, Delhi, 1982.

Saraf, D.N. In the journey of Crafts development, (1941- 1991), Sampark Publishing house, Delhi, 1992.

Elwin Verrier, The Art of Northeast Frontier of India, Northeast frontier agency, Shillong, 1959.

Hussain, Majid, Encyclopedia of India: Assam, Rima Publications, 1994.

Index

A

B

C